First World War
and Army of Occupation
War Diary
France, Belgium and Germany

20 DIVISION
Divisional Troops
Divisional Signal Company
20 July 1915 - 29 April 1919

WO95/2108/1

The Naval & Military Press Ltd
www.nmarchive.com
Published in association with The National Archives

Published by

The Naval & Military Press Ltd

Unit 10 Ridgewood Industrial Park,

Uckfield, East Sussex,

TN22 5QE England

Tel: +44 (0) 1825 749494

www.naval-military-press.com

www.nmarchive.com

This diary has been reprinted in facsimile from the original. Any imperfections are inevitably reproduced and the quality may fall short of modern type and cartographic standards.

© **Crown Copyright**
Images reproduced by permission of The National Archives, London, England, 2015.

Contents

Document type	Place/Title	Date From	Date To
Miscellaneous	2108/1		
Heading	20th Division Divl Engineers 20th Divl Signal Coy Jly 1915-Apl 1919		
Miscellaneous	20th Divisional Signal Coy-R E		
Miscellaneous	20th. Divisional Signal Company R.E.		
Miscellaneous	20th. Divisional Signal Company R.E.	21/07/1915	21/07/1915
Miscellaneous	Bar To Military Medal		
Miscellaneous	Died of Wounds (II)		
Heading	20th Division 20th Divisional Signal Coy Vol I 20-31-7-15		
Heading	War Diary of O.C. 20th Divisional Signal R.C. July 1915		
War Diary	Havre	20/07/1915	21/07/1915
War Diary	Lumbres	23/07/1915	27/07/1915
War Diary	Lynde	28/07/1915	28/07/1915
War Diary	Merris	29/07/1915	31/07/1915
Map	Appendix I		
Diagram etc	Map Showing Distribution Of Brigade Appendix I		
Miscellaneous	A Form. Messages And Signals		
Diagram etc	Circuit Diagram 61st Bde In Billets At Hallines		
Map	Merris H.Qs 20th Divn & H.Qs. RA. 20th Divn		
Diagram etc	Appendix II		
Miscellaneous	Div		
Diagram etc	Blue Line-Wire		
Diagram etc	Circuit Diagram of Signals 59th Infantry Brigade		
Diagram etc	61st Bde Billets July 30th 1915 Appendix II		
Heading	20th Division 20th Divl. Signal Coy Vol II Aug 15		
War Diary	Merris	01/08/1915	27/08/1915
War Diary	Nouveau Monde	28/08/1915	31/08/1915
Diagram etc	20th Division Circuit Diagram 31/8/15		
Diagram etc	20th Division Route Diagram		
Map	Maps		
Diagram etc	Merris		
Diagram etc	20th Lynde Co Rout Diagram Merris		
Diagram etc	Circuit Diagram Y T		
Heading	20th Division 20th Divl Signal Coy Vol 3 Sep 1 15		
Heading	War Diary For Sept 1915		
War Diary	Nouveau Monde	01/09/1915	30/09/1915
Diagram etc	20th Division Route Diagram September 1915		
Diagram etc	20th Division (YT) Circuit Diagram-12 Noon		
Diagram etc	20th Division (YT) Circuit Diagram-Brigades Moved To ARC From 3rd Corps		
Diagram etc	20th Division (YT) Circuit Diagram		
Heading	20th Division 20th Divl Signal Coy RE Vol 4 Oct 15		
Heading	War Diary of O C 20th Divisional Signal Co RE From Oct 1st & Oct 31st 1915 F.J.M Shalta		
War Diary	Nouveau Monde	01/10/1915	31/10/1915
Heading	20th Divl Signal Coy Vol 5 Nov 15		
Heading	War Diary For Nov 1915 of O C 20th Divisional Signal Co RE F J M Shalta		

War Diary	Nouveau Monde G 26.d.3.0	01/11/1915	16/11/1915
War Diary	Nouveau Monde	17/11/1915	23/11/1915
War Diary	Sailly	24/11/1915	30/11/1915
Diagram etc	20th Divisional (YT) Circuit Diagram		
Diagram etc	20th Divisional (YT) Circuit Diagram-29th Novr 1915. Appendix II		
Diagram etc	20th Divisional (YT) Circuit Diagram-30th November 1915. Appendix III		
Diagram etc	20th Signal Co R.E Nov 30th 1915 Circuit Diagram		
Heading	20th Signal Coy. Vol 6		
Heading	War Diary of 20th Divisional Signal Co RE For Dec 1915		
War Diary	Sailly G.32.b.2.9 Sheet 36	01/12/1915	31/12/1915
Diagram etc	Circuit Diagram XX Div		
Diagram etc	YT Indoor Wiring Diagram		
Diagram etc	YT Circuit Diagram 20th Dec 1915		
Heading	On His Majesty's Service.		
Heading	20th Divl. Signals Vol 7		
War Diary	Sailly G 32.b.2.9 Sheet 36	01/01/1916	12/01/1916
War Diary	Blaringhem B 23.a.8.9	13/01/1916	21/01/1916
War Diary	Oxelare O.17.b.3.5	22/01/1916	31/01/1916
Heading	War Diary of O C 20th Div Signal Co RE For Jan 1916		
Heading	War Diary of O C 20th Divisional Signal Co RE February 1916		
War Diary	Oxelaere O 17.b 3.5 Sheet 27	01/02/1916	03/02/1916
War Diary	Esquelbecq C8 c.2.8 Sheet 27	04/02/1916	14/02/1916
War Diary	Near Poperinghe A22.d 7.4 Sheet 28	15/02/1916	28/02/1916
Diagram etc	20th Division CCT Diagram 16 Feb. 1916		
Map	Maps		
Diagram etc	A B		
Map	Maps		
Heading	War Diary of OC 20th Divisional Signal Co RE For March 1-31 1916		
War Diary	A 22 d 7.4 Sheet 28	01/03/1916	11/03/1916
War Diary	A 22 d 7.4	12/03/1916	31/03/1916
Miscellaneous	D A G Base	03/06/1916	03/06/1916
War Diary	A 22.d.7.4	01/04/1916	13/04/1916
War Diary	A 22.d.7.4 Sheet 28	14/04/1916	18/04/1916
War Diary	C 8 c 2.8 Sheet 27	19/04/1916	28/04/1916
War Diary	C 8 c 2.8	29/04/1916	30/04/1916
Heading	War Diary of O C 20 Div Signal Co R C For Month Of April 1916		
Heading	War Diary of OC 20 Div Signal Co RE For Period May 1-31 1916		
War Diary	C 8 c 2.8 Sheet 27	01/05/1916	20/05/1916
War Diary	Sheet 28 G1 d 9.5.5	20/05/1916	27/05/1916
War Diary	Sheet 28 G1 d 9.5.5 (Poperinghe Town Hall)	28/05/1916	31/05/1916
Diagram etc	Y. T. Circuit Diagram 17/5/16		
War Diary	Sheet 28 G1.d.9.5.5 Poperinghe Town Hall	01/06/1916	12/06/1916
War Diary	Sheet 28 G1.d.9.5.5	13/06/1916	15/06/1916
War Diary	A 30 d 0.0	15/06/1916	20/06/1916
War Diary	G1.d.95.5	21/06/1916	30/06/1916
Heading	War Diary For 20th Div Signal Coy From June 1st To 30th 1916		
Diagram etc	Circuit Diagram		

Type	Description	From	To
Heading	20th Divisional Engineers 20th Divisional Signal Company R.E. July 1916		
War Diary	Sheet 28 G1.d.9.5.5 Poperinghe Town Hall	01/07/1916	13/07/1916
War Diary	A 25.d.1.6	14/07/1916	19/07/1916
War Diary	S 14.c.3.6 Sheet 28	20/07/1916	21/07/1916
War Diary	S 14.c.3.6 Bailleul Sheet 28	22/07/1916	24/07/1916
War Diary	Doullens Sheet 57d A16	25/07/1916	25/07/1916
War Diary	Bus Les Artois J 25 A Sheet 57D	26/07/1916	28/07/1916
War Diary	Covin J 1 d 4 8 Sheet 57 D	29/07/1916	29/07/1916
Heading	20th Divisional Engineers 20th Divisional Signal Company R.E. August 1916		
Heading	War Diary of O C 20th Divisional Signal Coy RE From 29.7.16 To 30.8.16		
War Diary	Covin J1.b.4.0 Sheet 57D	29/07/1916	14/08/1916
War Diary	Beauval Sheet 57D	15/08/1916	19/08/1916
War Diary	Treux J5.b.6.5	20/08/1916	21/08/1916
War Diary	F 26 d Sheet 57D	22/08/1916	22/08/1916
War Diary	Minden Post F18 C 5.3	23/08/1916	30/08/1916
Diagram etc	Route Diagram XXth Division Aug 1916		
Heading	20th Divisional Engineers 20th Divisional Signal Company RE September 1916		
Heading	War Diary of O C 20 Divl Signal Co RE For Period 31.8.16-28.9.16		
War Diary	Minden Post F18.c.5.3 Albert Sheet	31/08/1916	04/09/1916
War Diary	Minden Post F18.c.5.3 Albert Sheet Corbie	05/09/1916	10/09/1916
War Diary	Forked Tree F 26 c (albert Map)	11/09/1916	16/09/1916
War Diary	Minden Post F18.c.5.3	17/09/1916	17/09/1916
War Diary	Minden Post & Bernafay Wood	18/09/1916	20/09/1916
War Diary	Forked Tree F 26 c (albert) Treux J 5 b (62D)	21/09/1916	26/09/1916
War Diary	Aud 4.2 (Sheet Albert) Forkedtree	27/09/1916	28/09/1916
Heading	20th Divisional Engineers		
Heading	20th Divisional Engineers 20th Divisional Signal Company R.E. October 1916		
Heading	20th Divn Signal Company Vol 16		
War Diary	Forked Tree Camp F26 c 9 1 Bernafay Wood S 26 b 5.6	29/09/1916	07/10/1916
War Diary	Bernafay Wood S 26 b 5.6	08/10/1916	10/10/1916
War Diary	Treux	11/10/1916	15/10/1916
War Diary	Corbie	16/10/1916	18/10/1916
War Diary	Vignacourt	19/10/1916	20/10/1916
War Diary	Belloy-Sur-Somme	21/10/1916	30/10/1916
Heading	War Diary of O C 20 Div Signal Co RE Sep 29 1916-Oct 30 1916		
Heading	20th Divisional Engineers 20th Divisional Signal Company R.E. November 1916		
War Diary	Belloy Sur Somme	31/10/1916	31/10/1916
War Diary	Cavillon	01/11/1916	13/11/1916
War Diary	Corbie	14/11/1916	28/11/1916
Heading	20th Divisional Engineers 20th Divisional Signal Company R E. December 1916		
War Diary	Corbie	29/11/1916	11/12/1916
War Diary	A 4 d 4.8 Sheet Albert	12/12/1916	24/12/1916
War Diary	Corbie	25/12/1916	30/12/1916
Diagram etc	24 Left Group		
Diagram etc	Circuit Diagram 29 Signal Co Nov 23rd 1916		
Diagram etc	Route Diagram 29th Signal Co R.E. (T) 25.11.16		

Heading	War Diary of the 20th Divisional Signal Company January 1917 Vol 19		
War Diary	Corbie	31/12/1916	03/01/1917
War Diary	Arrow Head Copse S 30d 3.8 (albert Sheet)	04/01/1917	27/01/1917
War Diary	Heilly	28/01/1917	08/02/1917
War Diary	Briqueterie A 4 d 8 4	09/02/1917	14/02/1917
War Diary	Briqueterie A 4 d 4 2 (Sheet Albert)	15/02/1917	17/03/1917
War Diary	Guillemont T25 a 5.8	18/03/1917	30/03/1917
Diagram etc	Route Diagram 20th Div March 1917		
War Diary	Guillemont T25 a 5.8 Sheet 57c	31/03/1917	01/04/1917
War Diary	Rocquigny 0 27 a 7.5 Sheet 57c	02/04/1917	24/04/1917
War Diary	Little Wood Ytres P 26 b 2.3 Sheet 57c	25/04/1917	30/04/1917
War Diary	Ytres Little Wood P 26. b.2.3. Sheet 57 C	01/05/1917	23/05/1917
War Diary	H 15 c 3.6 Sheet 57c	24/05/1917	30/05/1917
Diagram etc	Local Lines of Diamond Bde Signal Offices		
Diagram etc	20th Division Circuit Diagram May 19th 1917		
War Diary	The Monument H 15 c 3.6 Sheet 57c	31/05/1917	28/06/1917
War Diary	Bernaville	29/06/1917	30/06/1917
War Diary	Domart	01/07/1917	20/07/1917
War Diary	Proven	21/07/1917	05/08/1917
War Diary	Dragon Camp	06/08/1917	14/08/1917
War Diary	Elverdinghe	15/08/1917	18/08/1917
War Diary	Proven	19/08/1917	10/09/1917
War Diary	Welsh Farm Elverdinghe	11/09/1917	19/09/1917
War Diary	Welsh Fme	20/09/1917	30/09/1917
War Diary	Proven	01/10/1917	02/10/1917
War Diary	Haplincourt	03/10/1917	03/10/1917
War Diary	Peronne	04/10/1917	09/10/1917
War Diary	Sorel-Le-Grand	10/10/1917	18/11/1917
War Diary	N Heudecourt	19/11/1917	19/11/1917
War Diary	Villers Pluich	20/11/1917	30/11/1917
War Diary	B Dug-Out Queens Cross	01/12/1917	02/12/1917
War Diary	Sorel-Le-Grand	03/12/1917	03/12/1917
War Diary	Biazieux	04/12/1917	05/12/1917
War Diary	Hucqueliers	06/12/1917	11/12/1917
War Diary	Blaringhem	12/12/1917	06/01/1918
War Diary	Westoutre	07/01/1918	16/02/1918
War Diary	Blaringhem	17/02/1918	21/02/1918
War Diary	On The Road	22/02/1918	22/02/1918
War Diary	Ercheu	23/02/1918	27/02/1918
Heading	20th Divisional Engineers 20th Divisional Signal Company R.E. March 1918		
War Diary	Ercheu	28/02/1918	20/03/1918
War Diary	Ercheu And Ham	21/03/1918	21/03/1918
War Diary	Ham	22/03/1918	22/03/1918
War Diary	Nesle	23/03/1918	24/03/1918
War Diary	Rethonvillers And Carrepuis	25/03/1918	25/03/1918
War Diary	Roye And Le Quesnel	26/03/1918	26/03/1918
War Diary	Le Quesnel	27/03/1918	27/03/1918
War Diary	Domart	27/03/1918	31/03/1918
War Diary	Cross Roads Boves-Gentilles And Boves	01/04/1918	01/04/1918
War Diary	Namps Au Mont	02/04/1918	02/04/1918
War Diary	Namps Au Mont Quevauvillers	03/04/1918	03/04/1918
War Diary	Quevauvillers	04/04/1918	10/04/1918
War Diary	Huppy Gamaches	11/04/1918	11/04/1918
War Diary	Gamaches	12/04/1918	17/04/1918

War Diary	Villers Chatel	18/04/1918	01/05/1918
War Diary	Villers Chatel Villers Au Bois	02/05/1918	02/05/1918
War Diary	Villers Au Bois	03/05/1918	06/05/1918
War Diary	Villers Au Bois Chateau De La Haie	07/05/1918	07/05/1918
War Diary	Chateau De La Haie	07/05/1918	05/10/1918
War Diary	Villers Chatel	06/10/1918	30/10/1918
War Diary	Cambrai	31/10/1918	02/11/1918
War Diary	Avesnes-Lez-Aubert	03/11/1918	05/11/1918
War Diary	Avesnes-Lez-Aubert Vendegies	06/11/1918	06/11/1918
War Diary	Vendegies	07/11/1918	07/11/1918
War Diary	Vendegies Wagnies-Le-Grand	08/11/1918	08/11/1918
War Diary	Wagnies Le-Grand Bavay	09/11/1918	09/11/1918
War Diary	Bavay	10/11/1918	10/11/1918
War Diary	Bavay Feignies	11/11/1918	11/11/1918
War Diary	Feignies	12/11/1918	22/11/1918
War Diary	Wagnies-Le-Grand	23/11/1918	25/11/1918
War Diary	Rieux	26/11/1918	27/11/1918
War Diary	Cambrai	28/11/1918	31/11/1918
War Diary	Cambrai Pas	01/12/1918	01/12/1918
War Diary	Pas	02/12/1918	27/02/1919
War Diary	Pas-En-Artois	28/02/1919	29/04/1919
Miscellaneous	History of 77th Bn.		
Miscellaneous			

21081/1

20TH DIVISION
DIVL ENGINEERS

20TH DIVL SIGNAL COY
JLY 1915 - APL 1919.

20th DIVISIONAL SIGNAL COY. - R.E.

The 20th. Divisional Signal Coy. was first formed at CHATHAM on October 14th. 1914. A nucleus of 75 men under Capt. F.J.M. STRATTON, R.E. 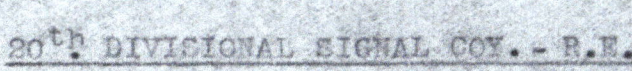 moved to Aldershot on October 19th., where they remained under canvas for several weeks. 2nd. Lt. P.W. CLARK and 2nd. Lt. F.A. SCLATER joined on October 25th. For lack of any technical gear, even arms, training at first was limited to squad drill, physical training, marching and semaphore, but instruments for giving instruction in 'morse' operating were quickly improvised and, contrary to the then existing orders, instruction in morse operating was soon commenced.

A few horses arrived about the 2nd. week in November (but no harness) and instruction in riding and horse-mastership was also commenced.

ALDERSHOT.

About the middle of November the Company, now about 120 strong, moved with the 20th. Divisional R.E., under Col. KENYON, to the married quarters at the Barracks at WOKING. In gradually growing quantities technical equipment such as flags, telephone gear, etc. began to arrive and training began to extend on more general lines. 2nd. Lts. F.P. REYNOLDS and W.R.N. TINGEY joined the Company at the end of November and by the middle of December it became possible to sort the Company out into Sections of which it was to be composed. 2nd. Lts. A.C.D. HANNEN and A.G. BRACE joined the Company in

-1-

December and January respectively and the Company was complete in officers and nearly so in men. The officers now took command of their respective sections, which they retained until the Company proceeded to France.

SHACKLEFORD.

In January, 1915, the Company moved to SHACKLEFORD, near GODALMING, where it was billeted for several weeks, one Bde. Section being at Peperharow, Lord Midleton's seat. Although the Company was now split up for the first time, the distances were not great and training could and did continue to be organized within the Company as a whole, though the Section Commanders were now beginning to take full charge of their section training. Equipment was still limited, one set of pack sadlery for cable work having to be shared by the three Brigade Sections, but the condition of the men as regards both equipment and clothing was steadily improving, as also was their knowledge of their work and their sense of the meaning of military discipline. A certain number of fire arms were now available for drill.

INSPECTION BY THE KING.

While the Company was at Shackleford and Peperharow the King and Queen inspected the Division at work. The Signal Company was inspected while carrying out a cable scheme between dug-outs which were made in the grounds of Peperharow Park! After a delightful month at Peperharow the Company moved into a comparatively unfinished camp at Witley. Here the first cable wagon an improvised one bequeathed by the 14th. Div. Signal

Division stayed whilst units carried out preliminary tours of duty in the line.

LAVENTIE.

Sept. 1915.

The Division took over the line in the Laventie sector in August, the Divisional Signal Office being in a cellar at the Chateau at NOUVEAU MONDE. The sector was a quiet one and no difficulty in maintaining communication was found. The only incident of note during this first tour of duty in the line was in the part played by the Right Bde. (60th.) of the Division in the fighting of Sept. 25th.

In the light of later experiences this was interesting. Adv. Bde. H.Q. was within 300 yds. of the front line and single trench cables were maintained without great difficulty up to the front line during the Battle. Behind Bde. H.Q. the lines were never once cut by shell fire and the shell fire was so local that no great difficulty was experienced forward of Bdes.

November 1915.

The first sideslip took place in November 1915 when the Division relieved the 8th. Div. at SAILLY-SUR-LA-LYS, handing over its previous sector to the Guards Division. Here again communications were easy and life on the whole uneventful for the Signal Company. Early in January 1916 the Division was relieved by the 8th. Division and withdrew to rest at BLARINGHEM.

Coy. now properly fitted out - was received and shortly afterwards proper cable wagons came to hand. The motor cyclists - of whom some had provided their own machines hitherto - also received machines and generally the Company's equipment began to near completion.

SALISBURY.
April 1915.

A further very useful experience came early in April in the form of a three days' march from Witley to Salisbury Plain. This was effected without a single member of the Company falling out. Here at Larkhill the later stages of training were completed, Bde. Sections working with their Bde. Staffs on Brigade and Divisional training scheme every week. Amongst the most valuable work done at this stage was the starting and organizing of signal offices at Divisional and Bde. Headquarters. This was done for the two months before the Company went overseas and most of the mistakes and difficulties arising from inexperience were overcome in that time.

The training of the Company was inspected for several weeks by Capt. C.H. PRICKETT, D.S.O., R.E. and by Capt. R.W. DAMMERS, Notts and Derby Regiment. As the time for proceeding overseas drew near a succession of inspections and reviews took place, culminating in a review of the whole Division by the King.

July 1915.

On July 20th. 1915 the Division embarked for France. The journey to LUMBRES (via Southampton and Havre) was uneventful as far as the Signal Company was concerned as also the further journey to MERRIS. Here the

THE SALIENT in February 1916.

About the end of January the Div. was transferred from the 1st. Army to 2nd. Army moving first to OXELAERE and then to ESQUELBECQ and on February 14th. took over the left-hand Sector of the British Line in the Ypres salient from the 14th. Division. It was soon evident that the Company was in for a very different type of warfare to that which it had so far encountered. The left Bde. (60th.) was attacked the very night of relief and the position remained very uncomfortable for a considerable time. Shallow buried cables inherited in the back areas and open trench cables forward of Brigades were all continually being cut and the work of the Signal Coy. rapidly became both heavy and dangerous. The forward communication trenches were so overlooked by the enemy from PILKEM Ridge that lines once broken could not be mended in daytime. As most of the subsidiary methods of communication since brought into practice were not then available, the Division and Brigade had perforce to be content with a lower standard of communication than in the quiet Laventie sector - an excellent preparation for all concerned for the days of active fighting to follow.

June 1916.

Two spells of serious fighting occurred while the Division was in the YPRES Sector, one in February when the Division was taking over the line and the second in June, when the Canadians on their right were heavily attacked and forced back from HOOGE and SANCTUARY WOOD. On this occasion the Canadian communications were badly smashed west of YPRES. By this time, however, the Division had some deep buried cables running up into YPRES and thro' the sewers of the town. Our lines held and the communications for two Canadian Brigades to the rear were all maintained for several days thro' our right Brigade (the 60th.)

Whilst in this sector the Division had its first experience of successful raids - a further useful experience.

Several changes of officers occurred whilst the Division was in the YPRES Salient, February to July, 1916. Capt. Ransford joined as 2nd. in Command, S.P.W. Clarke proceeding to England, Lt. F.A. Sclater joined the 8th. Corps Signal Company and 2nd. Lts. ROTHBATH, FRAMPTON and MALLETT were successively in charge of the 59th. Infy. Bde. Section. Lt. E.P. REYNOLDS was wounded and evacuated to England and was succeeded by 2nd. Lt. O.S. WEBB at the 61st. Bde. Section.

July 1916.

The Division pulled out of the line early in July 1916. The 60th. Bde. was immediately sent down to take over part of the line at FLEURBAIX and the rest of the Division, after a short interval, was sent to relieve the 24th. Division at BAILLEUL. The relief was hardly complete before the Division, now once more complete (the 60th. having rejoined after holding the flank of the Australians in their unsuccessful attack on AUBERS Ridge), was relieved by the 36th. and moved

down to the SOMME relieving the 38th. Division at
COUIN. Here two weeks' preparation for a coming
attack was carried out, the Signal Company being
largely occupied in an attempt to sort out a complex
system of buried cables left by the VIII Corps after
their unsuccessful attack on SERRE AND GOMMECOURT. Once
again the Division moved via BEAVAL, TREUX and Forked
Tree Camp (North of BRAY) to MINDEN POST on the ALBERT-
PERONNE road, where it relieved the 24th. Division and
prepared to carry out an attack on GUILLEMONT - a hard
position which had already been unsuccessfully attacked
many times.

        Continuous bad weather, trenches without cover
or dug-outs and much gas all combined to make the
conditions difficult. The attack was postponed again

GUILLEMONT. and again and in the end a Bde. of the 16th. Division
Sept. 3, 1916. had to be called upon to help the Division in the
Battle. The attack was launched on Sept. 3rd. and
was quite successful; communications held up very
well, although they had been giving a great deal of
trouble and had been very uncertain for some days
previously. In fact, this was one of the very few
occasions during the 1916 Somme battle where ground
communications beat the air for both speed and
accuracy.

        The Division was relieved after the attack but
was soon back in the line, relieving the Guards
Division at BERNAFAY Wood for 3 days - another short

rest then to the line again this time at BRIQUETERIE relieving the 5th. Division but the next night the French relieved the division and on the following night the Division again relieved the Guards at BERNAFAY wood. This continued change of Headquarters meant necessarily very hard work for all the personnel of the signal service under very difficult conditions - not rendered easier by continued rain and appalling mud.

GUEUDECOURT.   The final battle of the Somme fighting for the Division was the attack on GUEUDECOURT, here again good communication both up to and beyond Bde. H.Q. were maintained throughout the battle, although half an hour before zero half a mile of route on which dependence had been placed was carried away by a railway train.

After this battle the division retired to refit and train the many reinforcements required to complete units depleted in a month's continuous though successful fighting.

Captain Ransford left the Company for a tour of duty as instructor in England and Lt. Brace became 2nd.-in-Command, Lt. CARNEGIE taking over the 60th. Bde. Signal Section.

Little is to be said about the next tour of duty in the line at Bernafay wood, Dec. 1916, and at Arrow Head Copse in January, and again in February at BRIQUETERIE.

MORVAL-ROCQUIGNY Route.

A buried cable system existed most of the way to Brigades constructed during the last two tours of duty in the line to which the Division had contributed its share, and which was still being continued to SAILLEY-SAILLISEL when the German retirement of the spring of 1917 commenced, leading temporally to a more open type of warfare. In the very earliest stages of the advance the Signal Company brought off somewhat of a "tour de force" in building a 12-wire open route across a terrible patch of muddy crater-logged country between MORVAL and ROCQUIGNY; with this behind and decent country in front for cable waggons communication became for a time easier than at any previous stage since the Division left the FLEURBAIX sector in the previous year. For the first time since landing in France cable wagons were used whilst in the line. The Division moved first to GUILLIMONT then to a point near SAILLY SAILLISEL and as soon as the roads were fit for transport to ROCQUIGNY and later to YTRES. Signals generally required an advanced headqurters between Division and Brigades.

One battle (the attack on ROUALCOURT) was for the Signal Company an exact replica of the typical field day at home. Lines to a report centre were thro' a short time before the General and Staff arrived. Lines kept thro' during the battle, a string of messages describing the course of operations were received, the battle was won, the staff returned to their headquarters, and the Signal Office closed down. There was an air of unreality about the whole performance away behind the battle when compared with the more fierce conditions of the fighting the previous year.

YPRES AND HAVRINCOURT. May, 1917.

A pleasant month was spent at YPRES Wood with one Brigade in HAVRINCOURT Wood and one in GOUZEAUCOURT Wood.

2nd. Lt. Carnegie left for a Tank Bde. Signal Section 2nd. Lt. Ledingham taking over the 60th. Infy. Bde. Section from him.

A considerable addition to the direct responsibility of the Company occurred at this time, the R.F.A. Bde. Signal Sections previously administered by the Artillery coming under Div. Signals. The R.F.A. personnel being transferred to R.E. At the same time, these sub-sections were considerably increased in size and many N.C.O's. & men from the Div. Coy. were posted to them, as the reinforcements who arrived for this purpose were excellent material but almost entirely untrained.

LAGNICOURT. June, 1917.

The Division was relieved by the 42nd. Div. and moved north to relieve the 5th. Australian Division in the LAGNICOURT sector. Here things were quietening down, though the left of the line was close to BULLECOURT which was still in an unsettled condition after much heavy fighting.

It was here that the Signal Coy. lost its first O.C., Major Stratton leaving on June 22nd. to proceed to the 19th. Corps. He was succeeded by Captain A.G. Brace and Lt. E.P. Reynolds again joined the Coy. and became second-in-command.

<u>Wireless Sections become part of Div. Signal Coy.</u>

Another material addition to the Div. Signal Company occurred here, the Wireless Section, previously attached from Corps Signal Coy. as occasion demanded, was now included in the establishment of the Div. Signal Coy.

The Division was relieved at the end of June, 1917, by the 62nd. Div. and proceeded for a month's rest and training at DOMART before going north to take their share in the battle at YPRES in the summer 1917.

<u>YPRES, 1917.</u>

When the Division left the Salient exactly a year before the forward area in the same sector could only be approached at night or in dusk of dawn. Now after the greatest difficulty our guns, in spite of the initial disadvantage of position, every movement being visible from Pilkem had gained the mastery and the enemy's lines were kept under such a continuous fire that local retaliation was beyond him; so movement and work was possible by day.

Great work had been done on Buries by 14th. Corps who had been preparing for months, and up to "Cable heads" a good cable system was nearly completed. The 38th. Division were to attack and the 20th. were to pass thro' them after about 2 days' fighting, when it was expected that the line would be well beyond LANGEMARCK, open fighting was expected to follow.

The attack started well, the ridge and PILKEM were taken, but the advance stopped approximately on line just short of the STEENBEC stream. After weeks of fine dry weather the day of the attack and for days following it poured with rain, the shell-torn ground became impassable and ground conditions were rapidly as bad as on the Somme the year before. Such was the position when the Division took over with the object first of making good the line of the STEENBEC and then of attacking LANGEMARCK. The Company had learnt a lot from the 38th. Division and had all their experience to help them in laying their signal plans. Buried cable stopped at the old front line whence ground lines were laid as fast as they were blown to pieces. It was impossible to attempt to bury up to the front line both from the point of view of labour and material, but two short buries were dug each about half-a-mile long over the PILKEM ridge, where the heaviest shelling took place, one route in each Brigade front and so some protection was attempted over the worst shelled area. Night work of course and a most unpleasant job to tackle, working against time, on an area continually shelled and soaked in gas the working parties and the officers and men superintending did splendid work. Both jobs were successfully done and proved invaluable in the battle.

The communication scheme for this attack was necessarily the most complex that the Coy. had yet tackled. An officer on the Canal Bank (Lt. J. Hadden) had control of all the lines in the forward area and was in a position to put thro' alternative routes as necessity arose, breakdown parties were stationed with him (at "A" dugout) and also at two points further forward as well as at the two Brigade Battle Headquarters. Forward of the attacking brigades, in each case one main forward route was laid to ~~Bathes~~ Battalions and their continuation beyond the front line planned on settled routes. These were supplemented by visual, wireless and amplifiers to function on any section in the event of lines failing.

The scheme worked well practically uninterrupted, touch by wire was maintained to ~~Bathes~~ Battalions and Artillery O.P.'S. and thus in the first battle under 1917 conditions all went well with Signals.

After a few days' rest at PROVEN the division again relieved the 38th., objectives this time EAGLE TRENCH. The conditions were much the same as before, Div. H.Q. near ELVERDINGHE (at Welsh farm) Bdes. at STRAY FARM and ADELPHI. The 38th. Div. had buried lines from AU-BON-GITE, just over the Steenbec, to ALOUETTE Farm. But these were not connected back to STRAY FARM. This mile of bury over must sodden and difficult ground had to be tackled and was successfully accomplished before the attack.

Lt. Ledingham was out of action sick and Lt. Hadden took over the 60th. Bde. Section for the battle, Lt. Dunlop from 14th. Corp Signals taking charge of the important work at "A" dugout. Much the same procedure as in the previous attack was followed. But distances were longer and difficulties correspondingly increased. Communication was however uninterrupted and some idea of the pressure of signal work can be judged from the fact that in addition to continual telephone calls one thousand and ten telegrams were dealt with at the Div. H.Q. Signal Office on zero day alone, a record for the day of a battle when traffic is strictly curtailed to urgent operation messages.

Unlike the Somme in the previous year at YPRES the Division's experiences were not so long drawn out, after the second attack the 20th. were withdrawn from the line. Whilst it lasted the work for all ranks had been very severe and everyone was kept continuously at the highest pressure.

CAMBRAI, 1917. From YPRES the Division went south to peace it was thought, with the possibility even of a quiet winter, in practice they were quickly involved in one of the most dramatic adventures of the War. The Company took over the most complete system of communications in admirable order from the 40th. Division and settled down to enjoy them. But it was soon clear that "something was doing". A number of strange C.R.E's floating round and Army Commanders taking an unnatural interest in the front line and beyond. It was quickly known at first to those immediately concerned that preparations were to be made for a secret attack on a large scale. The present Divisional front to be divided between three Divisions, the 20th. holding the centre with a further Division in close reserve - artillery to match and a very large number of tanks. The task of providing communication for this was enormous and fell almost entirely on the 20th. who were however given gallant assistance by an Army Area detachment under Lt. HALSAL and also later by a section from the 29th. Division Signal Company. The time for preparation was limited to two weeks and all movement restricted as secrecy was all-essential. To bury cable was out of the question, it would be patently obvious from the air and moreover at least two months and battalions of labour would be required to construct it.

One buried cable route did exist, about $1\frac{1}{4}$ miles long, running from vicinity of QUEENS CROSS to the railway.

Half a mile south of VILLERS-PLUICH this fortunately came in the Divisional Battle Area and was invaluable, being indeed the backbone of the signal scheme. At the forward end of this bury a good dug-out existed named again (in memory of YPRES), "A" dugout; here a Divisional test station was planned and here, too, the working party lived during their two weeks' Herculean task of laying 137 miles of armoured cable in the trenches up to the Front line where two "cable heads" were to be constructed and to the various artillery positions. Lines for Cavalry, lines for Tanks, for heavy artillery and innumerable Brigades of R.F.A., for our own infantry and for the supporting 29th. Division, all were laid slowly and surely working to an iron-cast programme which could allow of no expansion in time. Testing, a slow and tedious process, was done at night after a full day's work. Truly the section at "A" dugout, under Lieut. Hadden, beat every record for hard and skilful work and looking back they really seem to have accomplished the impossible.

Meantime normal signal working continued but with an ever increasing volume of traffic; the normal five to seven hundred messages a day grew until over two thousand passed through the Divisional Headquarters Office at SOREL in one day. The Company was in fact doing the work of the 4 divisions concerned.

At length time was up. Divisional Headquarters moved to HEUDECOURT on "Y"day; at 12 midnight all Battle positions had been taken up and it was quickly reported from all stations "signals correct". The Division was working on the entirely new system built in 2 weeks and every pair was through!

The success of the attack next morning will be reported elsewhere; in the afternoon Divisional Headquarters was able to move to VILLERS-PLUICH. Communication now became most difficult. Forward of the old front line tanks simply cleaned up cables as quickly as they were laid and touch with the leading Brigade now 5 miles beyond the old front line seemed rather hopeless. As soon as possible ground lines were replaced by poled cables, one route to each Brigade, and the signal position again became staple; so ended a most successful venture.

<u>THE GERMAN COUNTER-OFFENSIVE, Nov.30th. 1917.</u>

The 20th. Division was still at VILLERS-PLUICH Brigade Headquarters in the Hindenburg support system about four miles ahead. The two main trunk routes of Poled cable gave direct communication to each brigade and Artillery in line - laterals between them providing alternatives in event of the main route failing. A manned test point was established on each route and the old "cable heads" of the attack were still maintained and linemen posted there. One point in the original preparations should be explained as it shortly became of supreme importance.

From HEUDECOURT to the beginning of the "Buried Cable" Corps Signals were responsible for laying and maintaining a poled multicorps cable. Both because it was felt that this was not entirely reliable, and also because if broken it would take days to mend; an alternative emergency route was laid by the Divisional Signal Company (2 pairs armoured on the ground) this took a circular route to avoid traffic and passed through the outskirts of GOUZEAUCOURT.

This was the position and general signal situation on November 29th. All night on the 29th. there was heavy firing and constant trouble with the overground lines. At dawn 30th. a heavy bombardment opened on the whole front. Quickly the forward land lines were cut one after another. The wireless station at Divisional Headquarters was knocked out by a direct hit almost at the outset - maintaining overground lines for the time being was out of the question. Messages by pigeon and runner gave confused and alarming reports - Germans were reported in VILLERS-GUISLAIN - GONNELIEU - and in GOUZEAUCOURT where the 29th. Divisional Headquarters was overrun. This was all very cheerful considering GOUZEAUCOURT was well behind; in fact between advanced and rear Divisional Headquarters at HEUDECOURT. It was now that the emergency lines back saved the situation. Of course the open routes and the Corps "multi" were as dead as if they had never been laid. But communication with Corps was maintained through these emergency lines, which actually passed into German hands and out again, for two most vitally important days. This communication not only served to   the 20th. Division but through them for the 6th., 12th. and 29th. Divisions, all of whose Corps communication was hopelessly broken. There is little doubt that but for these lines no news would have got back in time to arrange that timely help from the Guards Division which later in the day saved the most critical situation.

During the morning of the 30th. the position remained very obscure. Brigade Headquarters dropped back and lines were run to their new positions as quickly as possible. At about 11.00 the Company was ordered to send all transport and surplus signal personnel back to the vicinity of Queen's Cross and there to prepare a new Headquarters office as the Divisional Commander expected to move his Headquarters from Villers-Pluich at any moment. Capt. Reynolds with most of the signal office personnel and all the transport moved off. It was some hours before further news of them was heard. On arrival at Queen's Cross they were rather taken aback to find themselves under machine gun fire. Capt. Reynolds got his party into trenches round Queen's Cross "strong point" and awaited developments, the transport taking cover in the sunken road near by. Germans could be plainly seen in Gouzeaucourt not much over a mile distant - no other troops anywhere in sight.

Then one of the grandest incidents of the War occurred - advancing from Gouzeaucourt Wood - in open order as on parade. - the Irish Guards passed through the Signal detachment and in perfect formation without a check went straight for the village, cleared it of the enemy and advanced beyond.

That evening at midnight advanced; Division Headquarters moved to a sunken road near Queen's Cross. The situation was still bad, but clearer. The two Brigades in line now had their Headquarters at Villers-Pluich and lines to them via "A" dugout had to be maintained. As the Germans got up their guns this proved to be an ever increasingly difficult task. The parties at "A" and at Villers-Pluich under Lt. C.K. Moore did most splendidly, especially when it is remembered that every officer and man for two days and nights had been working "all out".

This was the position when the 20th. was relieved by the 61st. Division brought up in haste from rest near Arras. It was a sadly reduced Division who eventually drew out of the line.

During the two days of the attack, Nov. 30th. and Dec. 1st., maintenance of the open routes from Villers-Pluich called for the greatest gallantry. Corpl.THOMPSON, the N.C.O. in charge of the detachment at left cable head, bore some of the heaviest part of this work with the small number of men at his station. Not once or twice, but continually, shells blew great gaps in his lines. (At one time 3 bays (150 feet) of poled cable was set ablaze with phosphorus shell). He mended and relaid continuously but the task seemed really beyond hope. Somehow it was done - Corpl. Thompson organized his men in reliefs but went out himself with them each and every time - nothing but his courage and most splendid example made this task possible. The Military Medal subsequently awarded for this action was indeed most thoroughly deserved.

After some weeks' rest and refitting at BLARINGHEM the Division were back again in the Salient, rather different to their hopes on leaving it only so few months before.

2nd. Lt. R.L. Holmes joined the Coy at this point and Lt. Wenham took command of the 60th. Brigade Section in place of Lt. Ledingham who was wounded.

An ordinary normal winter in the Salient followed ordinary but rather complicated buried lines, very long. Brigades being nearly 12 miles from Divisional Headquarters at WESTOUTRE.

Capt. Reynolds left here to take command of the 37th. Division Signal Coy. and Capt. H.E.L.PORTER joined as Second-in-Command in his place.

Early in February 1918 the Division moved south, being relieved by the 37th. Divisoon -"Chosen" for the 5th.Army. What followed will be remembered in every detail by all who took part.

At ERCHEUX the Division was in G.H.Q. reserve (in 18th. Corps). Talk of the coming German offensive was continuous and plans for meeting every possible situation were arranged. All these different schemes entailed numerous signal preparations. The form the attack eventually took was one for which a pre-arranged signal scheme had been the most possible and this had been thoroughly arranged.

The battle opened on the morning of March 21st. and the Division moved to H.Q. in HAM. that afternoon. Next day it was clear that it would be necessary to fall back - arrangements were quickly made to connect the two Bdes, (the 3rd. (61st.) had been despatched to assist the 36th. Division to whom they were attached for some time), and Corps to EPPEVILLE, a central advanced Div. Exchange being cited across the Canal in an isolated farm building. This was all successfully accomplished in the afternoon of the 22nd. and the test station was manned by Lt. Badden and 3 linemen.

Things moved more speedily than was anticipated and it happened that neither Brigade went to the positions expected but the scheme was fortunately adaptable and they "came on" all right. From this second day until the end of the Divisions share in the action, 10 days ahead, cable carts, teams and detachments worked continuously, horses being in some cases "hooked in" for days on end.

Division moved to EPPEVILLE at 9.30 p.m. on 22nd. as soon as Bdes. were on the move HAM. office closed, the Signal Lorry was easily the last M.T. to cross HAM. Bridge. During the night orders came for all troops to be clear of the Canal before dawn and the first of many occasions when the question how long to leave an outstation "out" had to be settled. Lt. Hadden rang through about 11.0 p.m. with the pointed report that he alone of his party could swim. The 60th. Bde. Wireless Detachment got astray about this time, they were established at the position where the Bde. H.Q. was to have gone but didn't - when eventually tracked down they were found comfortably billeted! - awaiting the Bde. They only got away by minutes. At this time Hun machine gun fire could be heard at Div. H.Q. and seemed rapidly to be getting nearer. The most comforting sign, strange to say, was that the Germans continued to shell between HAM and EPPEVILLE, evidently searching for the station - nasty big stuff - but it gave an indication of his position.

Bdes. closed in the early hours of the 23rd. The test station got in safely by way of HAM Bridge and at dawn the Coy. with full transport moved off to NESLE - a small advance party had gone forward at midnight, to struggle with the leavings of the 5th. Army Signal Office, a more difficult task than picking up the lines you want from the inevitable chaos can hardly be imagined. Various Bdes. of Artillery and Infantry from other Divisions were now being attached to the Division, all needing lines, few had any Signal personnel or stores. The 5th. Army Signal Store at NESTLE proved invaluable, cable wagons worked continuously and very shortly after the Division arrived at NESTLE all Bdes. and Artillery were "on". Quick moves were the order of the day, but with very few exceptions it was only when units were actually on the move that line communication did not exist. Everyone seemed possessed of a physical strength for work which was beyond belief. Time for sleep was absolutely nil.

Next move to RETONVILLERS on the 25th. Here no lines existed but within 20 minutes of taking over separate lines were out to Bdes., and that night communication was normal. The following day about 2.30 p.m. on again to CARAPUIS, in the early morning some French troops had come up and a big counter-attack that afternoon was spoken of, but it did not materialise. At CARAPUIS the 61st. Bde. rejoined, lines were again quickly improvised, but the same evening the Division moved to ROYE, the Carapuis Office remaining open until all Bdes. had closed. At ROYE all Brigades were in the Town and early next morning the march to LES QUESNIL commenced.

What was thought to be the end proved only the commencement of this long-drawn battle. On arrival at LES QUESNIL the Division found itself at once in action. Up to date cable wagons had refitted at Army or Corps dumps but now shortage of cable was getting serious. Lines were laid to 59 and 61 Bdes. but 60, who were in the opposite direction, had to rely on wireless and motor cyclists. Wireless functioned successfully from here, an excellent aerial being arranged from the Church spire.

Next H.Q. was at DOMART where already two other Divisions were in possession, nobody liked DOMART very much. The Signal Coy. mess was "shelled out" practically on arrival and the so-called "horse lines" met the same fate in the afternoon and the Divisional Staff were literally blown out of the H.Q. when they finally left, but that was two days ahead yet.

At DOMART Signals repeated previous experience and rapidly got lines arranged to Infantry Bdes. On the second day Div. moved back to BOVES but the Signal Office remained at DOMART and prepared a Battle H.Q. in readiness for the next day. At about 2 p.m. a heavy bombardment of the village commenced and it became untenable. H.Q. moved to a ruin a mile outside the village and it was here for the first time that Signals were for the time being really beat for lines. All had been irretrievably smashed in the bombardment of the village and until this to some extent subsided, relaying was hopeless. Later in the day advanced H.Q. was moved back to a cross road a mile and a half outside BOVES whence the usual laying of lines took place, but this was nearly the end. In 2 days' time the Division was relieved by the 14th. Division and withdrew for rest and reinforcement.

The Signal casualties had been heavy. The 59th. Bde. Section lost all senior N.C.O.'s and their officer, Lt. JACKSON, who was badly wounded. Sgt. THOMPSON was killed at DOMART with 3 others of his Section.

After a month's rest at GAMASCHE and later at VILLERS-CHATEL the Division took over from the Canadians at LENS and VIMY. Here they remained all the Summer and Autumn of 1918 without serious incident. A great amount of work was done on the communications of this area and finally a complete and practically perfect buried system for trench warfare was constructed.

During the early summer heavy attacks were anticipated and much counter-preparation kept the Signal Company very busy. Heavy concentrations of gas shell caused serious casualties, in one night the Section Officer and all N.C.O.'s (except 1 Sgt.) of the 61st. Bde. becoming casualties.

Lt. WEBB left to take over 57th. Div. Artillery Signals and Lt. MALLET went to a similar post with the 8th. Div. and Capt. HANNEN went as 2nd. in Command to 39th. Division Signal Coy., Capt. J.S. PARSONS, D.S.O., joining to command the Divisional Artillery Signals.

Shortly after the German retirement in Autumn, 1918, commenced, the Div. was withdrawn and proceeded to CAMBRAI area in 3rd. Army and had just taken over from the 24th. Division on the MONS-MAUBERGE road when the Armistice came. So ended three years and 4 months of active service.

The conditions under which a Signal Company works do not tend to great dramatic incident. Their work in trench warfare in attack and in retirement, though vitally necessary to every arm of the Service, may pass almost unnoticed <u>unless they fail</u>. The object of their existence can be summed up in one sentence - communication must be maintained without interruption. That the 20th. Divisional Signal Coy. did this whenvever it was humanly possible to do so, and sometimes when it was not, is what they trained to do and what they claim to have accomplished by the most loyal co-operation of Drivers, Linemen and Operators.

[signature] RE

20th. DIVISIONAL SIGNAL COMPANY R.E.

HONOURS AND AWARDS. (WITH COMPANY).

OFFICERS.

"DISTINGUISHED SERVICE ORDER".

Rank.	Name.	Date.
Major	F.J.M.Stratten.	June 1917.

"MILITARY CROSS".

Major	A.G.Brace	January 1917.
Lieut.	C.S.Webb	January 1918.
Lieut.	F.J.Mallett	April 1918.
Lieut.	J.Hadden	January 1918.
Lieut.	J.R.Patten (R.F.A)	

"BAR TO MILITARY CROSS"

| Lieut. | F.J.Mallett | June 1918. |

"MENTIONED IN DESPATCHES",

Major	F.J.M.Stratten	January 1916.
ditto.	ditto.	June 1916.
Major	A.G.Brace	June 1916.
ditto.	ditto.	June 1918.
Lieut.	J.Hadden.	January 1918.
Captain	L.C.D.Hannen	January 1919.
~~Lieut~~	~~C.S.Webb~~	

20th. DIVISIONAL SIGNAL COMPANY R.E.

HONOURS and AWARDS.

21st. July. 1915 to date.

DISTINGUISHED CONDUCT MEDAL. (5)

No.	Rank.	Name.	Date.
45651	Sergeant.	McLaren, W.	1/6/18.
49447	"	Sargent, S.J.	1/6/17.
107435	"	Stockdale, G.W.	10/5/18.
46682	2/Corpl.	Goode, W.	15/4/16.
560227	Sapper	Baker, F.	16/1/16.

MILITARY MEDAL. (28)

50798	Sergeant.	Bearn, C.H.	5/9/16.
47189	"	Dilley, W.R.	/18.
40450	"	Marshall, J.P.	30/9/16.
56596	"	Nash, J.	27/10/16.
44837	"	Sanders, J.H.	17/8/17.
107435	"	Stockdale, G.W.	27/10/16.
66017	"	Thompson, S.E.	5/1/18.
47005	"	Tyrrell, F.L.	3/10/17.
58236	"	Wolfe, W.	23/4/18.
54152	MC Cpl.	Crummack, E.S.	
106666	MC Cpl.	Parker, C.	22/4/18.
73592	MC Cpl.	Robson, D.	25/4/18.
66106	Corpl.	Wimpey, E.W.	27/1/18.
311436	2/Cpl.	Bridle, F.E.	17/8/17.
311468	2/Cpl.	Bailey, J.R.	26/8/17.
311440	L/Cpl.	Bartley, R.	1/10/18.
75584	L/Cpl.	Powell, G.	27/1/18.
45258	L/Cpl.	Ralls, J.S.	28/8/17.
311451	Sapper.	Blacka, J.	5/1/18.
43737	"	Banham, G.W.	28/8/17.
50007	"	Buxton, A.E.	3/10/17.
45325	"	Delby, D.T.	3/6/16.
76732	"	Fergus, T.	1/6/18.
46681	"	Hellands, H.J.	10/7/16.
45659	"	Pemberton, H.	27/10/16.
311443	"	Rayner, H.	17/8/17.
46978	"	Waugh, W.	27/10/16.
58236	"	Wolfe, W.	23/4/18.

BAR TO MILITARY MEDAL. (1)

107435	Sergt.	Stockdale, G.W.	5/ 1/18.

MERITORIOUS SERVICE MEDAL. (2)

14496	Sergt.	Denton, T.N.	~~1/ 1/18~~ 1/ 1/19.
46939	Sergt.	Gibson, W.	1/ 1/19.

MENTIONED IN DESPATCHES. (3)

45651	Sergt.	McLaren, W.	1/ 1/17.
165927	MC Cpl.	Morris, J.	17/ 5/18.
56585	Sergt.	Ross, J.	18/ 5/19.

FOREIGN DECORATIONS. (2)

45651	Sergt.	McLaren, W. Belgian Decoration Militaire. 1/1/19
47326	2/Cpl.	O'Neill, W. French Medal Militaire. 13/7/17

2D Air Sig. Coy. R.E.

DIED OF WOUNDS. (11).

No.	Rank.	Name.	Date.
49423	Sergt.	Peart, J.	30/ 8/16.
47300	Spr.	Fortunate, T.V.	17/ 3/17.
45230	Spr.	Browning, T.	12/ 8/17.
93683	Spr.	Lyon, W.	23/ 9/17.
546935	Spr.	Westwood, J.H.	24/ 3/18.
32 5471	Pnr.	Stewart, A.M.	7/ 7/18.
311457	Spr.	Morgan, C.E.	9/11/18.
311462	Dvr.	Jones, A.	13/11/18.
50007	Spr.	Buxton, A.E.	28/ 5/16.
64996	Spr.	Golding, H.	) Died in Hospital in
211147	Spr.	Wildman, J.T.	) England, results of Gas Poisoning. July. 1919.

KILLED. (7).

No.	Rank.	Name.	Date.
77707	M C Cpl.	Bowring, A.H.	15/ 5/16.
50008	Spr.	Coleman, T.H.	26/ 6/16.
48261	Spr.	Taverner, R.	29/ 8/16.
41745	Spr.	Carter, C.	5/ 9/16.
2890	Spr.	Flack, G.J.	20/11/16.
66067	Sgt.	Thompson, S.E.	31/ 3/18.
267669	Spr.	Beetius, E.A.	31/ 3/18.

MISSING. (7).

165468	Pnr.	Wheeler, G.A.	30/11/17.
66106	Cpl.	Wimpey, G.A.	30/11/17.
56289	Spr.	Backhouse, S.R.	30/11/17.
147998	Spr.	Houlten, J.J.	30/11/17.
127596	Spr.	Greenwood, A.H.	30/11/17.
25222	Spr.	Ringe, E.B.	24/ 3/18.
546935	Spr.	Westwood, J.H.	24/ 3/18.

20th Division.

"Divisional Signal Coy."
Vol. I.
20-31-7-15

181/6250

Confidential

War Diary of
O.C. 20th Divisional Signal Coy R.E.
July 1915.

WAR DIARY or INTELLIGENCE SUMMARY

Army Form C. 2118.

Place	Date	Hour	Summary of Events and Information	Remarks and references to Appendices
HAVRE	20/7/15	11.30pm	Left Bucknall by train for SOUTHAMPTON and embarked on SS Kwankoiton Importer	77ny
HAVRE	21/7/15	9.0pm	Landed at HAVRE, day in rest camp No 5. Drew 1 R2 to complete to establishment. Entrained at night	7 ny
LUMBRES	23/7/15	10.0pm	22nd July 5.1st in train. LUMBRES reached turning night H4 at CHATEAUD LUMBRES wire to 55th BDE on WHRRAS, HCRA at LUMBRES HQ & BDE RFA at BETENGHEM. Wire to 6/10/56 at 17.00. 14.53 Laid ready the arrival line from GHQ taken over & internal telephone by rural? homes in LUMBRES	77 ny
LUMBRES	24/7/15	10.0pm	Wire to 61st completed turnover: 60th BDE helipo + on G HQ work. SS cable section. Light 2nd Lt JD Andrew arrived in morning. Fixed PO officials. Manned HQs P.O. bureaux.	77 ny
	25/7/15	11.0pm	Line to 19th BDE RFA continued BDK at HEFRINGUES also wire continued from HQ RB HQ K 91 + 92 – BDE RFA at MERCK and to 93rd BDE RFA at WROULT.	77 ny
	26/7/15	9.0pm	Circuit unsatisfactory	77 ny
	27/7/15	10.0pm	Wire to artillery 59th BDE General's house + PO thereafter from town	77 ny
LYNDE	28/7/15	11.0pm	Office moved to General's house. Gasoline light other brigade line taken down	Appendix I

A.D.S.S./Forms/C.2118.

WAR DIARY
or
INTELLIGENCE SUMMARY

(Erase heading not required.)

Army Form C. 2118.

Place	Date	Hour	Summary of Events and Information	Remarks and references to Appendices
LYNDE	28/7/15	early	HQ moved to LYNDE, office established in school room, wires to 4 HQ taken into use.	
MERRIS	29/7/15	10 pm	HQ established at convent at MERRIS. Wire to CO wanting in office. Arranged for CO line placed into his school. Service of 6½" TBDE at MONTE BOON & 8" BDE at BERTSESM	FF Park
"	30/7/15	11 pm	60" BDE tapped in to 8" BDE line. Line run to 5½" BDE at LE VERRIER. CO lines along autobus loaned for infantry telephone went from CRA in MERRIS Hqs 2nd BDE (PRET IT SER Bois) and DK at AU SOUVERAIN. Another line laid from CRA to 9th & 43rd Btys at RUE PRINST and VERTE RUE.	FFM
"	31/7/15	10 pm	Office moved from convent to ECOLE MUNICIPALE DE FILLES close by.	FFM / Appendices I

Appendix I

July 24, 1915
-29

92nd + 91st Bde RFA. Merck - St Liévin RFA.

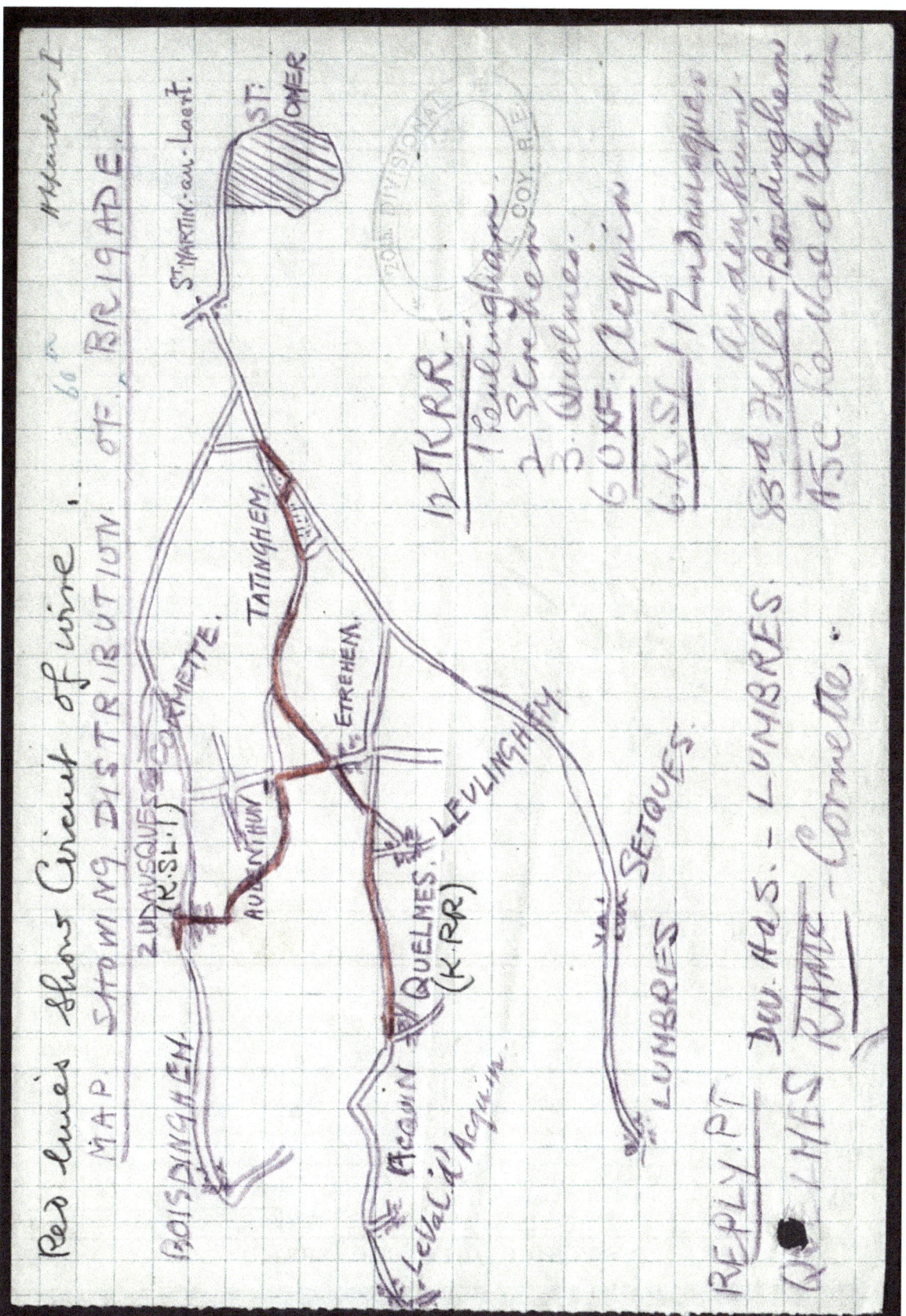

"A" Form. Army Form C. 2121.
MESSAGES AND SIGNALS.
No. of Message.

Prefix	Code	m.	Words	Charge		This message is on a/c of	Recd. at	m.

Office of Origin and Service Instructions.

Sent At ... m. To ... By ...

......Service.
(Signature of "Franking Officer.")

Date ......
From ......
By ......

TO

Sender's Number.	Day of Month	In reply to Number	A A A

From
Place
Time

The above may be forwarded as now corrected.   (Z)

Censor.   Signature of Addressor or person authorised to telegraph in his name.

This line should be erased if not required.

(688-9) — McC. & Co. Ltd., London. — W 14142/641. 225,000. 4/15. Forms C 2121/10.

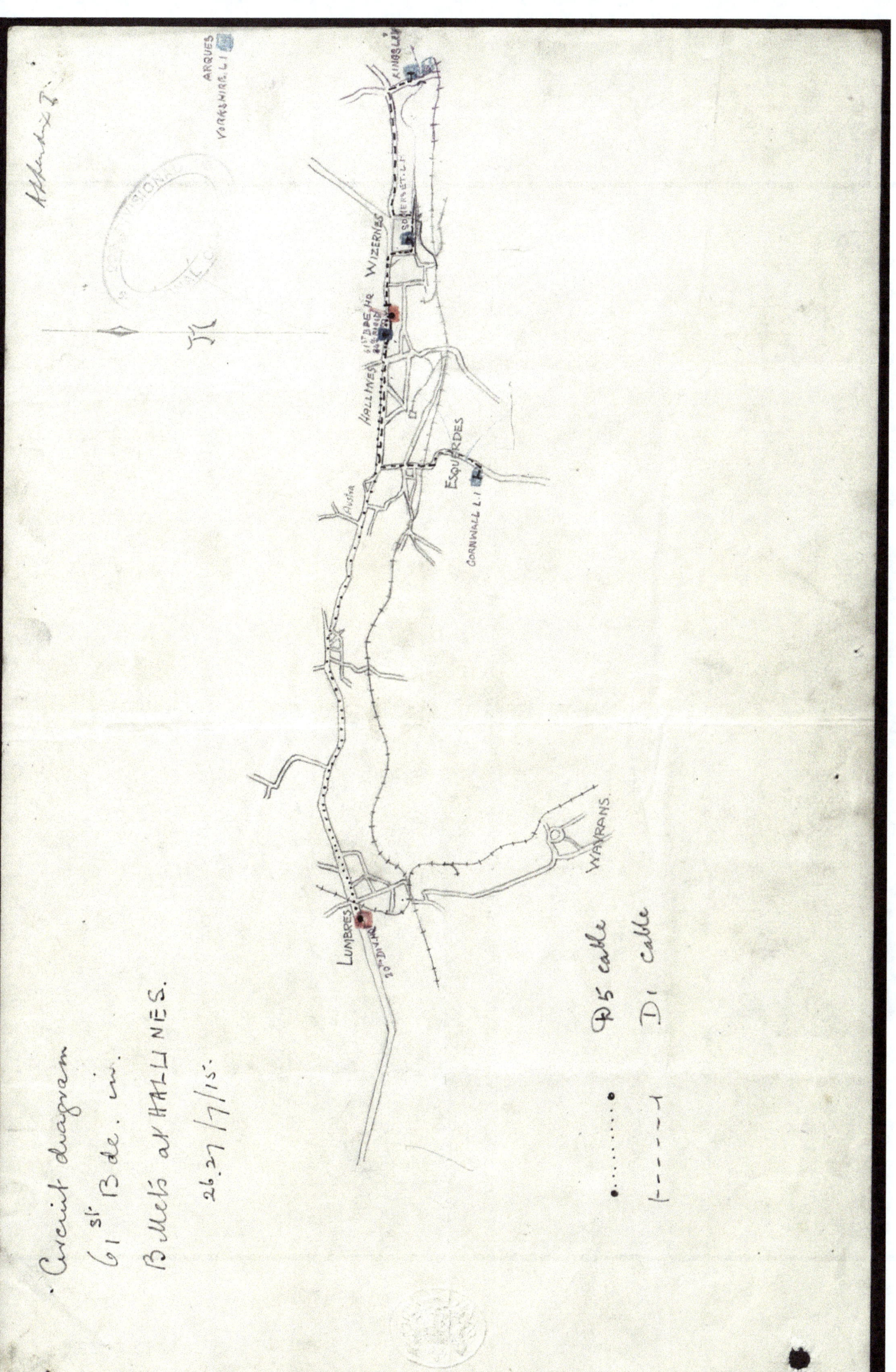

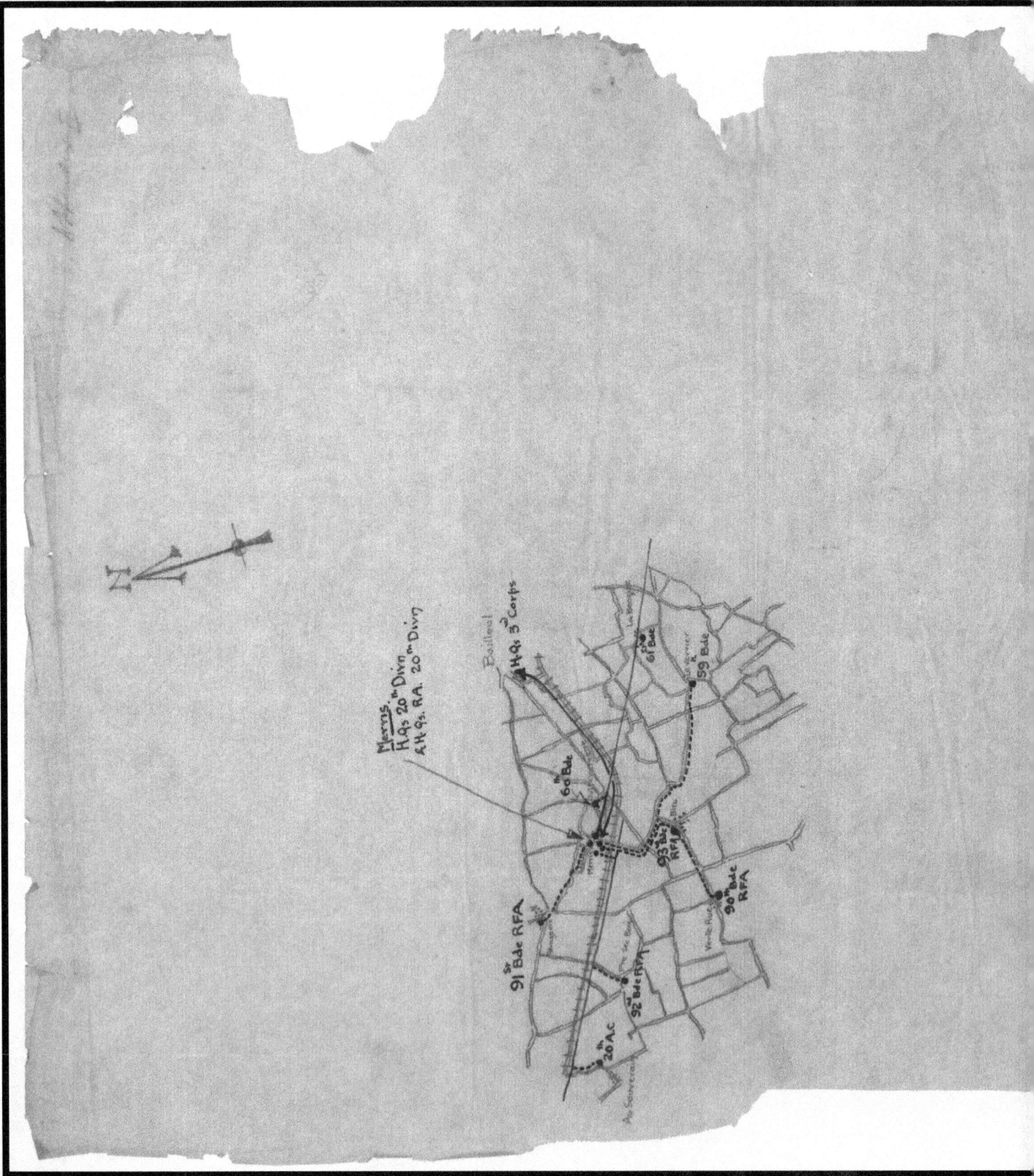

Appendix D

MERRIS
GSO.
Signal Office
CRA.
DLI
60th Bde.
61st Bde.
To Bailleul
92nd Bde RFA.
Pt. Sec Bois.
Amm Col.
Au Souverain
93rd Bde
Bleu
59th Bde.
Le Vernier
90th Bde R.F.A.
Verte Rue.

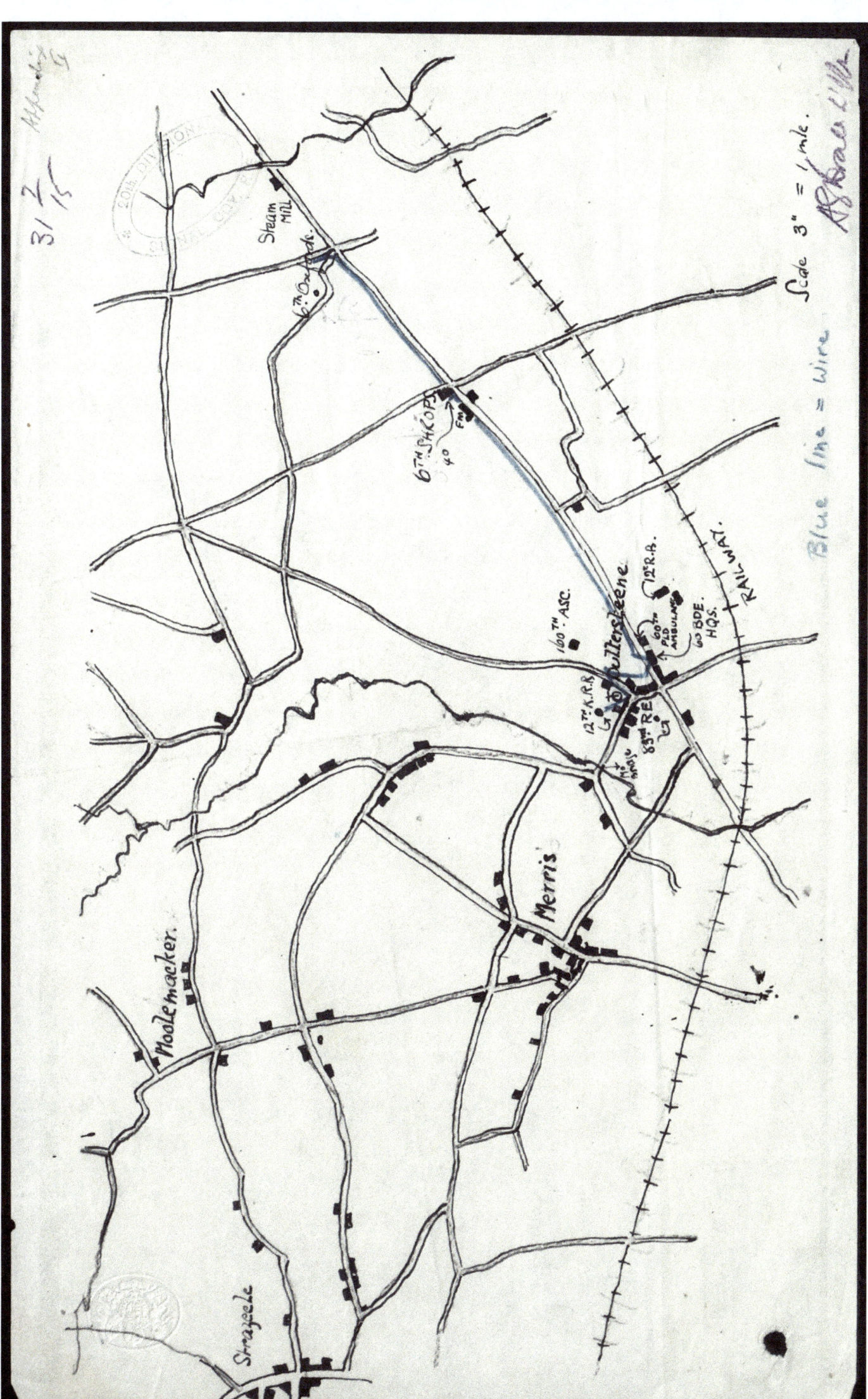

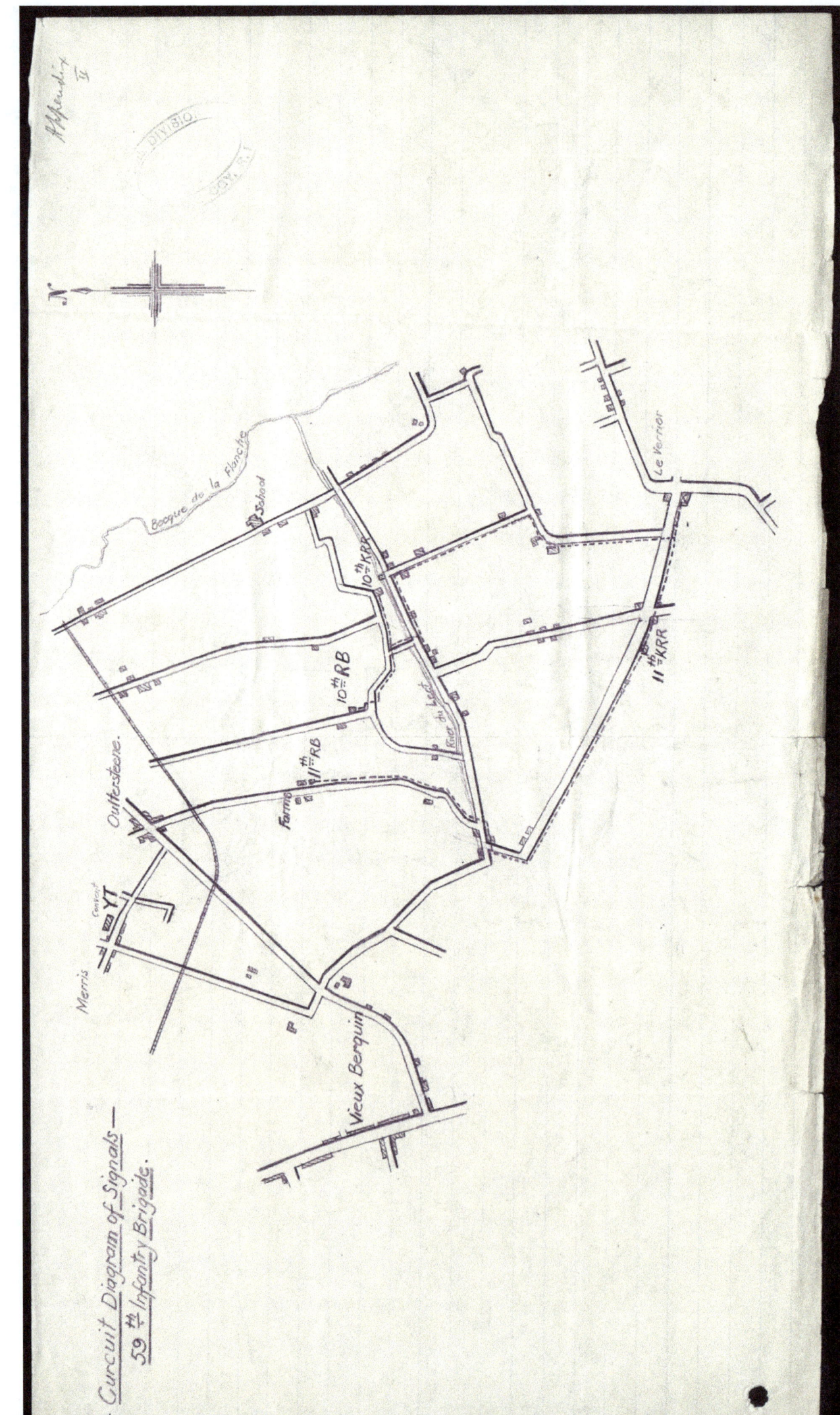

61st Bde. Billets July 30th 1915
Appendix I

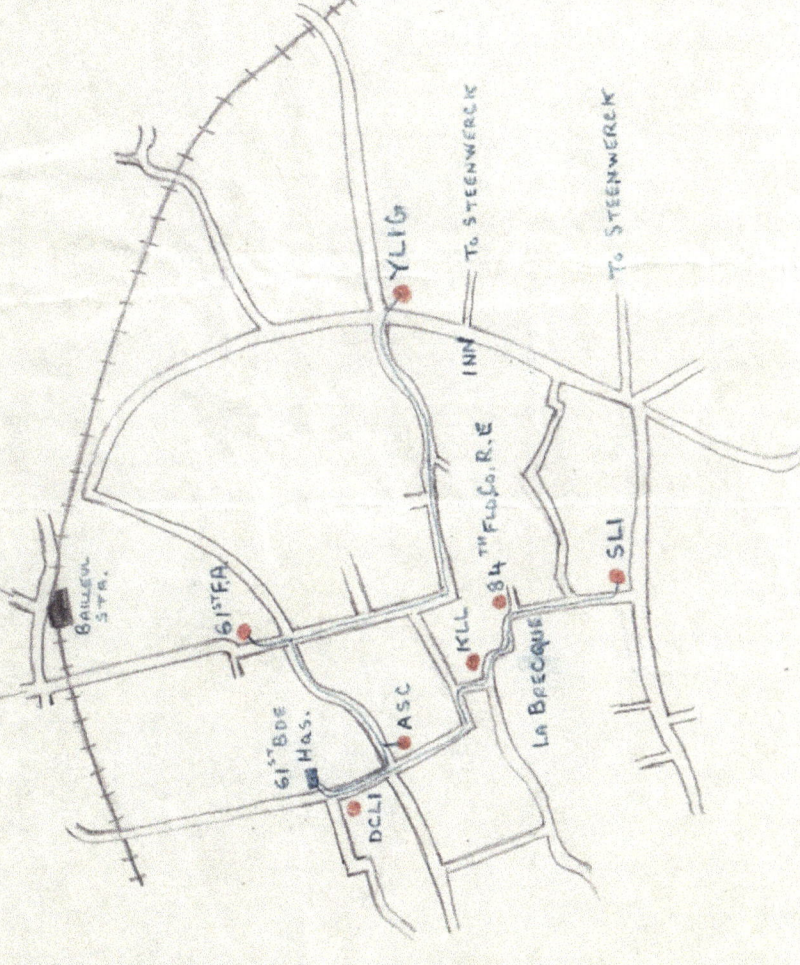

121/6787

20th Hussars

20th Bork: Signal Coy:
Vol II
Aug 15.

WAR DIARY or INTELLIGENCE SUMMARY

Army Form C. 2118

2nd Corps Signal Company

Place	Date	Hour	Summary of Events and Information	Remarks and references to Appendices
MEAULTE	1/8/15	11.30pm	Wire laid to 87 & 88 BDE RE from C.R.A. strowing matter	77ms
"	2/8/15	10.30pm	circuits unchanged. Speaking telephone received from base	77ms
			well	
"	3/8/15	10.55pm	Speaking telephone just installed from signal office to office S.S.	77ms
"	4/8/15	6.0pm	circuit unchanged	77ms
"	5/8/15	11.50pm	11th Durham L.I moved near HA then line dis at 4.0pm. SS cable broken left	77ms
			with corps pullers to join new corps HQ at Chateau de la Motte	
"	6/8/15	11.0pm	new wire laid to Durham Div. Very Busy now.	77ms
"	7/8/15	11.30pm	Preparations for moving new switchboard 20 line	77ms
"	8/8/15	11.50pm	corps moved to CHATEAU DE LA MOTTE & new lines working 11.40 am. Set up	77ms
			new 20 line tel. exchange in signal office. line to S&MR, corps staff rear H: front spm	77ms
	9/8/15	10.30pm	no change	77ms
	10/8/15	11.30pm	wire fixed to C.R.E. and to SH the F.D. Coy R.E	77ms
	11/8/15	11.30pm	no change	77ms
	12/8/15	11.50pm	no change	77ms
	13/8/15	11.50pm	no change	77ms
	14/8/15	11.50pm	no change	77ms
	15/8/15	11.40pm	no change	77ms

Army Form C. 2118

WAR DIARY
or
INTELLIGENCE SUMMARY.
(Erase heading not required.)

Instructions regarding War Diaries and Intelligence Summaries are contained in F.S. Regs., Part II. and the Staff Manual respectively. Title pages will be prepared in manuscript.

Place	Date	Hour	Summary of Events and Information	Remarks and references to Appendices
MERRIS	16/8/15	11.45pm	Line to Le Verrier (55th Bde) interrupted & BLEU for 19th Bde: 19 Bde also attacked alarm & came to duplication. Le Verrier in 55 Bde wire: while circuit out to OUTTERSTEEN for 20 Bde officer there warned etc.	7 July
MERRIS	17/8/15	11.55pm	84th a/op moved to MERRIS: had b-L-A because needed in and head office for 84th established. Came with 8th DIV on 19th BDE wire.	7 July
MERRIS	18/8/15	11.15pm	Bell telephone established 8.15pm. B/b p.m.	7 July
MERRIS	19/8/15	11.30pm	On departure of 19th BDE from LE VERRIER arts across by poled line L.t. DOUGLAS on 48 DIV station	7 July
MERRIS	20/8/15	11.30pm	No change	7 July
MERRIS	21/8/15	11.30pm	Divisional supply column Head of march coming move of DIV beliebre MEEKUT DIV. {this from MARSEILLES will replace this from BORRE, established temporarily}	7 July
MERRIS	22/8/15	11.15pm	No change	7 July
MERRIS	23/8/15	11.30pm	Repaired spare wire K66 to 151st Bde HA completed	7 July
MERRIS	24/8/15	11.30pm	Running line to STEENWERCK removed line to D.L.I.	7 July
MERRIS	25/8/15	11.30pm	Removed line to supply column. 91st Bde arty H.A. district are	7 July
MERRIS	26/8/15	11.30pm	Cut second half thought to house made runway artillery were picked up	7 July
MERRIS	27/8/15	11.45pm	Cleaning up lines	7 July
NOUVEAU MONDE	28/8/15	11.55pm	Moved to new HQ; between HQ of MEERUT DIV La, Pt R, CCA, CRA, CDS, 5th & 160 Rfs Bde at works. (a) takings for 2 brigades + officers	7 July

1577 Wt. W10791/1773 500,000 1/15 D. D. & L. A.D.S.S./Forms/C. 2118.

WAR DIARY
or
INTELLIGENCE SUMMARY.
(Erase heading not required.)

Army Form C. 2118

Instructions regarding War Diaries and Intelligence Summaries are contained in F. S. Regs., Part II. and the Staff Manual respectively. Title pages will be prepared in manuscript.

Place	Date	Hour	Summary of Events and Information	Remarks and references to Appendices
NOUVEAU MONDE	29/8/15	11.30pm	Wire to CRA Bde told telephone: other lines held. Artillery wire to DAC & 23rd Bty	77np
NOUVEAU MONDE	30/8/15	11.30pm	23rd Bde 18th moved. Other lines held. 2nd Div 155th division lines failures	77np
NOUVEAU MONDE	31/8/15		lines which were cut from line to Rowell Bde were mollified; maintenance work done	77np

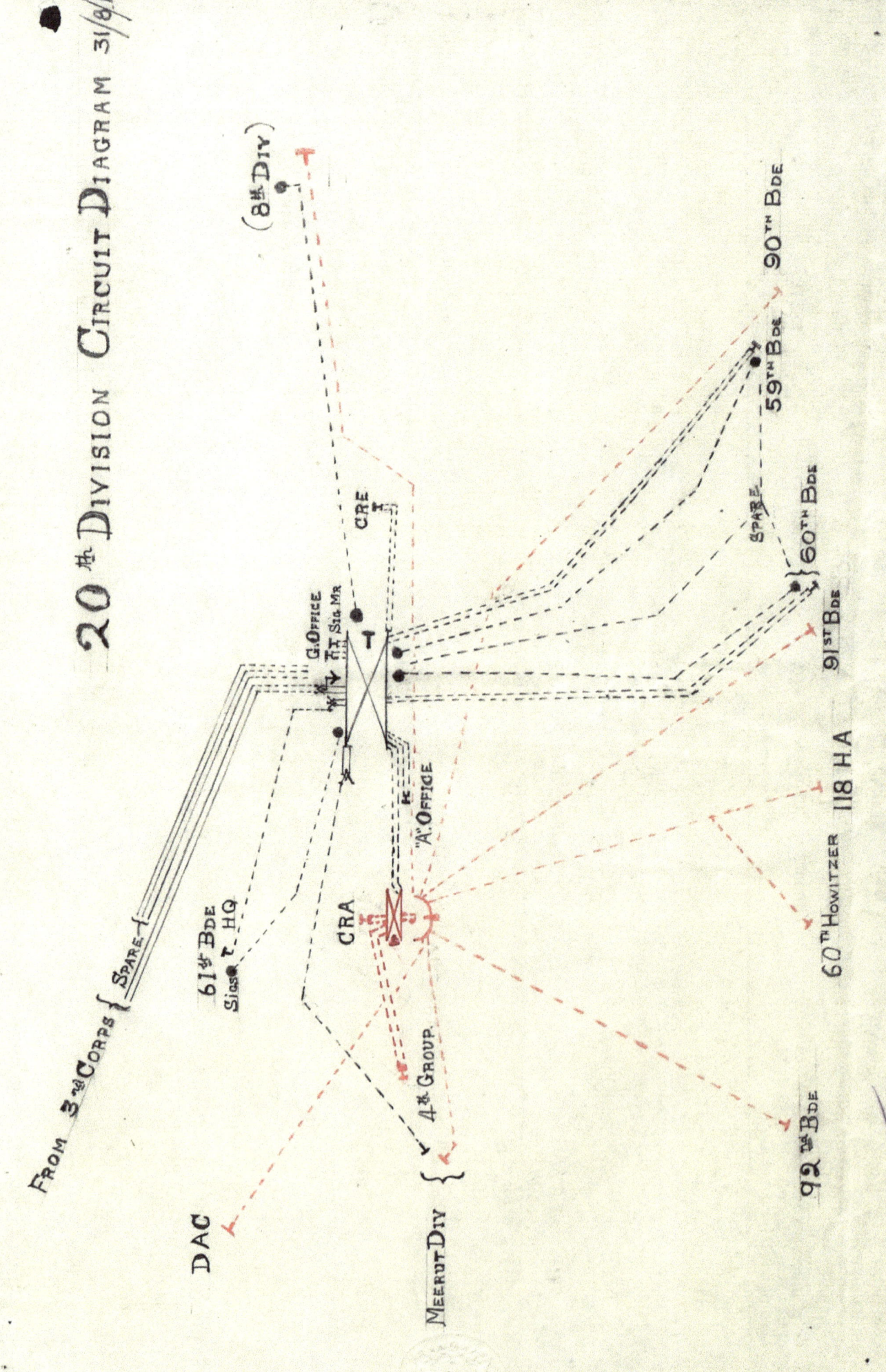

20TH DIVISION ROUTE DIAGRAM

NOTE
ARTILLERY LINES
BRIGADE LINES
DIVISIONAL LINES

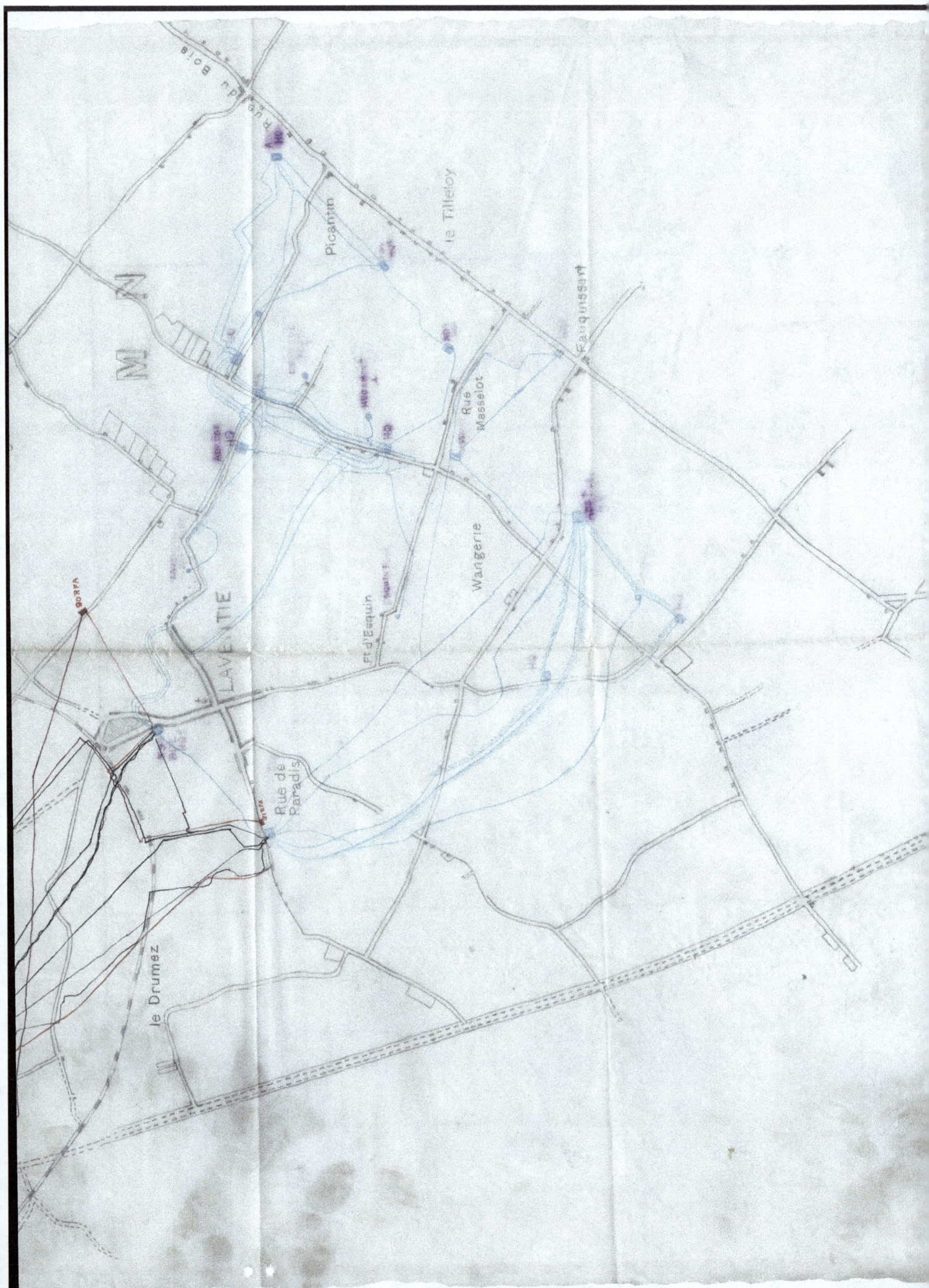

MERRIS "20th April"
18/15

91st RFA

84th Coy RE

60th Bde

To 61st Bde

Sig M.
G Q
T A
CRE
CRA

93rd RFA

92nd RFA

Amm Col

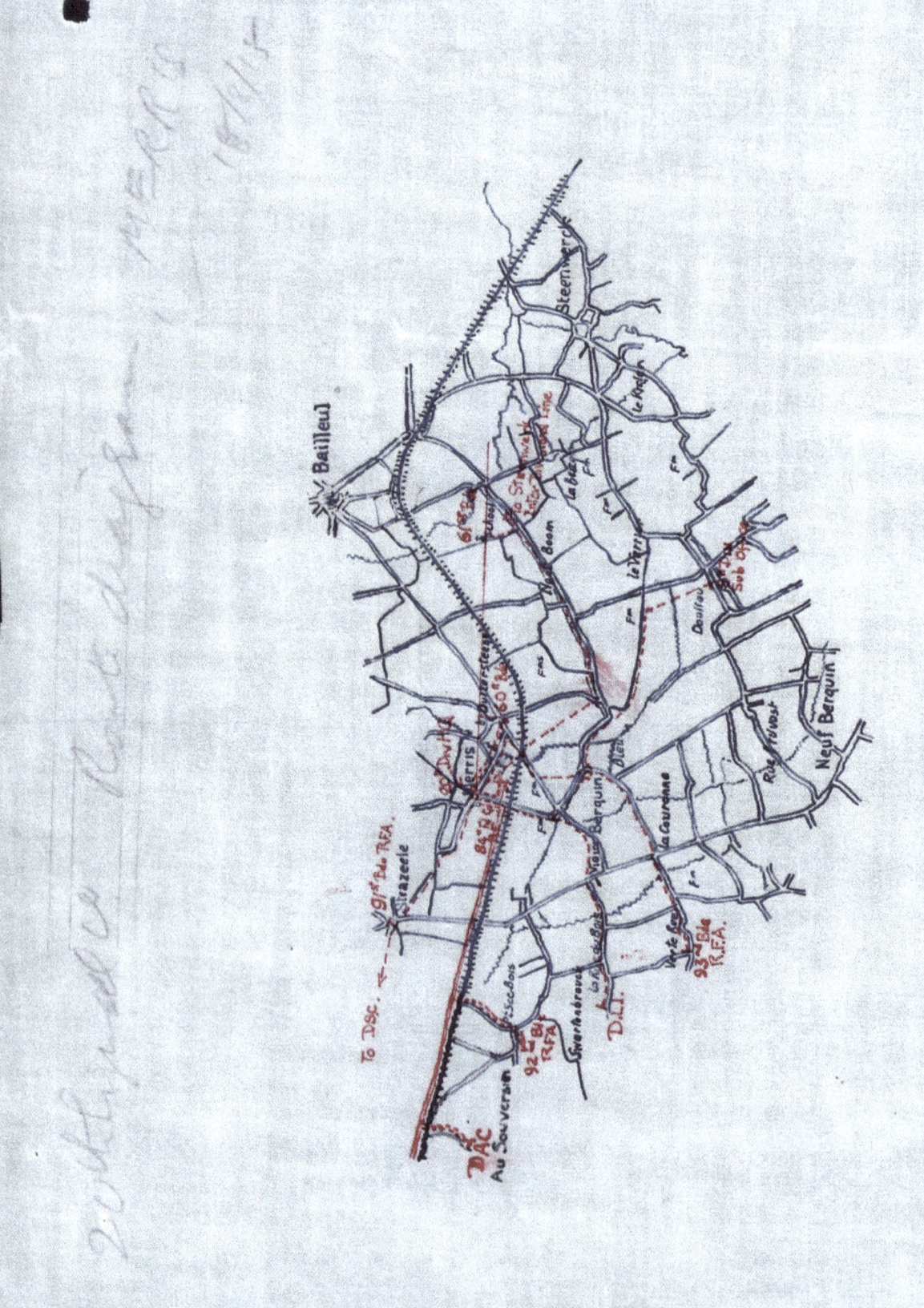

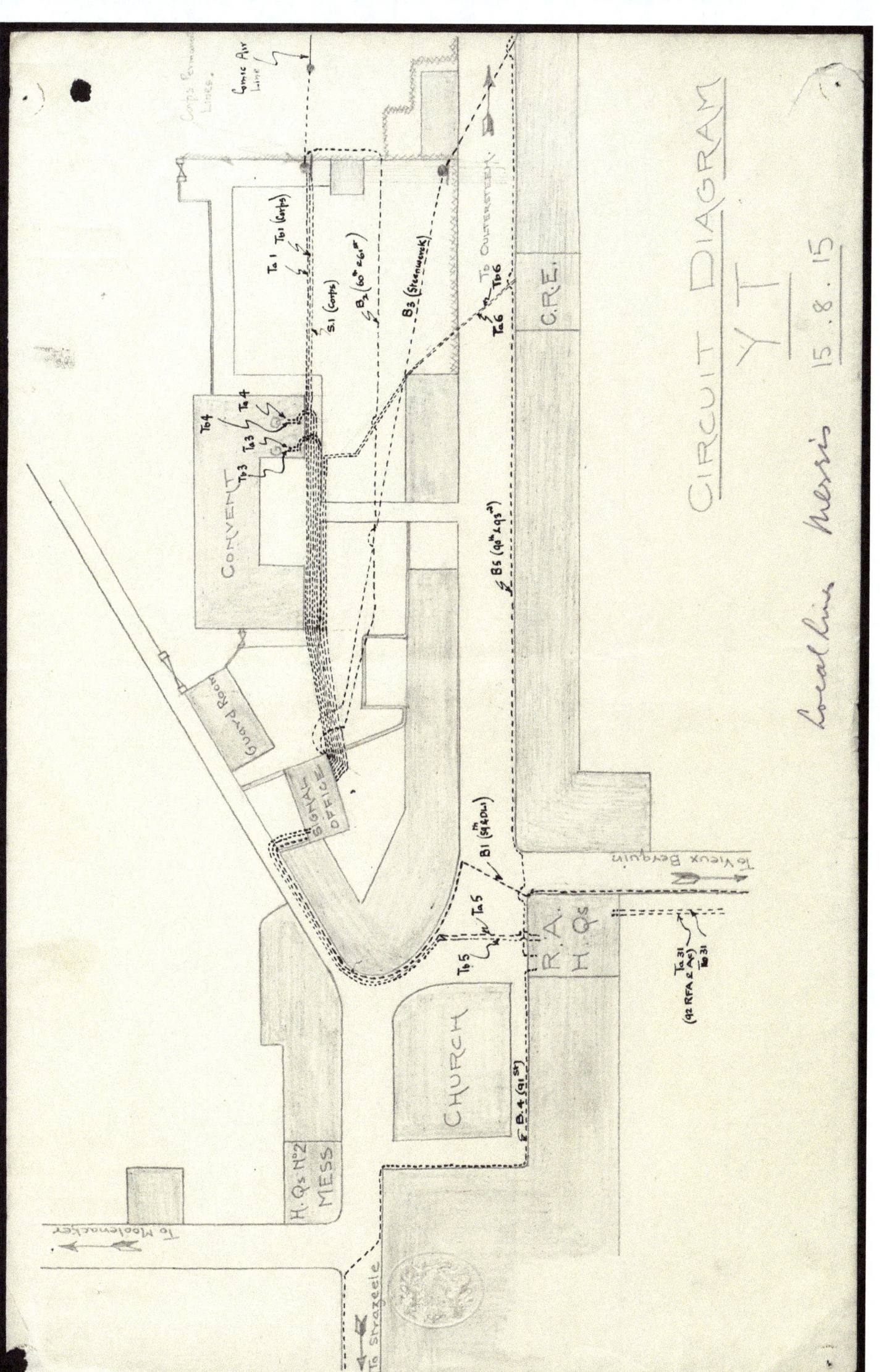

20th Division

26E Arty: Spec El:
Vol 3

Sept. 15

Confidential

War Diary for Sept. 1915

F.J.M. Stratton
Capt. R.E.
O.C. 20th Divisional Signal Coy. R.E.

WAR DIARY / INTELLIGENCE SUMMARY

20th April 1915
Army Form C. 2118

Place	Date	Hour	Summary of Events and Information	Remarks and references to Appendices
MORBECQUE	1.7.15	11.45pm	Saloing old line. Laid line to 61st Bde Hd & 2nd Fd Amb Dressing Station from 60th Bde & St François	77M/1
MORBECQUE	2.7.15	11.30pm	Received advanced report centre in RUE DE PARADIS. Airline from DIV HQ to MRC. Got on old line	77M/1
—	3.7.15	11.30pm	Took over burial line from MRC to 57th Bde & 57th Bde A.C. new line from 61st Bde to ENGINEERS & 61st Fd Ambulance	77M/1
—	4.7.15	11.30pm	2 lines laid from Div HQ to 23rd Bde HQ ready for move of 61st Bde HQ	77M/1
—	5.7.15	11.30pm	Work on buried line to 57 Bde A.C. continued & French RA to their own artillery group. Rear of 61st Bde new line to 61st Fdl Amb & Div Mtd Troops Hd Qrs (R.W. Taylor)	77M/1
—	6.7.15	11.30pm	Took over 39th Bde buried line & an CROSSROADS group continued buried line Army/F	77M/1
—	7.7.15	11pm	event unchanged	77M/1
—	8.7.15	11.30pm	New line laid from 57th Bde to 1st Bde. also from MEERUT Div Reporter to MD DIV HQ	77M/1
—	9.7.15	11.15pm	New buried line from MRC to 61st Bde to Adv Reports to 61st Bde. line 61st 57th Unchecked	77M/1
—	10.7.15	11.30pm	The Pm line from MRC to DIV HQ we ran in to the office. New line laid from 60 Bde to 60 Bde Adv HQ. Post started on line from CROSSROADS group R.F. to O.H. Trunk cable tested	77M/1
—	11.7.15	11.45pm	Work continued on above lines. Line to DIV Mtd Troops recld	77M/1

WAR DIARY or INTELLIGENCE SUMMARY.

Army Form C. 2118.

30th April 1915

(Erase heading not required.)

Place	Date	Hour	Summary of Events and Information	Remarks and references to Appendices
NOUVEAU MONDE	12/9/15	11.40pm	Telephone lines completed. Photograph of huts from CRA BEROX BLANCHE received in	77My
"	13/9/15	11.30pm	Orvillers hut land from a office front. Cable of entablement hem but land to 60th from 37th and hut land obligation	77My
"	14/9/15	11.30pm	land from CRA to Heavy artillery station	77My 77AP
"	15/9/15	11.30pm	Maintenance and cabling of lines	77My
"	16/9/15	11.30pm	communication unaltered	77My
"	17/9/15	11.30pm	communications unaltered	77My
"	18/9/15	11.30pm	communications unaltered	77My
"	19/9/15	11.35pm	Lines laid from 61st APC to CROIX BLANCHE artillery front, & also RC 25th Bde & BMA or SANDERS's farm	77My
"	20/9/15	11.30pm	no change	77My
"	21/9/15	11.30pm	lines laid from 91st Bde RE to 60th APC from 60th APC to 58th APC	77MyS
"	22/9/15	11.45pm	line laid from 37th MRE to 61st APR E	27My
"	23/9/15	11.30pm	no change	27My
"	24/9/15	11.30pm	no change. Brown wood forward to MRCs	77My
"	25/9/15	11.30pm	no change. trench for switching over circuits to movements of HQ	77My

WAR DIARY or INTELLIGENCE SUMMARY.

26th Signal Coy RE   Army Form C. 2118.

(Erase heading not required.)

Place	Date	Hour	Summary of Events and Information	Remarks and references to Appendices
NOUVEAU MONDE	26/9/15	11.40pm	No change in communication, wire to ESTAIRES for 68th Bde, temporary attack made	FS/AJ
	27/9/15	11.30pm	68th Bde removed. Infantry Bde moved back to normal line	FS/AJ
	28/9/15	11.40pm	68th Bde back in Estaires. 60 Bde took over hut of Meerut Division, communication maintained through Meerut ADC. Wires handed over	FS/AJ
	29/9/15	11.15pm	New wires built to 93rd Bde RFA + to 13th Battn's RDx from CRA to DiS	FS/AJ
	30/9/15	11.30pm	No change same	FS/AJ

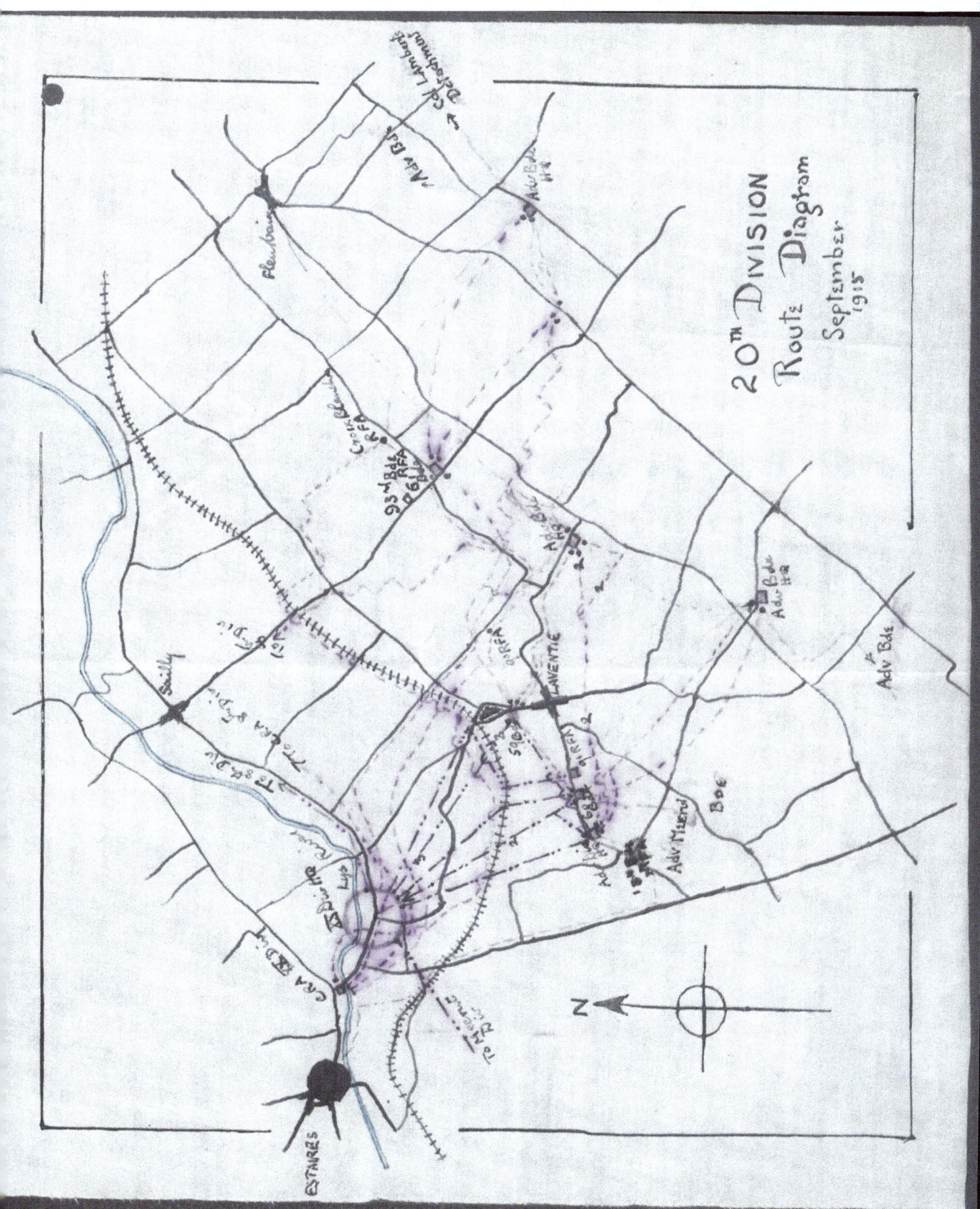

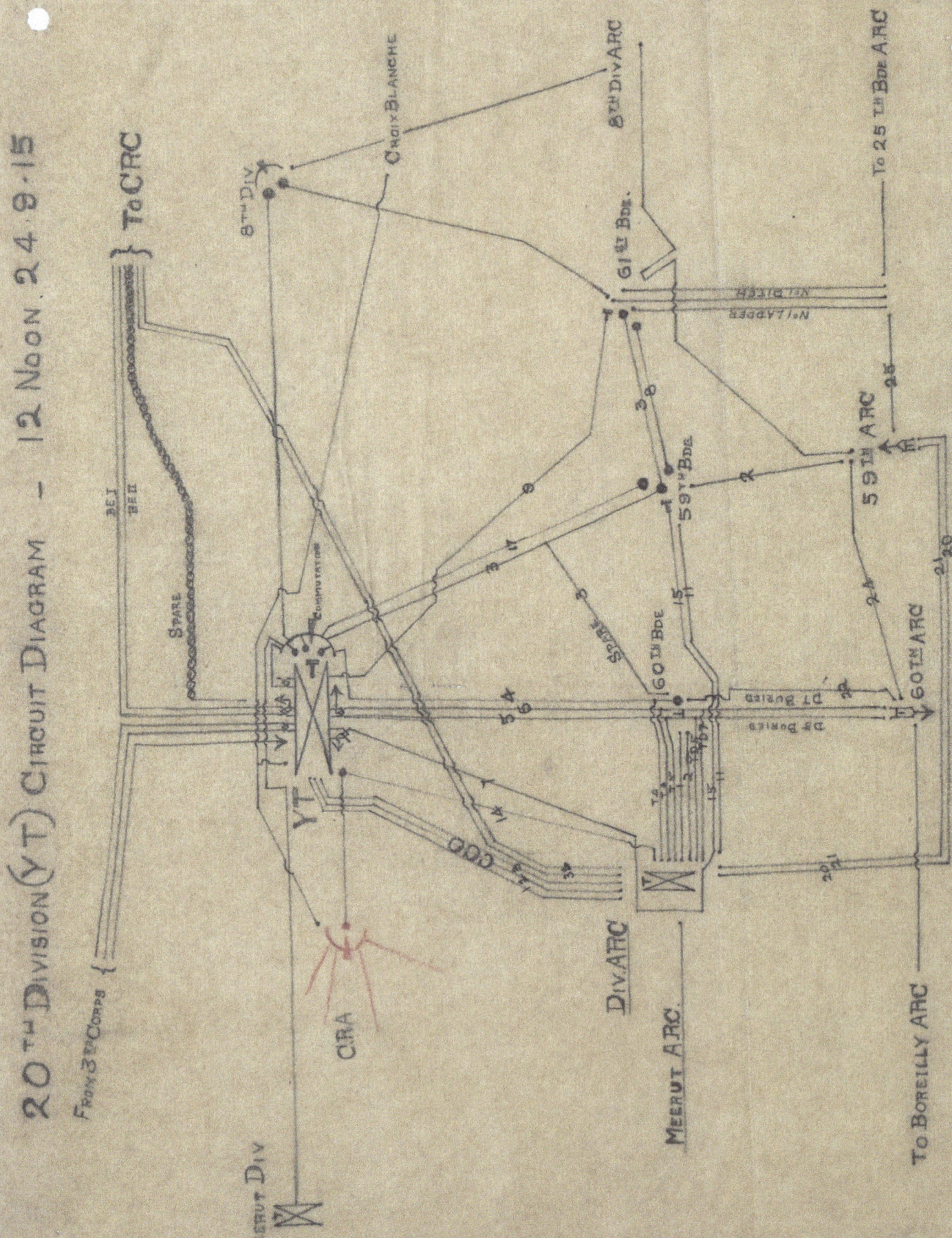

20th Division (YT) Circuit Diagram – Brigades Moved to ARCs From 3rd Corps

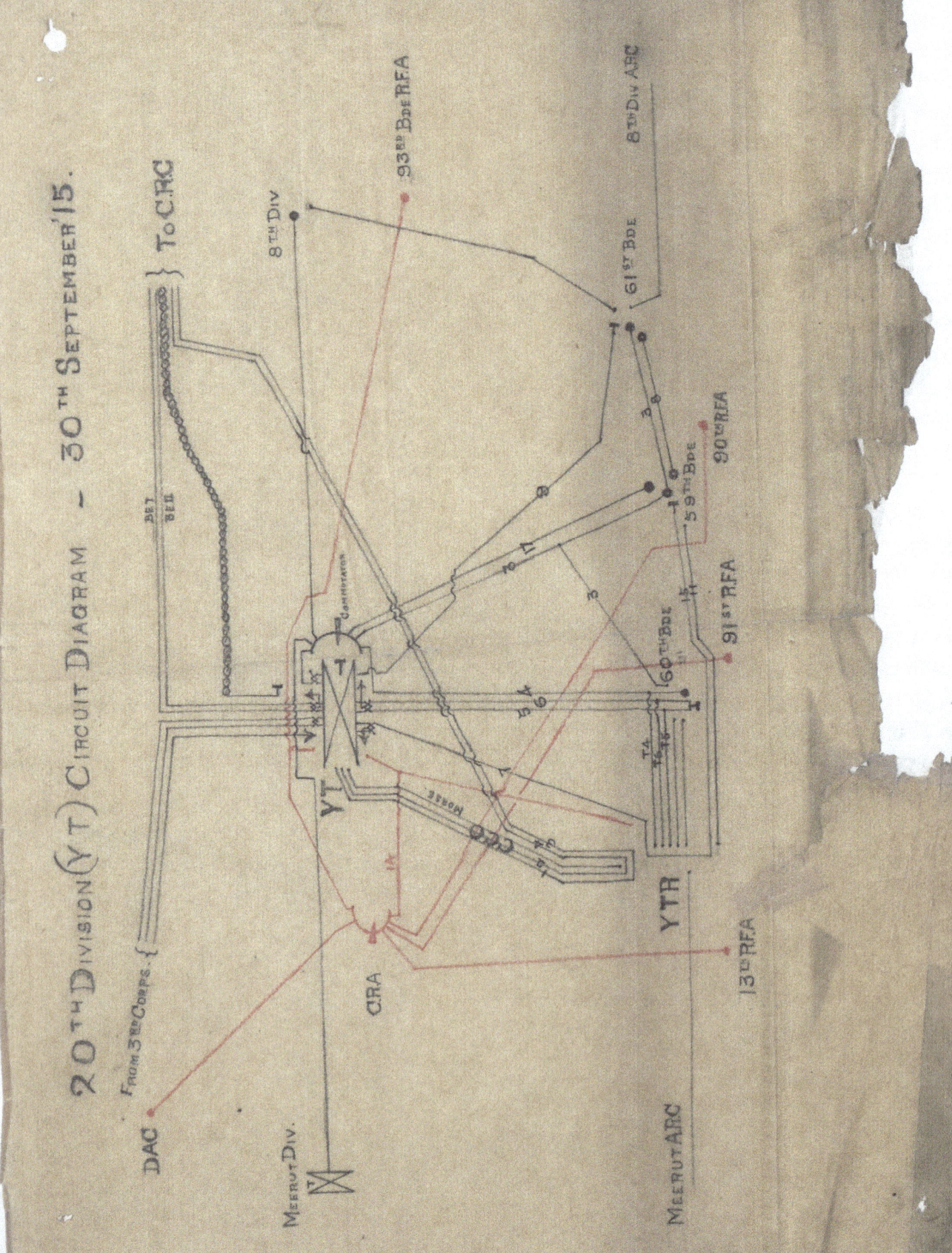

D/
7596

20th Division.

20th Div.: Signal Coy R.E.
Vol: 4
Oct 15

Confidential
―――――――

War Diary for
Oct. 1915 of
O.C. 20th Divisional Signal
Co. R.E.
from Oct 1st to Oct 31st, 1915
F.J.M Stratton

Army Form C. 2118.

2nd Australian R.E.

WAR DIARY
or
INTELLIGENCE SUMMARY.
(Erase heading not required.)

Instructions regarding War Diaries and Intelligence Summaries are contained in F. S. Regs., Part II. and the Staff Manual respectively. Title pages will be prepared in manuscript.

Place	Date	Hour	Summary of Events and Information	Remarks and references to Appendices
NOUVEAU MONDE	1/10/15	11.0 p	No change in camp	7 July
	2/10/15	11.0 p	Line to Div Supply Column, Neuf Berquin	7 July
	3/10/15	11.30 p	Line b/o of Bde ARC laid new	7 July
	4/10/15	11.30 p	Line laid from 60 "Bde to 50 "Bde subsection from Col Ricardo's HQ front	7 July
		11.30 p	to some place. Line laid from 93rd Bde HQ to 60th new ARC	7 July
	5/10/15	11.40 p	Anchor to 61st BDE HQ	7 July
	6/10/15	11.30 p	No change	7 July
	7/10/15	11.40 p	Road to 173rd Tunneling Co RE	7 July
	8/10/15	11.45 p	Line from 59th new ARC to 60th new ARC laid	7 July
	9/10/15	11.0 p	No change	
	10/10/15	11.30 p	Line from 90th Bde RE to 59th new ARC	7 July
	11/10/15	11.30 p	No change	7 July
	12/10/15	11.0 p	Line from HQ 1st Bde RE to 59th new ARC 1870th Bde RE	7 July
	13/10/15	11.10 p	New cable line from YT & YTR	7 July
	14/10/15	11.30 p	New airline from YT & YTR	7 July
	15/10/15	11.0 p	No change	7 July

Army Form C. 2118.

WAR DIARY
or
INTELLIGENCE SUMMARY.

(Erase heading not required.)

20th April 1916

Instructions regarding War Diaries and Intelligence Summaries are contained in F. S. Regs., Part II. and the Staff Manual respectively. Title pages will be prepared in manuscript.

Place	Date	Hour	Summary of Events and Information	Remarks and references to Appendices
NOURBAU MONDE	16/10	11.10 p	no change except relaying cable by airline	77 M.J
	17/10	11.0 p	no change	77 M.J
	18/10	11.0 p	no change	77 M.J
	19/10	11.0 p	no change	77 M.J
	20/10	11.0 p	no change	77 M.J
	21/10	11.0 p	no change	77 M.J
	22/10	11.0 p	no change	77 M.J
	23/10	11.0 p	no change	77 M.J
	24/10	11.0 p	new line laid to 20 no 24 Battn Hours	77 M.J
	25/10	11.0 p	no change	77 M.J
	26/10	11.30 p	no change	77 M.J
	27/10	11.30 p	no change	77 M.J
	28/10	11.30 p	no change	77 M.J
	29/10	11.0 p	no change	77 M.J
	30/10	11.0 p	new line laid from 69 H.Q. to 1/1st de RFA for use of Liaison Officer between RFA & Divn	77 M.J
	31/10	11.0 p	no change	77 M.J

20 h Oktbr. Sig. Reg.
vol. 5

84/7678

Nov. 15.

Confidential

War diary for Nov. 1915
of
O.C. 20th Divisional Signal Co. R.E.

F. J. M. Stratton
CAPT. R.E.
O.C. 20th DIVISIONAL SIGNAL COY. R.E.

WAR DIARY
or
INTELLIGENCE SUMMARY.

Army Form C. 2118

20th Divisional Signal Co. R.E.

(Erase heading not required.)

Place	Date	Hour	Summary of Events and Information	Remarks and references to Appendices
NOUVEAU MONDE	Nov. 1	11.0 pm	No change in communication; maintenance work on lines	F.J.Inf
	Nov. 2	11.0 pm	no change	F.J.Inf
	Nov. 3	11.0 pm	no change	F.J.Inf
	Nov. 4	11.55 pm	no change	F.J.Inf
	Nov. 5	11.0 pm	no change	F.J.Inf
	Nov. 6	12.15 pm	no change	F.J.Inf
	Nov. 7	11.30 pm	no change	F.J.Inf
	Nov. 8	11.30 pm	no change	F.J.Inf
	Nov. 9	11.30 pm	no change	F.J.Inf
	Nov. 10	11.0 pm	Picked up lines 2 PP from 2FZ towards LAHORE area. Also picked up line C from 2FZ	F.J.Inf
			Brigade DV signal office took over from LAHORE 11 am	
	Nov. 11	11.30 pm	Line 9 tied into 90th Bde. RCA to commence work 2PA+2FAR. Forward parapet Y street	F.J.Inf
			on to new parapet 9 to make telephone line to ZP4 from YT street 33, line 4.	
			tied with 281	
	Nov. 12	11.0 pm	Line laid for 60th Bde. from HQ to Station to button HA to reserve billets	F.J.Inf
	Nov. 13	11.30 pm	Line from 90 Bde. to 2 FIR and 93rd Bde to 2 FAR picked up	F.J.Inf
	Nov. 14	11.0 pm	60th BDE moved to reserve in ESTAIRES relieved by 2nd 83rd GUARDS BDE. See app. 2	F.J.Inf
	Nov. 15	11.0 pm	Line from 93 Bde Rucks 905 pump picked up	F.J.Inf
	Nov. 16	11.0 pm	Line from 2FIR to ZFMR also lies from 9 and 3 to 2 FMR picked up	F.J.Inf

Army Form C. 211

WAR DIARY
or
INTELLIGENCE SUMMARY.
(Erase heading not required.)

Instructions regarding War Diaries and Intelligence Summaries are contained in F. S. Regs., Part II. and the Staff Manual respectively. Title pages will be prepared in manuscript.

Place	Date	Hour	Summary of Events and Information	Remarks and references to Appendices
NOUVEAU MONDE	Nov 16	11 am	Line from 9th Inf Bde to 251 R picked up, also the from 33 units to 2 FAR	77 Inf
	Nov 16	11:30 pm	No change in communication	77 Inf
	Nov 17	11:30 pm	Line 36 picked up from YT to YTR. Also line laid from 2 FA to new 2 FA, & rugby line to HQ nightfall	77 Inf
	Nov 20	11:30 pm	No change	77 Inf
	Nov 21	11:30 pm	Line 9 to 62 FA picked up	77 Inf
	Nov 22	11 pm	No change	77 Inf
	Nov 23	11:30 pm	Sect testing of 3 + 4 picked up. At 11 pm change of instruments & operators made with 62 Bde. 76 & Bde Hq are working day & night during morning. Communication with them thro' JH	77 Inf
SAILLY	Nov 24	11 pm	At 10 am took over Y Hughes Bridge. Moved into tpr office with communication apparatus transport on Flv + Blrws lines. Had thoughts of getting in between hands	77 Inf
	Nov 25	11 pm	No change. Nothing to cover billets	77 Inf
	Nov 26	11:30 pm	No change	
	Nov 27	11:30 pm	Batallion moved between 8th RM. Communication established by 11 am	77 Inf
	Nov 28	11:30 pm	Picked up line 33 from NOUVEAU MONDE to POUR E DEPOT	77 Inf
	Nov 29	11:10 pm	Picked up 23 R2A to MIDDENMUDE	77 Inf
	Nov 30	11:40 pm	Lancaster active brigade to relieve old cable line	77 Inf
	Nov 30	11:30 pm	Picked of letter line in station	See appendix III & IV

Appendix. I

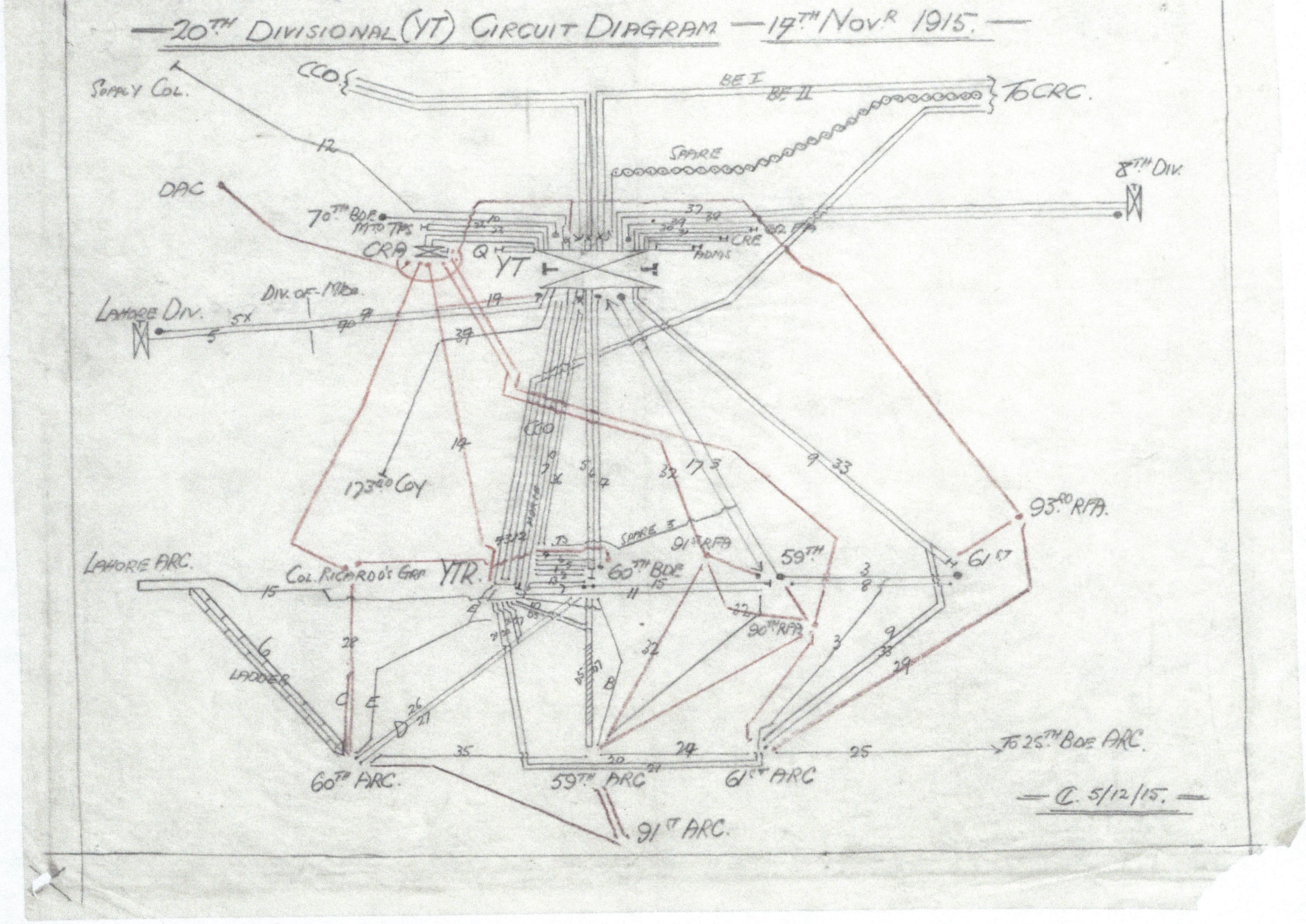

—20TH DIVISIONAL (YT) CIRCUIT DIAGRAM — 17TH NOVR 1915.—
SUPPLY COL.
CCO
BE I
BE II
TO CRC.
SPARE
8TH DIV.
DAC
70TH BDE
MTD TPS
CRA
Q
YT
CRE
ADMS
LAHORE DIV.
DIV. OF MBO.
173RD COY
CCO
SPARE 3
91ST RFA
59TH
61ST
93RD RFA.
LAHORE ARC.
COL. RICARDO'S GRP
YTR.
60TH BDE
90TH RFA
LADDER
TO 25TH BDE ARC.
60TH ARC.
59TH ARC
61ST ARC
91ST ARC.
— C. 5/12/15. —

Appendix IV.

20TH DIVISIONAL (YT) CIRCUIT DIAGRAM. — 27TH NOVR 1915.

C. 4/12/15.

20th Divisional (YT) Circuit Diagram – 30th November 1915.

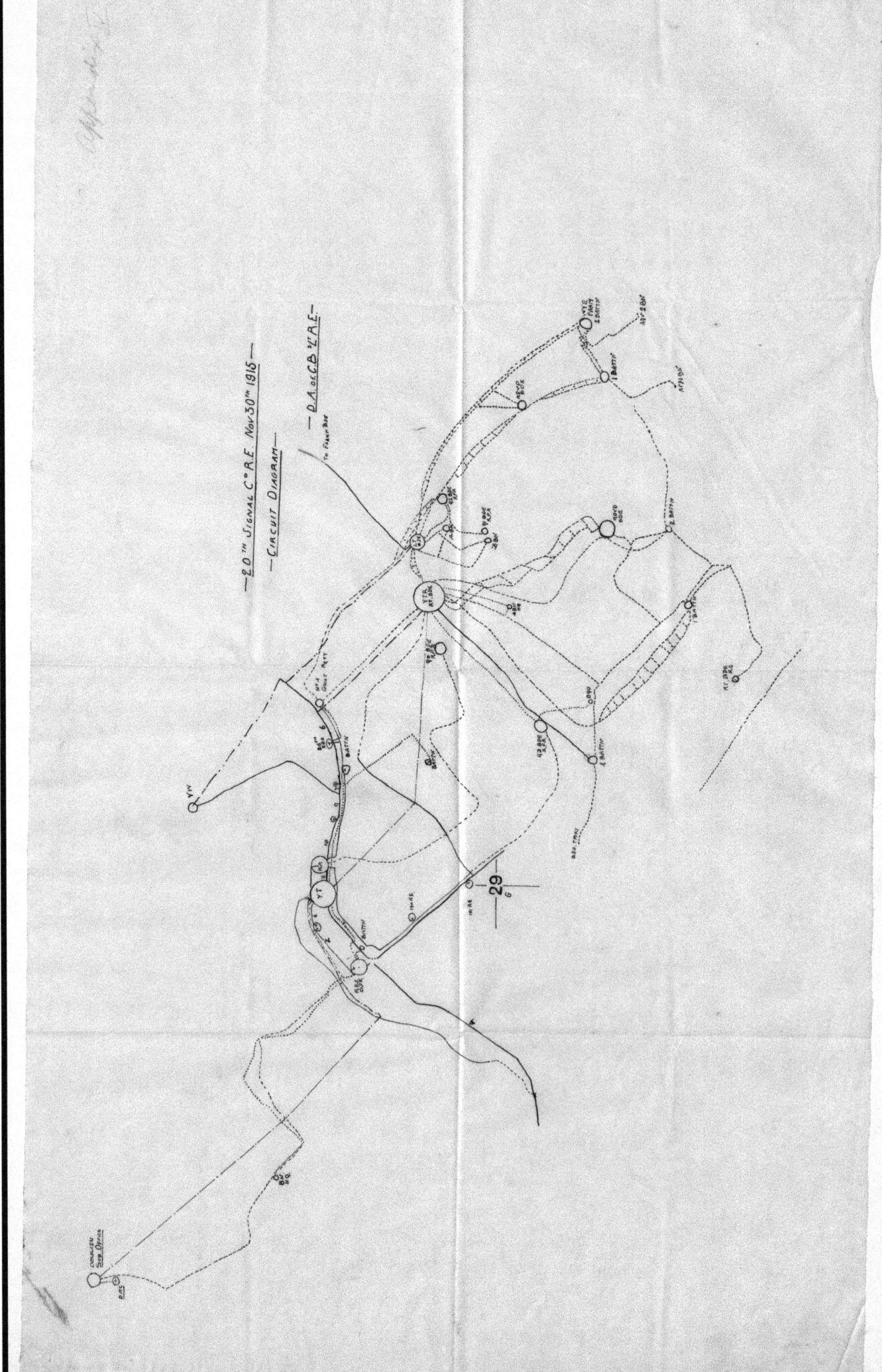

20 th Serial log.
vol 6

12/7931

Confidential

War Diary
of
20th Divisional Signal Co R.E.
for Dec. 1915

F J M Stratton
Capt R.E.
OC 20th Signal Co R.E.

20 August C.R.E.

WAR DIARY
or
INTELLIGENCE SUMMARY.
(Erase heading not required.)

Army Form C. 2118

Instructions regarding War Diaries and Intelligence Summaries are contained in F. S. Regs., Part II. and the Staff Manual respectively. Title pages will be prepared in manuscript.

Place	Date	Hour	Summary of Events and Information	Remarks and references to Appendices
SHELY G.32.c.2.9 Sheet 36	1/7/15	11.30pm	Laid lines round old HQ pulled up	77M4
	2/7/15	11.30pm	New lines to brigade completed	77M4
	3/7/15	11.20pm	Cable lines to Brigade and Croix Blanche R.E.A. pulled up	77M4
	4/7/15	11.40pm	New line started to 91, 92, 93, 94 Bdes R.F.A.	77M4
	5/7/15	11.30pm	93 Bde shifted H.Q. 7 Bn information to hectrs	
	6/7/15	10.0pm	No change. Construction and maintenance work continued	77M4
	7/7/15	10.30pm	Line to 91st Bde RFA finished	BWB
	8/7/15	10.15pm	New line to 93rd Bde R.F.A. begun. New telephone line to RA HQ begun & finished. Old line to Bauleu pulled up.	BWB
	9/7/15	10.20pm	No change, construction and maintenance continued	BWB
	10/7/15	10.30pm	No change, construction and maintenance continued	BWB
	11/7/15	10.40pm	Running lines from Y.T. to Sidley Cross.	BWB
	12/7/15	11.0pm	New line to 90th RFA started. Continued. Roads improved.	77M4
	13/7/15	11.0pm	Line to 90th RFA finished	77M4
	14/7/15	11.5pm	General maintenance	77M4
	15/7/15	11.0pm	Artillery and Infantry advanced lines. 91 & Bde relieved by 96 Bde & left area.	
	16/7/15	11.10pm	Laid a new line from 96 & 91 Bde R.H.A. through our trenches	77M4
	17/7/15	11.20pm	Laid new line - forward one of our lull from line HA to edge of crater from which fr	
			attack on enemy's line was launched	
	18/7/15	11.30pm	Work of previous days completed	77M4
	19/7/15	11.0pm	Artillery and maintenance	77M4

WAR DIARY or INTELLIGENCE SUMMARY.

Army Form C. 2118

20th Signal Co. R.E.

(Erase heading not required.)

Place	Date	Hour	Summary of Events and Information	Remarks and references to Appendices
SAILLY A 32 b 2 9 Sheet 36	20/12/15	11.0pm	Line BDKE to Farine, relaid with comic airline by Infantry cable	77 Army
	21/12/15	11.0pm	Testing and maintenance work	77 Army
	22/12/15	11.0pm	2Lt ROTH and 17th joined for duty. Maintenance and clearing of events. HERBERT	77 Army
	23/12/15	11.0pm	Picked up old disused cable leading in to VTR + F26R	77 Army
	24/12/15	11.30pm	Clearing of old cable. 66th Bde relieved 48th in front area	77 Army
	25/12/15	11.0pm	Xmas day. No parade other than battle Programme which drive is evening	77 Army
	26/12/15	11.40pm	Went round artillery exchange	77 Army
	27/12/15	11.10pm	Clearing everyway out.	77 Army
	28/12/15	11.20pm	a.m. 27, the with further replacing of cable by airline along the Rue de la hop	77 Army
	29/12/15	11.0pm	Work of two previous days completed	77 Army
	30/12/15	10.40pm	New line from front to G.0.45th K22 telephone old cable line	77 Army
	31/12/15	11.20pm	General maintenance, clearing & labelling.	77 Army

F.J.M. Stratton Capt. R.E.
OC 20th Signal Co. R.E.

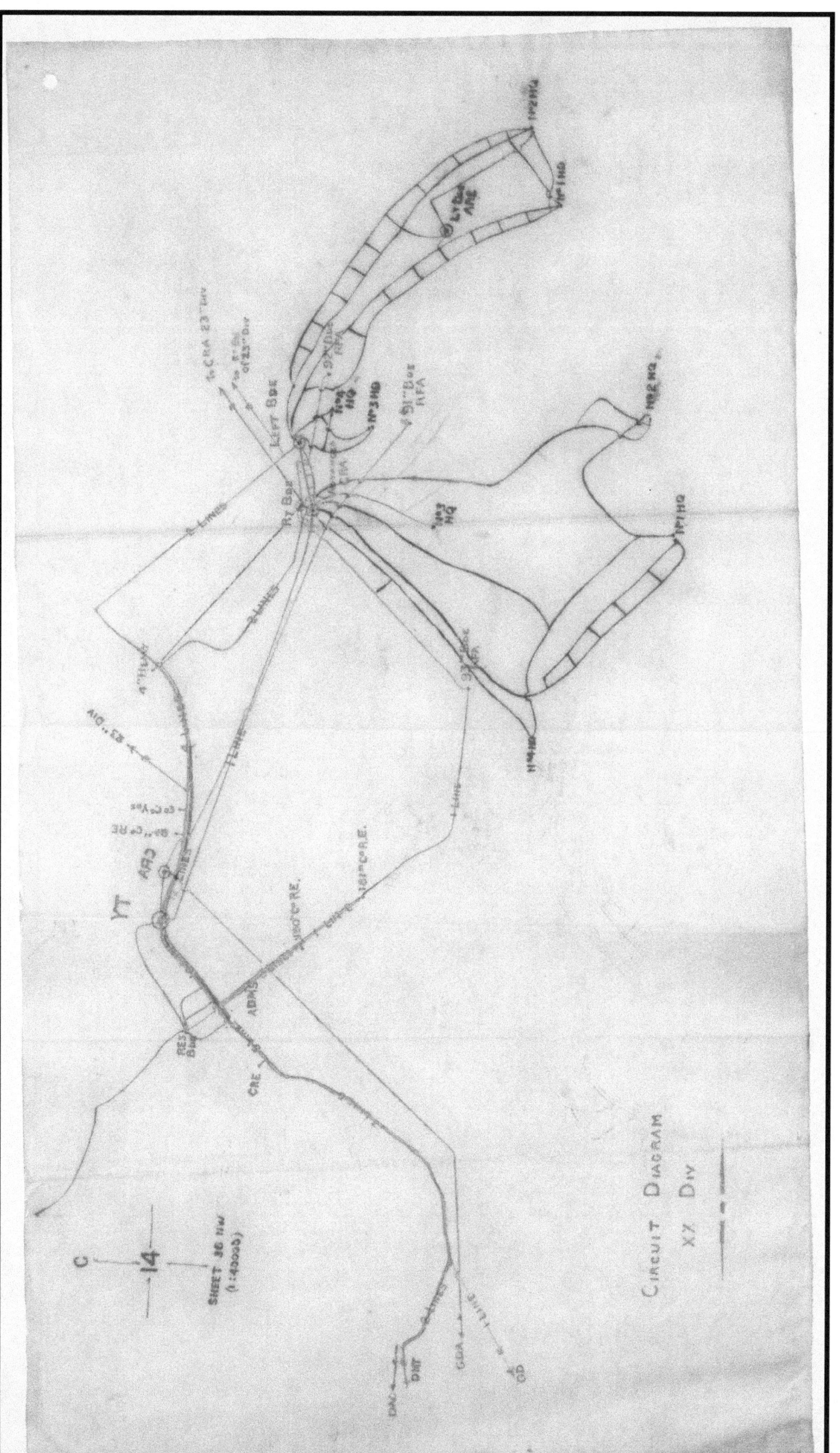

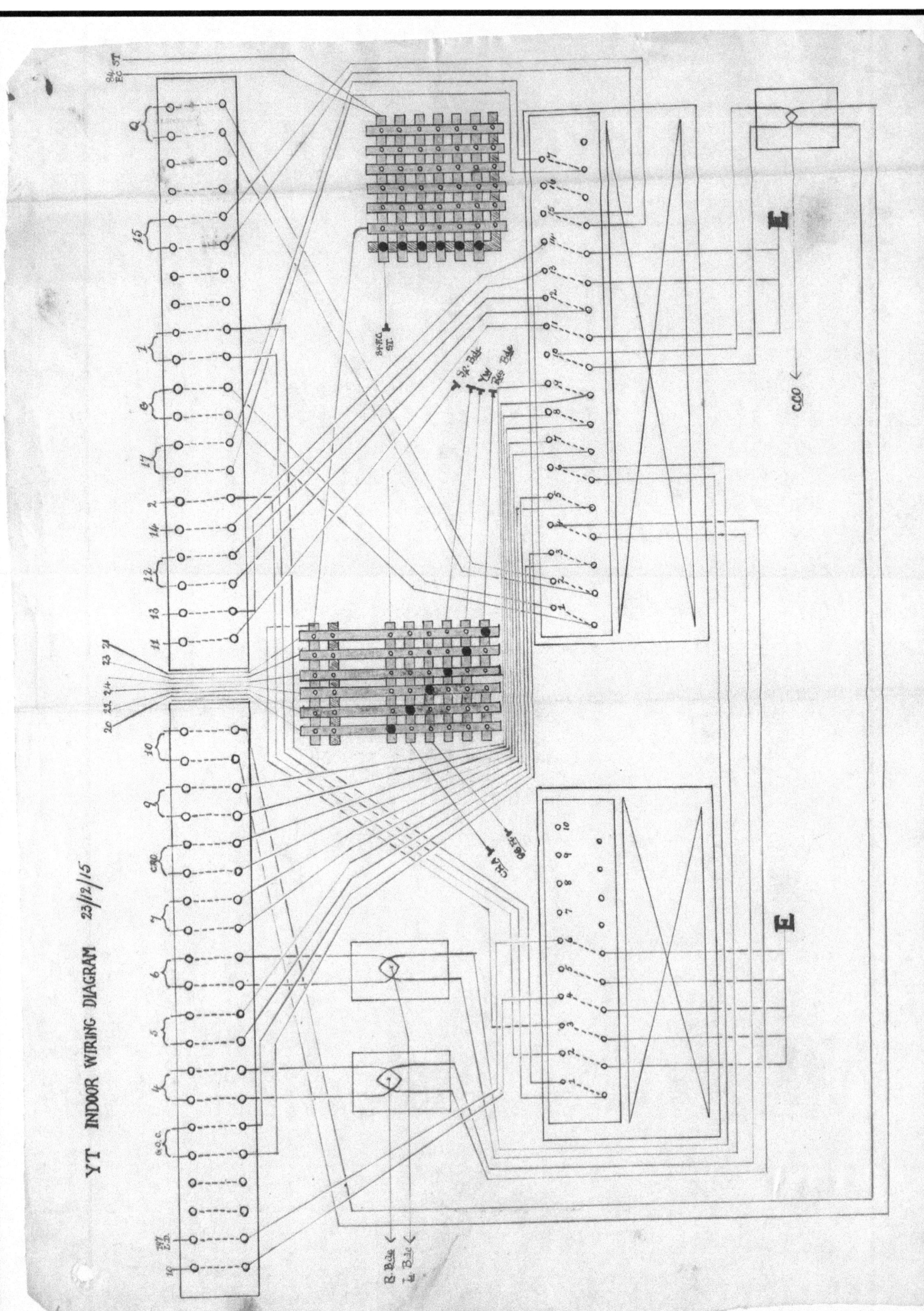

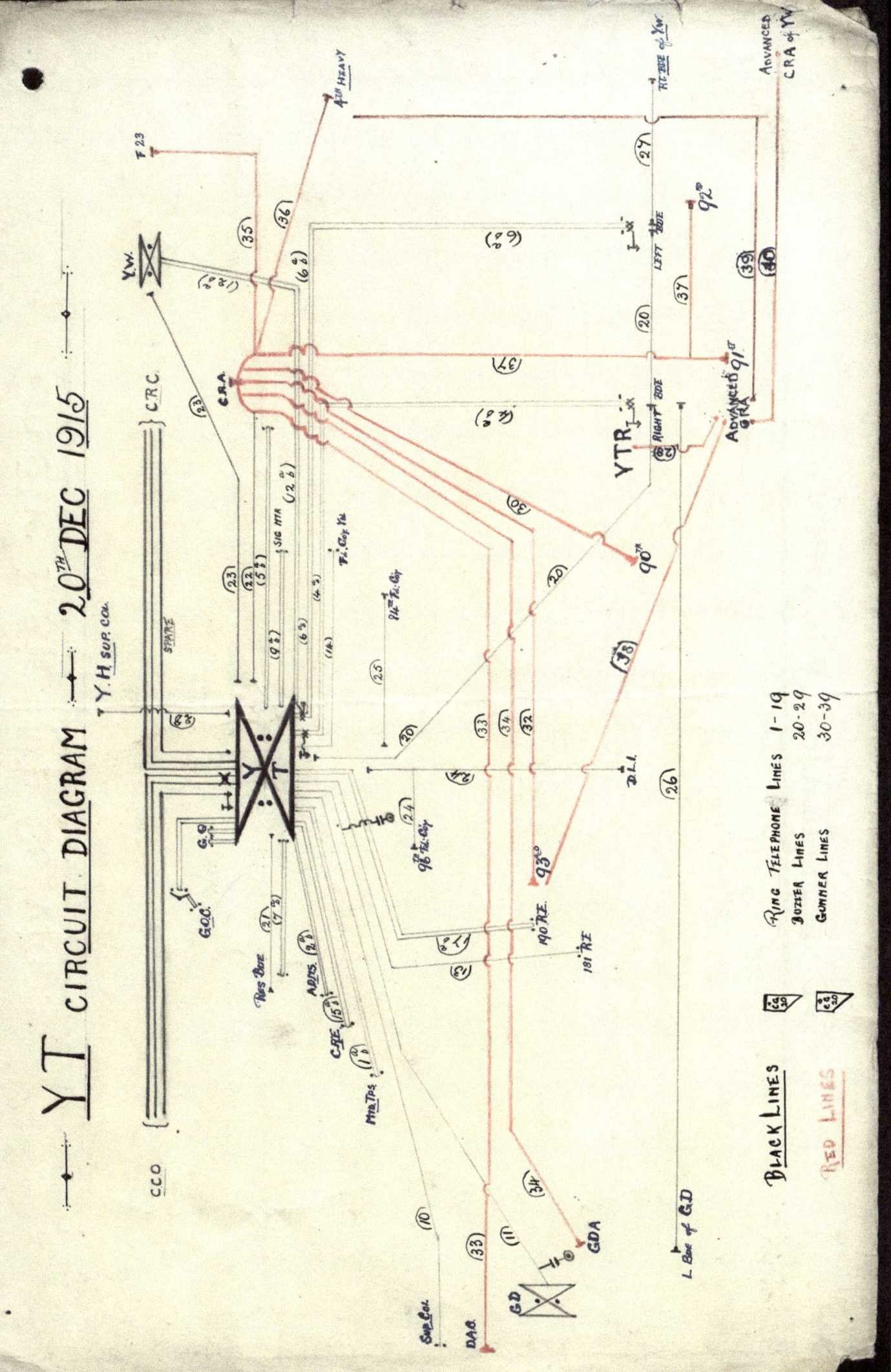

On His Majesty's Service.

20ten Sink: Serials
Vol: 7

WAR DIARY or INTELLIGENCE SUMMARY

Army Form C. 2118.

Place	Date	Hour	Summary of Events and Information	Remarks and references to Appendices
SMLW	1/7/6	11.45p	Labelling mentioned and clearing of emergency rails.	77nd
632.6.2.9 Sheet 36	2/7/6	11.30p	Lt Purchase RE left for Ryland to find new army units. Lt Richards transferred from No 2 B.S.A Section. 2 Lt H. Rothkauts (joined 22 7/5) took command of No 2 section. Line from u Bde RFA run to advanced artillery exchange	77nd
	3/7/6	11.0p	No change in comms.	77nd
	4/7/6	11.30p	Permanent pole the main road to Souilly, enlarged and lines repeated	77nd
	5/7/6	11.0p	No change	77nd
	6/7/6	11.0p	Worked in branches.	77nd
	7/7/6	11.0p	Heat to advanced artillery exchange completed	77nd
	8/7/6	11.0p	New hut erected at front	77nd
	9/7/6	11.30p	Cable attack in am. J. Special lines to front trench from Major's head hell post. No incidents. 6.0am D.R. later with No 1 & 3 Detachment moved off to Blanzy-les- advanced cart. Branches & Lt Allen arrived with two detachments for Bdce new office (EE) opened at 3.25pm at Letomis and D.R. office for own remaining behind a self	77nd
	10/7/6	11.0pm	No change in communication	77nd
	11/7/6	11.30pm	No mums with remaining detachments and horse transport left for Blanzy from am afternoon, marching through the night	77nd

WAR DIARY
INTELLIGENCE SUMMARY

(Erase heading not required.)

Army Form C. 2118.

20th Signal Coy R.E.

Place	Date	Hour	Summary of Events and Information	Remarks and references to Appendices
SAILLY LABOURSE HULLOCH	12/6	11.30p	a/gun bombardone Signal office to 8th Div. Signal Coy moved up from with reinf. officer Thompson	
			by ca. lorry, arr'd about BARLINGHEM to CHQ reserve. Signal office opened 9am at B.23 a 8.9. Bullets relative lightly set around.	77 Mg
BARLINGHEM	13/6	11.30p	Telegraph office and wireless	77 Mg
B.23 a 8.9	14/6	11.30p	9th Bde moved HQ attached but from SERCUS to C.H.Q.S.	77 Mg
	15/6	11.0p	General maintenance work	77 Mg
	16/6	11.0p	laid lines for R.A.8. 90 + Bde + 9th ant Bde by day	77 Mg
	17/6	11.0p	Took rd and lines laid by returning signals from D.hrs/ka rechar'd to BERGUETTE STEENBECQUE. Ripped up.	77 Mg
			SERCUS + off. Busga line to D.L.I at new POSITION and picked up lines of withdrawn lines to STEENBECQUE	77 Mg
	18/6	11.30p	lines new laid 7, 8, 9, 14th Bde 4, 5 Dis line (5 mile line)	77 Mg
	19/6	11pm	Picked up Capt F.M. Sclater went to G.H.Q wireless School for course of instruction. Lieut F.A Sclater assumed command of Heron party	FAS
	20/6	11pm	Picking up D5 line disused	FAS
		11pm	Picked up disused D5 lines to 60th and 61st bdes (6 miles)	FAS
	21/6	11pm	Packing stores and recharged switchboard with 1st Bn 3/4K sh95 & Coy	FAS

Army Form C. 2118.

WAR DIARY
or
INTELLIGENCE SUMMARY.

(Erase heading not required.)

20th Div'l Signal Coy R.E.

Place	Date	Hour	Summary of Events and Information	Remarks and references to Appendices
OXELARE O17 63.5	22/7/18	11 pm	Moved by march route to OXELARE. Small advance party opened office at 11 am. Communication obtained by means of 2nd ARMY lines and DR's	FAST
	23/7/18	11 pm	Laid cable line to 59th Bde and carried on a 2nd ARMY permanent line to RA at NORDPEENE	FAS
	24/7/18	11 pm	Laid cable lines to 61st Bde & at ARNEKE by adding to RA line. Also laid line to 60th Bde at EECKE by adding to 59th Bde line at LE HAUT EN BAS. D3 Telephones used on all these lines.	FAS
	25/7/18	11 pm	Running through cable and overhauling equipment and harness.	FAS
	26/7/18	11 pm	Laid lines from RA to 90th Bde at OEHTZEELE and party to KENIEPOF	FAST
	27/7/18	11 pm	Laid line from RA headquarters to artillery bde at OOST HOUCK	FAS
	28/7/18	11 pm	Line finished to le NIEPPE and OOST HOUCK line carried on to AMN COLUMN at LE DERZEELE.	FAS
	29/7/18	11 pm	Lt SCLATER and Lt AANNEN visited 49th Sig'l Co RE at ESQUELBECQ with a view to taking over with exception of one	FAST
	30/7/18	11 pm	CAPT STRATTON returned from GHQ and assumed command of the Company	FAS
	31/7/18	11 am	Visit to 14 DIV. HQ with a view to taking over telephones, events, etc	

J.H. Stratton Capt.
O/C 20 Div Signal Coy

Confidential

War Diary
of 1st Div. Signal Coy.
for
Jan. 1916

signature
Captain

20th Signals
Vol: 8

Confidential

War Diary of
OC 20th Divisional
Signal Co R.E.

February 1916

F J M Stratton
Capt. R.E.
O.C. 20th Divisional Signal Co

WAR DIARY
or
INTELLIGENCE SUMMARY
(Erase heading not required.)

Army Form C. 2118.

2nd Divn Cyclists

Place	Date	Hour	Summary of Events and Information	Remarks and references to Appendices
CASSEL	1/2/16	11.30pm	Returned for night. Became 6th Corps reserve	7/2/16
O/703/5 Cluster	2/2/16	11pm	No change. DCCA Glanville RS and 2nd Lt W H Brampton K joined from 6th Berks's N Div unit.	7/2/16
	3/2/16	11.30pm	Moved HQ to ESQUELBECQ 61. Btte moved to WORMHOUDT. 2/Lt Harman returned Y2 front at HQ. Capt Shelton stayed at BASSÉE 63. 2/Lt Brampton took charge of R Btte section; 2/Lt H Rothwell heat 7h 2nd Army defrosts. Lagd him to 6th Btte	7/2/16
ESQUELBECQ	4/2/16	10.30pm	lines laid to 5th Btte at HERZEELE and RA HQ at ZEGGERS-CAPPEL	D.H.
E & C 28 Sheet 27	5/2/16	11pm	Telephone list lines completed to 5th and 31st Bdes Cyclists and N° 3 detachment. Line laid to RA Btte at ARNEKE 93 & DAC Run party ½ at GLANVILLE arrived from OXELAERE	D.H.
	6/2/16	11.30pm	Picked up remaining artillery lines in old area.	D.H.
	7/2/16	11pm	Bell telephone line to Bdes altered to reduce induction	D.H.
	8/2/16	11pm	No change. Lt GLANVILLE and our detachment left for New HQ at A22d	D.H.
	9/2/16	11pm	No change. Office opened up at new HQ. A22 c.8.4 Sheet 28	D.H.
	10/2/16	11.30pm	Party of civilian under Lt Maclean sent forward to Trois Tours Chateau Workstatement arrived at new HQ from RAVELSBEEQ	7/2/16
	11/2/16	11.0pm	Line to laid for Trois Tours (YTM) to Lt brook R/o 40 M B R SH Sheet 28	7/2/16
	12/2/16	11.20pm	Rain of lines laid to Reserve Bde HQ at DIPERINGHE from our dist 64	7/2/16

WAR DIARY
or
INTELLIGENCE SUMMARY.

Army Form C. 2118.

Place	Date	Hour	Summary of Events and Information	Remarks and references to Appendices
F.S.O ENDER	13/6	11.0 pm	Work on front line as [illegible] thousands of company works [illegible] HQ	
GR c 2.8 slow	14/6	11.30 pm	Battn in [illegible] from [illegible] stayed at RR at dawn. Considerable difficulty with train to right of [illegible] [illegible] adrift in another front. Had to work some time to extricate [illegible]. Runs [illegible] with heavy fire.	
Near POPERINGHE A22/74 Stood	15/6	10 pm	Considerable trouble with new levering to shells & other [illegible] explosive reporting lairs to Infantry like rand other [illegible] not all working together after letting our stiff legend. Lead hind cattle kept with by down road & other [illegible] withstand line during night. 15/6 status before starts in camp	
	16/6	11.30 pm	General maintenance work on road line	
	17/6	11.0 pm	Ditto. Wireless station installed in adjoining field	
	18/6	11.0 pm	Maintenance of lines. Clearing earth and contents	
	19/6	11.30 pm	Ditto	
	20/6	11.0 pm	Ditto 500 men new comm par to reserve the [illegible] D3 cable [illegible]	
	21/6	11.0 pm	— Comm par to recover telle taken into our cattle [illegible] new burial took	
	22/6	11.0 pm	part in Br N6 ast. Buried stellar area 20 hit on this burial area in 3 days [illegible] maintenance	

WAR DIARY
or
INTELLIGENCE SUMMARY

(Erase heading not required.)

Army Form C. 2118

20th Div. Signal Co. R.E.

Instructions regarding War Diaries and Intelligence Summaries are contained in F.S. Regs., Part II. and the Staff Manual respectively. Title Pages will be prepared in manuscript.

Place	Date	Hour	Summary of Events and Information	Remarks and references to Appendices
France Sheet 8	23/1	11 a.m.	Maintenance continued. Have been busy in rather considerable trouble with shells	F/My
	24/1	10.30 pm	wind & snow bad lines	F/My
	25/1	11.0 pm	Wire being Hargreaves. all leave cancelled	F/My
	26/1	4.30 pm	Discovered that not more but to Rd-Blue Mr, intended for a firing job with 24 to 32 R. Div. lines of 6th Div. Considerable interference. Demand Trunk be away from enemy wire to work comdr through the line. On into gale highly damaged by shrapnel & brought back from easket bank shell burst, its aspect office at our town. Small cable lines established not damage. Speech, Ig buried w. office nowts afford deeper	F/My
	27/1	11.59 pm	ditto. hand maintenance and repair work.	9/My
	28/1	10.0 pm	ditto. Corps own line into office & one balloon section	R/My

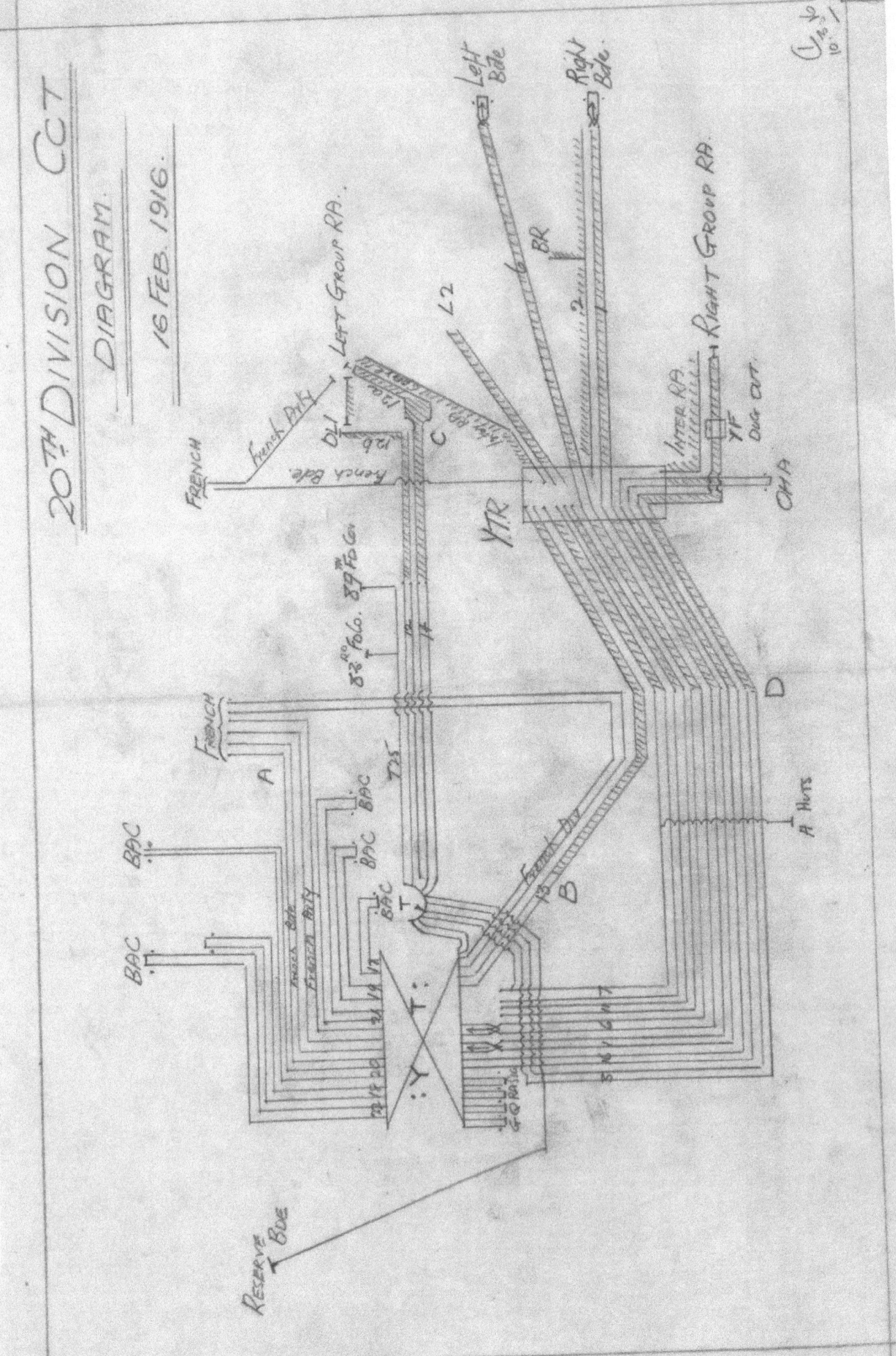

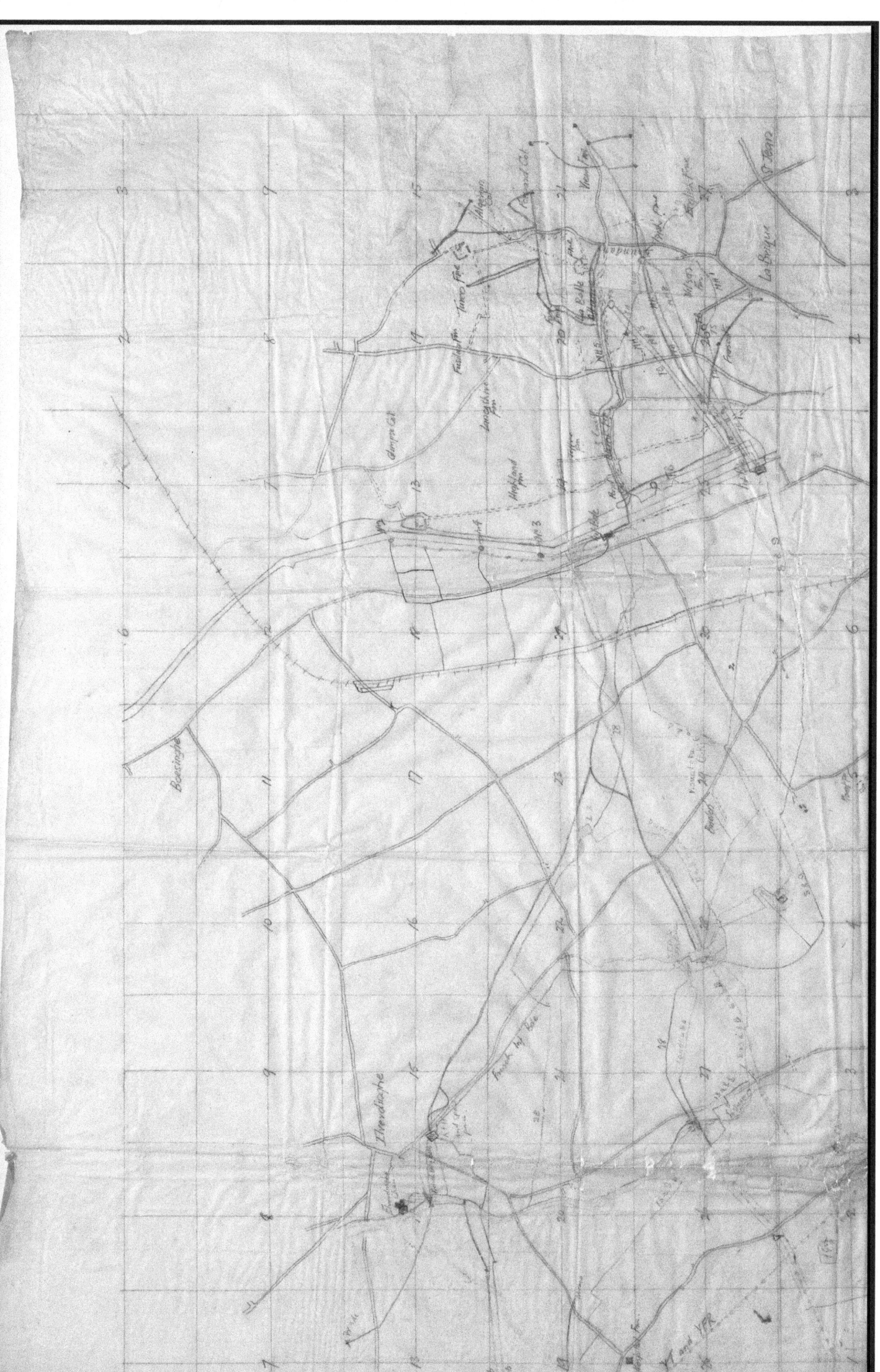

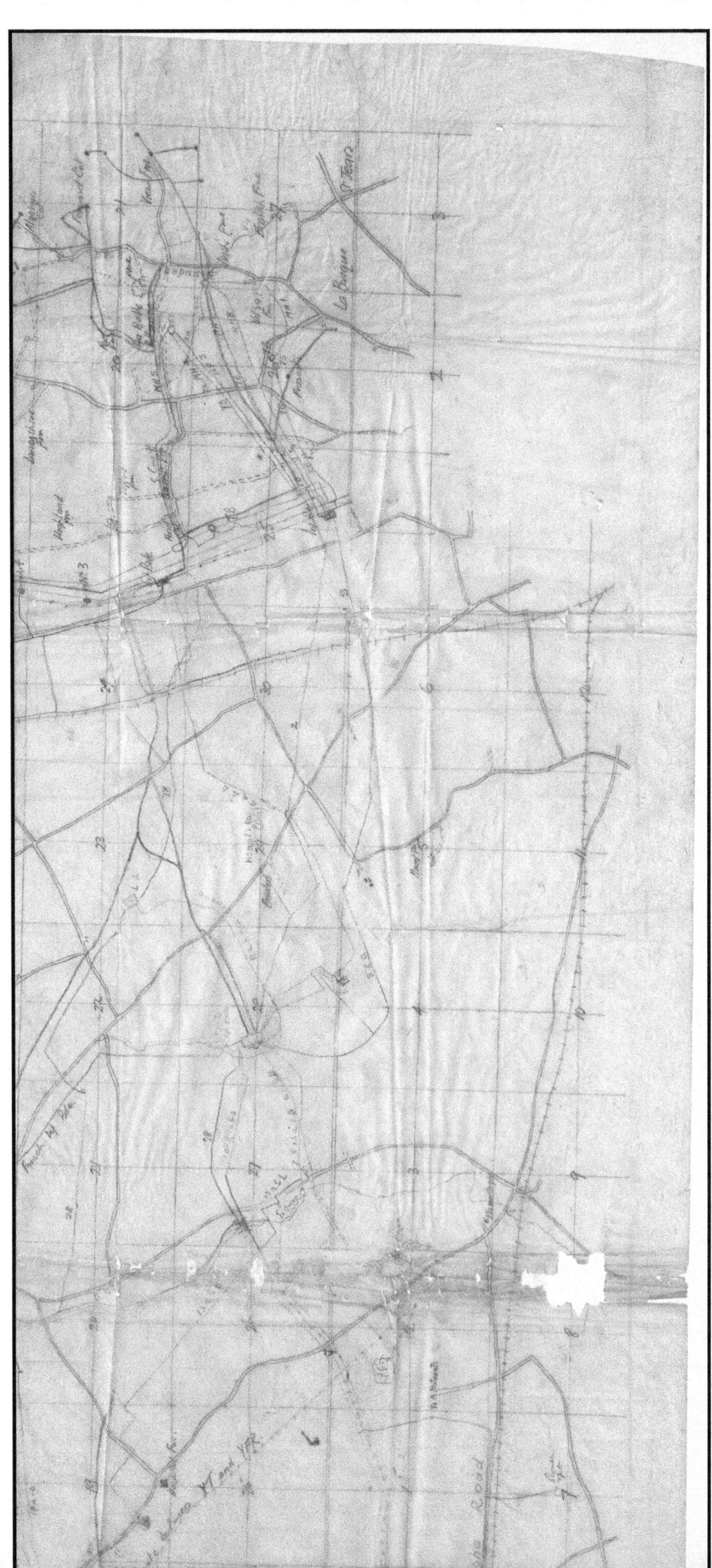

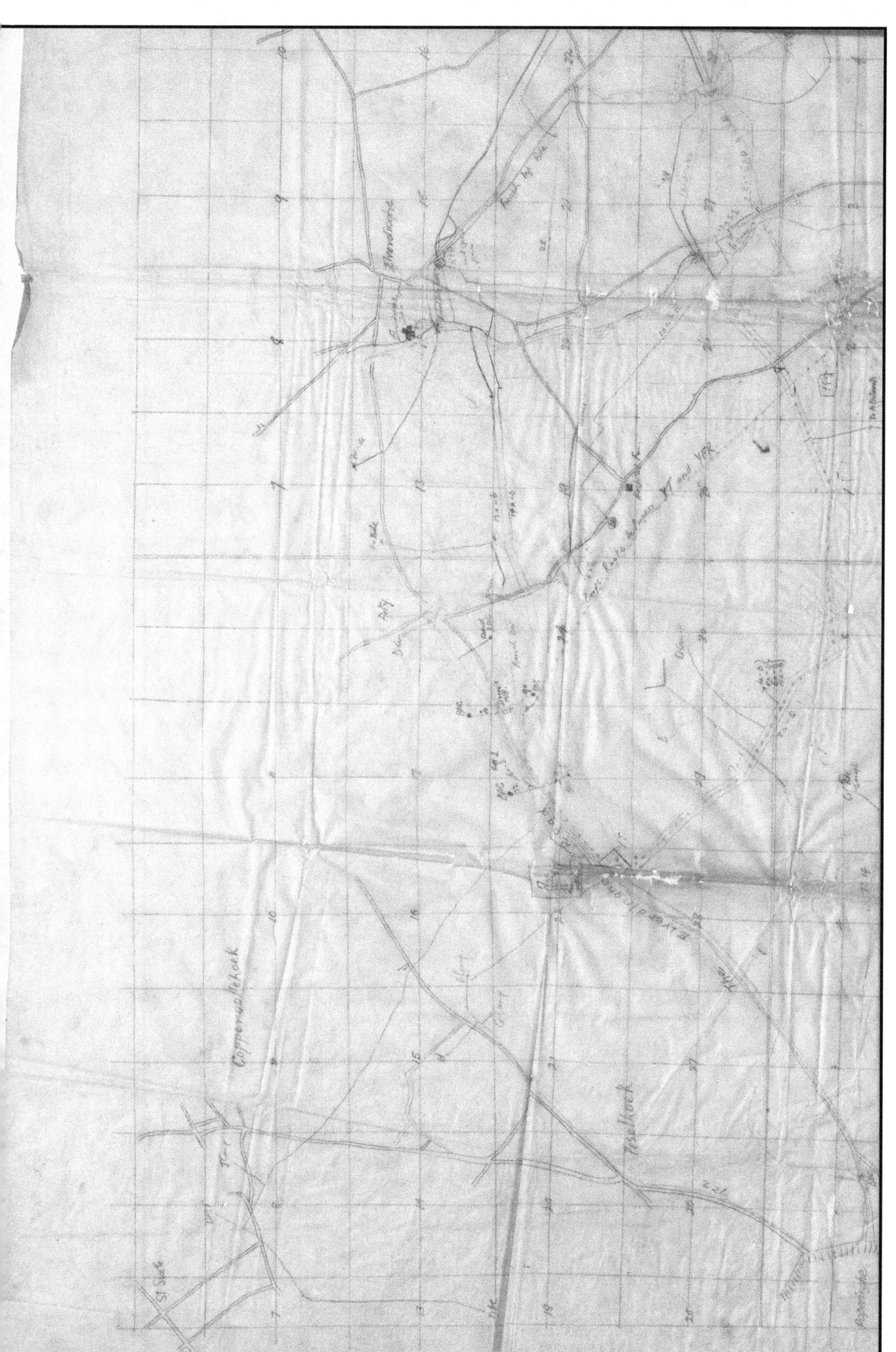

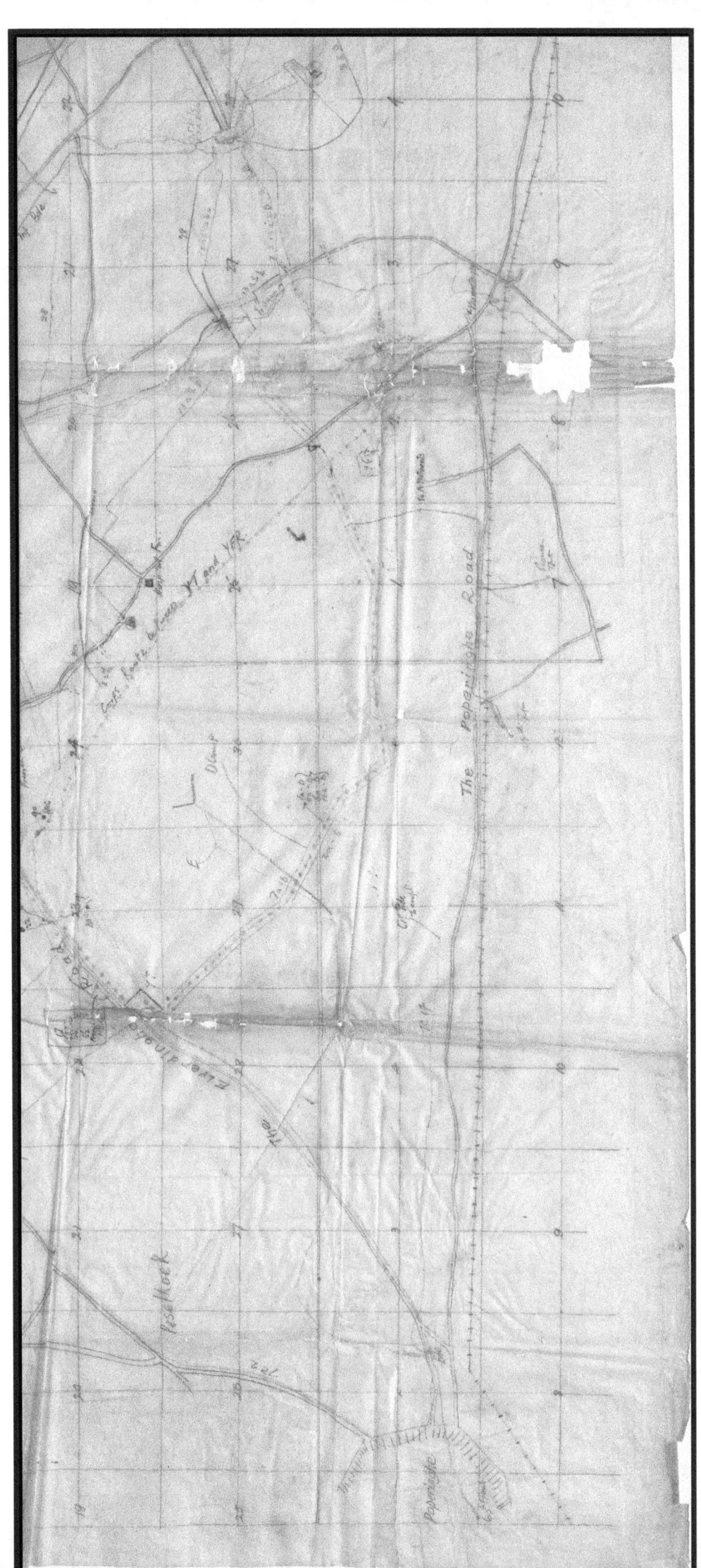

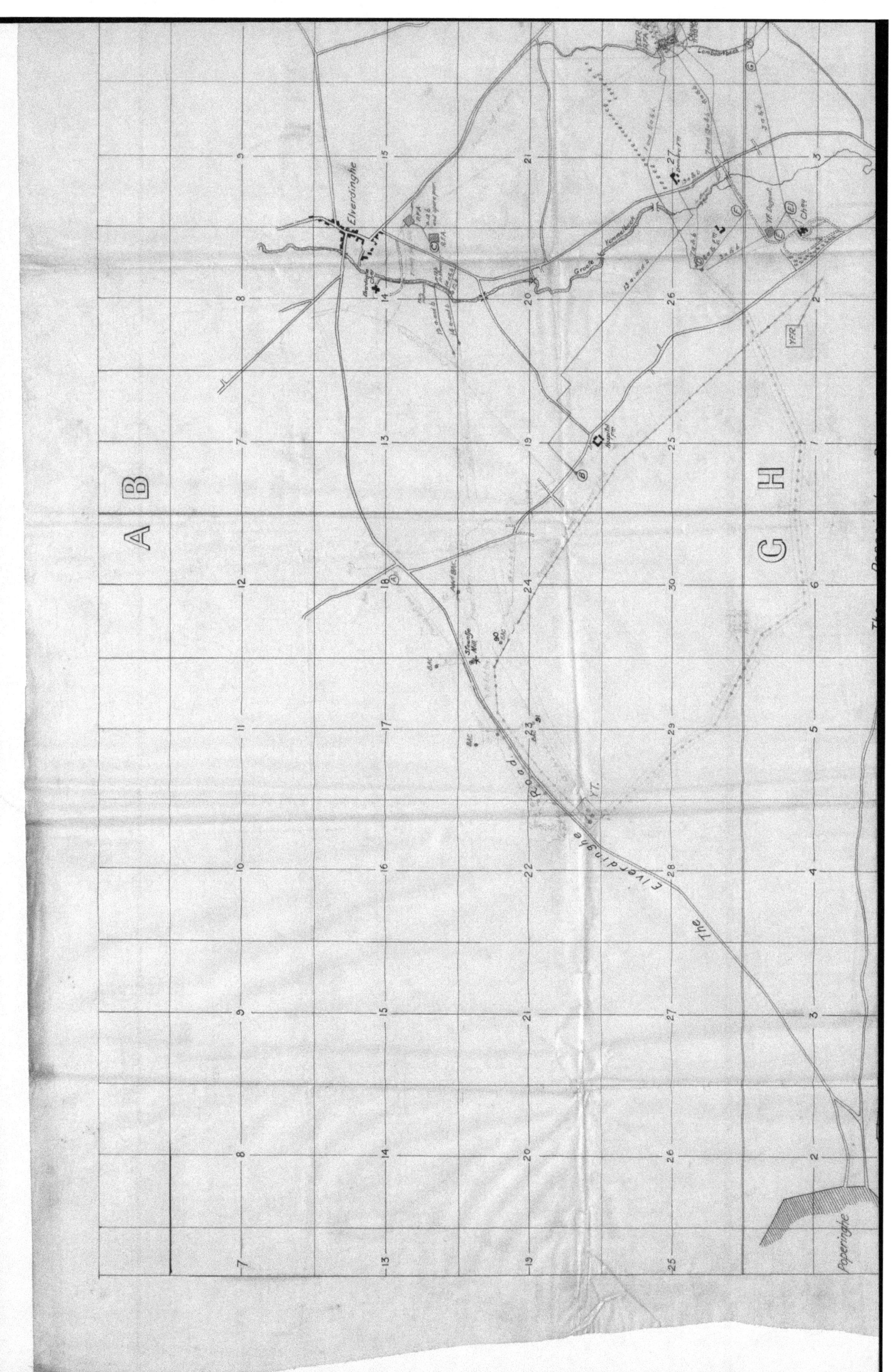

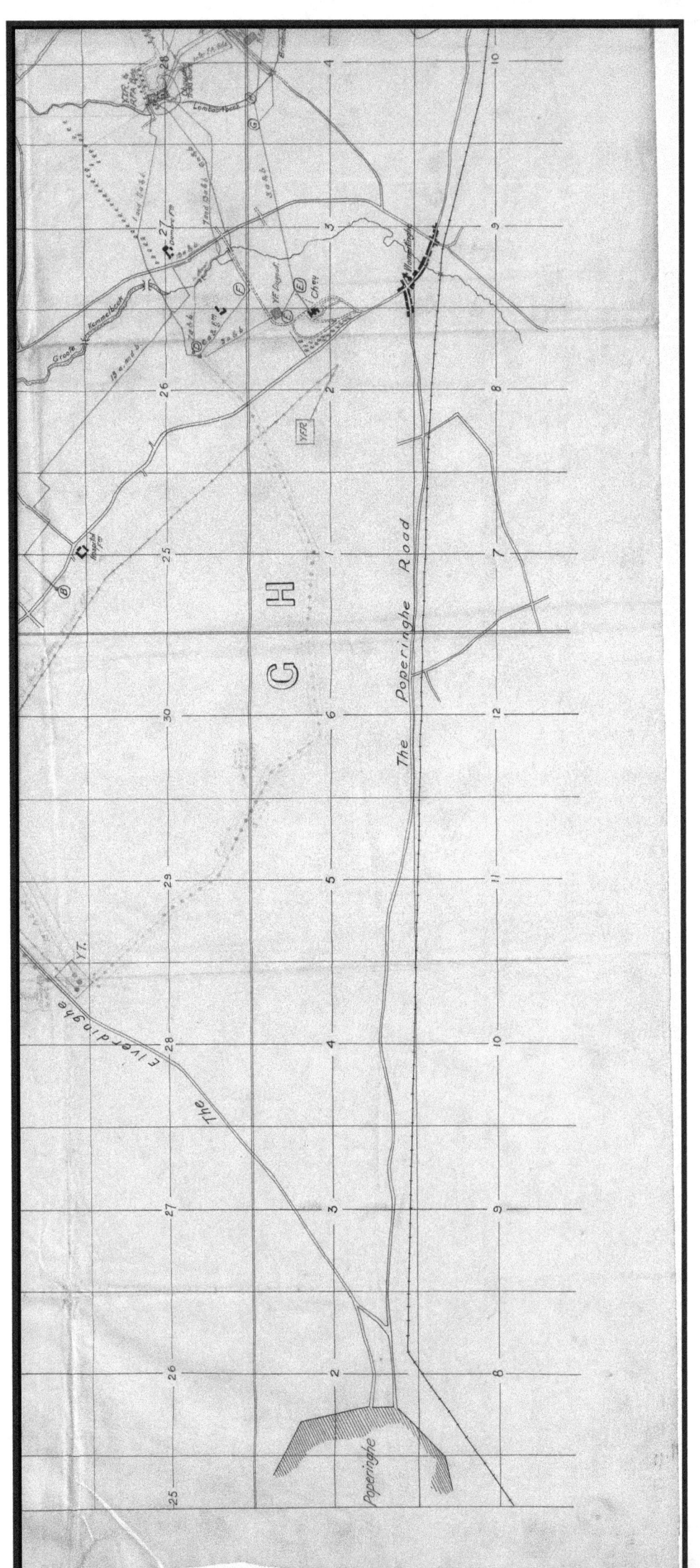

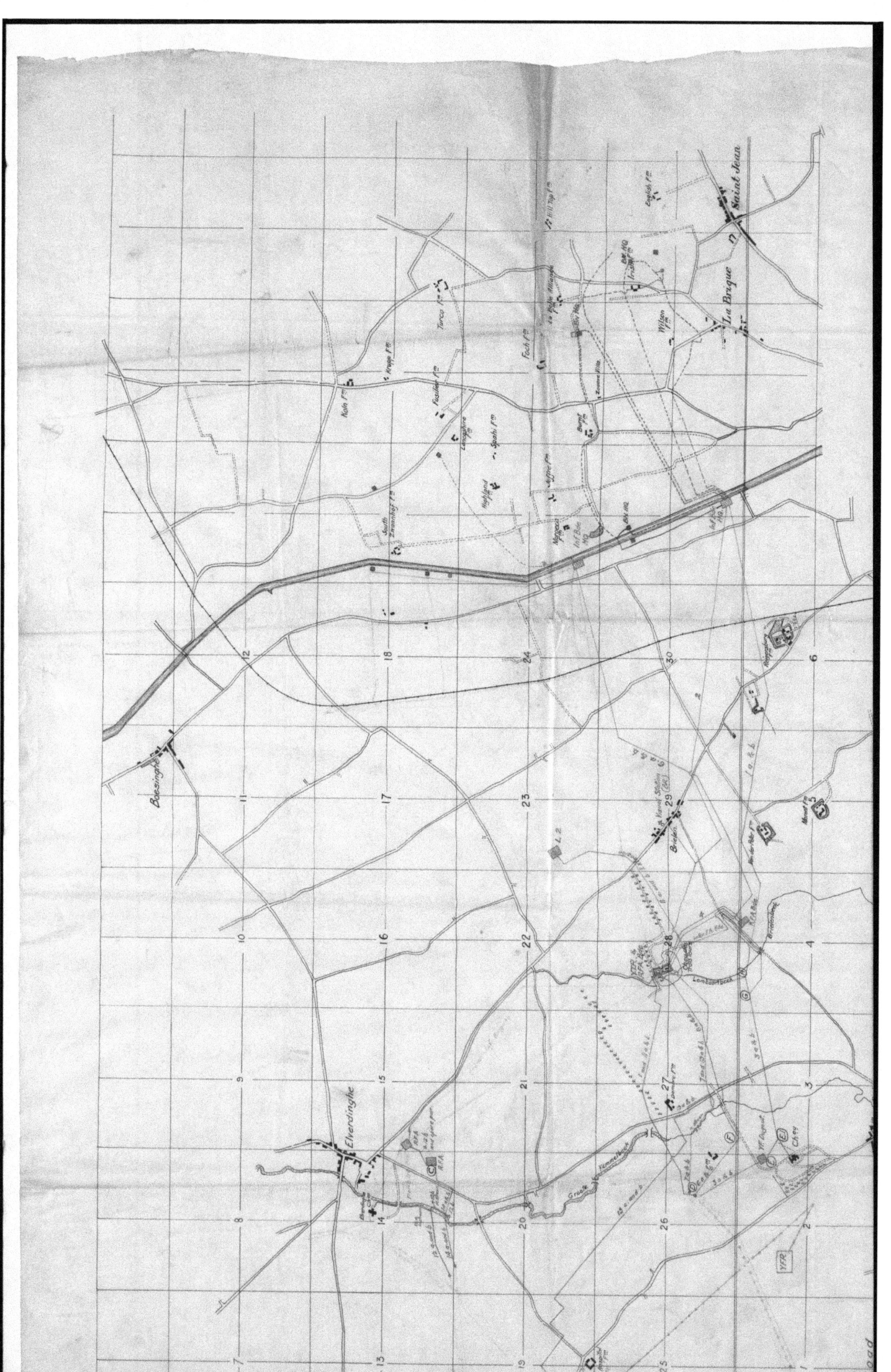

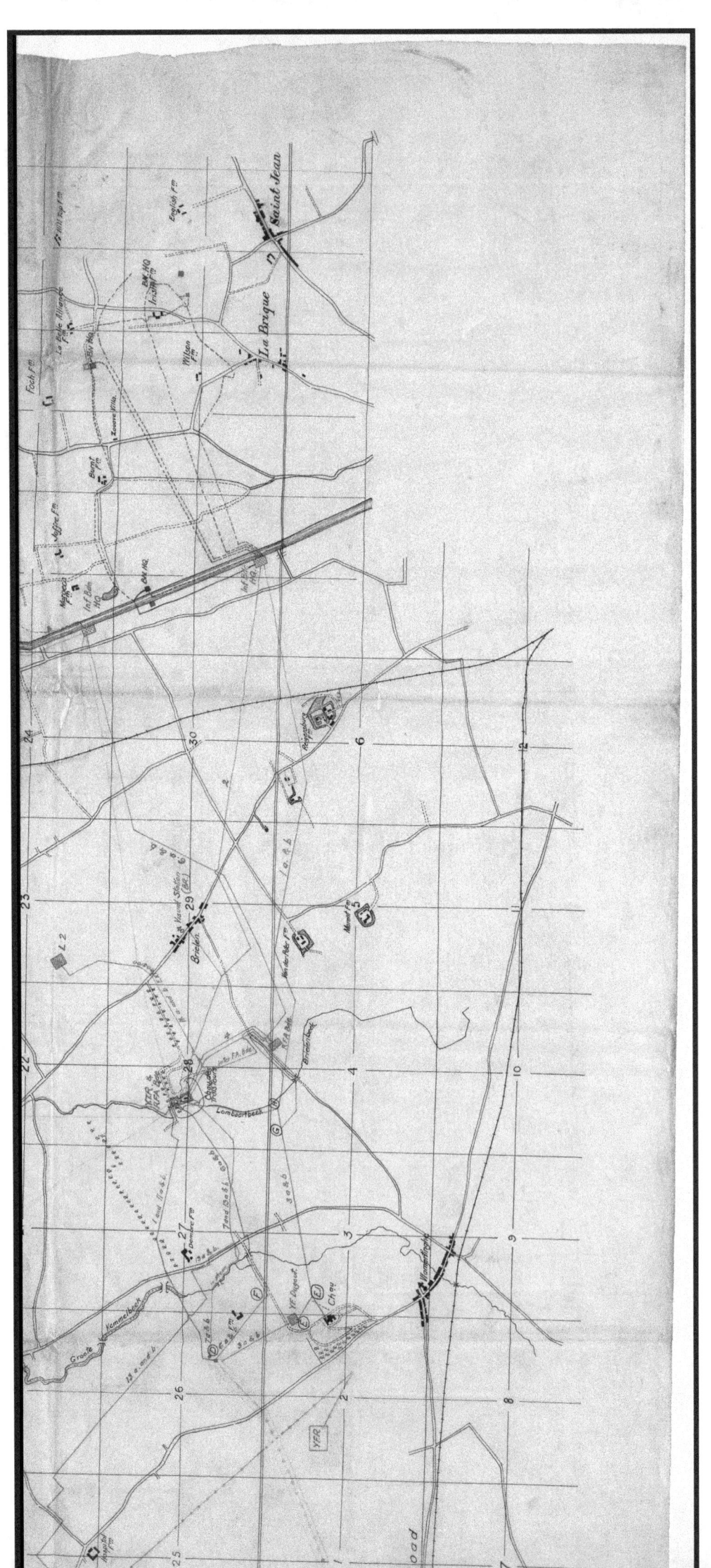

Secret
20th Signals
Vol G

War Diary of
OC 20th Divisional
Signal Co R.E.
for March 1- 31, 1916

FJM Shuter
Captain
OC 20th Div. Signal CoRE

20TH DIVISION
4/4/16
SIGNAL COY.

WAR DIARY
or
INTELLIGENCE SUMMARY

Army Form C. 2118

Place	Date	Hour	Summary of Events and Information	Remarks and references to Appendices
AZZd ?H Rules 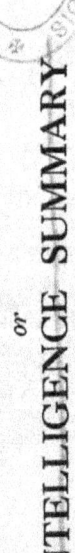	1/3/76	11.30pm	Maintenance work Line to RE Bde continues out night. 2/Lt & Lt Broadwood smokes	
	2/3/76	11.6pm	Intercepts point. 8th Divn left wireless comm of GHQ. Maintenance work. Ditto, but much enj use of pin additional at TT. trebles	
	3/3/76	11.40pm	Ditto. Maintenance line continues	
	4/3/76	11.0pm	DWB relieved RE. Debt Offrs of 2/7 Bde sent for instruction. Line & maintce. brigade broken wires to shellfire. 2/7 Bde	
	5/3/76	11.30pm	In the first two hours action, before the artillery brigade wanting to reach them. State of affairs existed 24 hours when Sig began ago again.	
	6/3/76	11.30pm	In of Sig cable on march line resorted to toughen 2 pulley schemes erected for final Deflector in wards a necessity party Heavy rainfall. First wireless weakening brigstern on cased burnt area 5 pole.	
	7/3/76	11.30pm	Bde HQ Heart. Two cables worth of somewhere firm, and lightly and wet/Buster/Work on buried line continued all lines handed over with some traffic between 60 & Bde	
	8/3/76	11.30pm	Several lines down with snow. All lines remade a/pull night	
	9/3/76	11.30pm	After run off but from two tons to truck Brigade manual. To avoid electrolysis where line is buried man constantly damp out. One line has interrupted been on arrival in the area 10% very defective of lend to British D30 the but numerous remakes made of these together	
	10/3/76	11.50pm	Maintenance work. Buried line continued. Received 2 Fuller phone from BAR	
	11/3/76	11.30pm	Fuller phones tried successfully bet/2 Bde with Wld telephone superimposed thought harmonic Buried great cable T8. T.T. completed + working with a 2/har/h N/P. Evasion = 1/pm signaller pms 9/pm	

Army Form C. 2118

WAR DIARY
or
INTELLIGENCE SUMMARY
(Erase heading not required.)

Instructions regarding War Diaries and Intelligence Summaries are contained in F. S. Regs., Part II. and the Staff Manual respectively. Title Pages will be prepared in manuscript.

Place	Date	Hour	Summary of Events and Information	Remarks and references to Appendices
A22 d 7.4	12/3/16	11.0pm	Cable laid and maintenance. Class for R.E. hierer commenced under Lt Moore	77 maf
	13/3/16	11.0pm	Tee run to French Pdt line at Shrewsbury forest  and to carpenters log	77 maf
			sketch of road cable running round van Shrewdinghe	
	14/3/16	11.30pm	The new tie to French line taken into use and allowed pass through and working OK for the first time for a month. A new tie run from line N2 across to left tree on road bank	77 maf
	15/3/16	11.20pm	Maintenance.	77 maf
	16/3/16	11.30pm	Stayed back towards Grands Div Signal Cd about 11 went into the line	75 maf
	17/3/16	11.30pm	VTT test put on line to CDR working well. line had been cut by our artillery an hour	77 maf
			Cd from Grande and line GT continued GT to VTT Transport	
	18/3/16	11.20pm	Maintenance. Relaying work with Guards. New buried pair from Shrewdinghe two towers	77 maf
			and VTT able commenced	
	19/3/16	11 pm	Maintenance. Night work continued	77 maf
	20/3/16	11 pm	New class for Infantry signallers at 6 each week Shrapnel commenced. Work on	77 maf
			buried line from Shrewsbury to 2 towers continued.	
	21/3/16	11 pm	R.E. Bde hut badly shelled. D. Delmar taken to Poperinghe wounded	77 maf
	22/3/16	11.20 pm	Signallers repot to YTR Lieut Moore for considerable time. Trouble turned to work in Hopfield being knocked about	77 maf
			Short periods & cutting all lines. 2nd Lt Antonio 3/1st Home Counties D Signed Co R.E. (T)	
			joined for temporary duty	77 maf

1875 Wt. W503/826 1,000,000 4/15 J.B.C. & A. A.D.S.S./Forms/C. 2118.

Army Form C. 2118

WAR DIARY
or
INTELLIGENCE SUMMARY
(Erase heading not required.)

Instructions regarding War Diaries and Intelligence Summaries are contained in F.S. Regs., Part II, and the Staff Manual respectively. Title Pages will be prepared in manuscript.

Place	Date	Hour	Summary of Events and Information	Remarks and references to Appendices
ADA 4	23/7/16	11.6pm	Maintenance. Work on buried line continued	7 July
	24/7/16	11.30pm	New portion of T.8 run towards Trois Tours from Kemmel back. Cpl Reynolds on leave OCK 24.31. L/Cpl S. Glanville took charge of section	7 July
	25/7/16	11.40pm	Wire laid to Sleaze from route to DAT & J camp. DCM awarded L/Cpl Boodle W.A. L/Glanville considered with scarlet fever. 2nd Antoine to hospital as contact	7 July
	26/7/16	11.05	Air patrols returned from wireless course at H.Q. maintenance & buried line	7 July
	27/7/16	11.30pm	Air patrols returned to respective brigades not maintained, when 7 artillery joined up. Howlins BD & 17 FDK took movement route later into Brigade Grenade dump on line at 7 late	7 July
	28/7/16	11.10pm	Spr 27 Hallett A.S., T. joined for duty. Ambulance park spinal telegraph work Buried line at right. Stained off the line to DAT. 2nd R.E. class started	7 July
	29/7/16	11.10-	General maintenance & buried work. Burry work at night	7 July
	30/7/16	11.30pm	New line run from R camp m.g. D camp in readiness for our division. Spr buried line began. Spr Budd for the Bn to Poland going on 4th cont. Chayst on Hof Resent Uh.	7 July
	31/7/16	11.40pm	Buried work & maintenance	7 July

F.J.M.Scott Capt R.E.
O.C. 20 Signal Co. R.E.

DAG Base

Herewith war diary for April 1916
of OC 20 Div Signal Co. RE.
Delay in forwarding regretted

F J M Strutt Major RE

O.C. 20th DIVISIONAL SIGNAL COY. R.E.

20 Div Signals
Vol 10

WAR DIARY or INTELLIGENCE SUMMARY

Army Form C. 2118

(Erase heading not required.)

Instructions regarding War Diaries and Intelligence Summaries are contained in F.S. Regs., Part II. and the Staff Manual respectively. Title Pages will be prepared in manuscript.

Place	Date	Hour	Summary of Events and Information	Remarks and references to Appendices
Fouquereuil	1/7/16	11.0pm	Work in Wagon wpt Hospital & in SUPERIEURE dugouts returned from leave	Appx
	2/7/16	11.0pm	Dugout work & tramway & bulk pair feed T2B completed. Roadwork continued	Appx
	3/7/16	11.30pm	Completed running Tab wire to about A2d	Appx
	4/7/16	11.0pm	Work on Tapping office continued (Intelligence cont.) Off on leave to UK appd 4 in 11	Appx
	5/7/16		2Lt Crombie O/C No 3 section	
	5/7/16	11.30pm	Maintenance Lineout work started. New System of code names for units and local calls from signal stations informed area canal bank and States system worked	Appx
	6/7/16	11.0am	Satisfactorily. Bgr Station start. Test classes started at J Camp. D.H.P + T2B Ltante new pack set for testing ready.	Appx
	7/7/16	11.0pm	Maintenance Lineout & W/T on. Camp and road intelligibility late afternoon. Signals hear (N°3) blown up by H.E. shell. No one damaged. Lines broken & repaired indicated by the target Regt morning. 2 Repairs broken.	Appx
	8/7/16	11.30pm	Lineout work. Pack jd. Damage repaired morning new bgr office	Appx
	9/7/16	11.0pm	Roofers L & R wing emplacement at B12C1.2 lead on JHR 9/10	Appx
	10/7/16	11.0pm	Lineout work. Damaged in W/T station. S f headqts. Dig-out office empl expt	Appx
	11/7/16	11.0pm	Welling & maintenance work Repairs to war frame	Appx
	12/7/16	11.30pm	Maintenance work and work on cable wagon	Appx
	13/7/16	11.0pm	Ditto. Lt Potter in town of instruction from by last journal prdcts	Appx

Army Form C. 2118

WAR DIARY
or
INTELLIGENCE SUMMARY
(Erase heading not required.)

Instructions regarding War Diaries and Intelligence Summaries are contained in F.S. Regs., Part II. and the Staff Manual respectively. Title Pages will be prepared in manuscript.

Place	Date	Hour	Summary of Events and Information	Remarks and references to Appendices
Hazebrouck	14/5/16	11.40pm	Air attack returned from front. Staff 7 miler joined in advance party from 6th Div with party of linesmen.	7 May
	15/5/16	11.30pm	Greatly fund damaged by hostile artillery. Two lines re-established. Several lines on main routes to Thames totally destroyed. Advanced party. Relief of Bde brigade commenced.	7 May
	16/5/16	11.0pm	6 pm Bde to Calais	7 May
	17/5/16	11.0pm	Cable section went across to gallery on arrival of 6th brigade with Capewell. 3/5th Bde relieved in accordance with 16th Inf Bde	7 May
	18/5/16	11.0pm	Relief in progress. 10.0pm handed over signal office to 6 Div Sigs. 10.0pm Div Relief completed	7 May
C&C 2.8 Sheet 27	19/5/16	11.0pm	Relief of 5th Div completed 12.45am. Move to Reserve area completed	7 May
	20/5/16	9.0pm	Heavy rain & everything down	7 May
	21/5/16	7.0pm	Cable from Wormhoudt to Herzeele gleaned. New airline hung through	7 May
	22/5/16	11 pm	Bn HQ at Herzeele. Air line previously laid by Army led into Arty Wdge at Zegger Cappel and D.A.P. at Rubronck	7 May
	23/5/16	11 pm	Local lines improved and slight extensions removed	7/5
	24/5/16	11 pm	Cable line to R.A. replaced by airline, picked up and run through	7/5
	25/5/16	11 pm	Two cable detachments on field work. Major Statter went on special leave. Lt Schakr commands in his absence	7/5
	26/5/16	11 pm	Other two cable detachments on field work. 2nd Lt Mallet left for Sig 6th Div	7/5
	27/5/16	11 pm	W.Bde company halted at Zeggers Cappel, one detachment laid 5 mile line to Bollezeele for one night while 1 sect Bde wireless there	7/5
	28/5/16	11 pm	Line to Bollezeele picked up and run through	7/5

Army Form C. 2118

WAR DIARY
or
INTELLIGENCE SUMMARY
(Erase heading not required.)

Instructions regarding War Diaries and Intelligence Summaries are contained in F. S. Regs., Part II. and the Staff Manual respectively. Title Pages will be prepared in manuscript.

Place	Date	Hour	Summary of Events and Information	Remarks and references to Appendices
Q 8 C 2 8	29/4/16	11 pm	All ferm detachments on field work.	
	30/4/16	11 pm	Cleaning up for Inspection tomorrow	

F J McKenzie Major
O.C. 2nd Canadian Div. Cyc. Co.

1875 Wt. W593/826 1,000,000 4/15 J.B.C. & A. A.D.S.S./Forms/C. 2118.

Secret

War Diary of
O.C. 20 Div. Signal Co.
for month of April 1916

FJM Stark
Major

O.C. 20th DIVISIONAL SIGNAL COY R.E.

20 Div Signals
Secret
Vol II

War Diary of
20 Div Signal Coy R.E.
for period May 1 – 31, 1916

F J M Statter
Major R.E.

Army Form C. 2118

WAR DIARY
or
~~INTELLIGENCE SUMMARY~~
(Erase heading not required.)

Instructions regarding War Diaries and Intelligence Summaries are contained in F. S. Regs., Part II. and the Staff Manual respectively. Title Pages will be prepared in manuscript.

Place	Date	Hour	Summary of Events and Information	Remarks and references to Appendices
C&C 2.8 Sheet 27	1/5/16	11 pm	Major General W D Smith C.B. the divisional commander inspected the company transport in the morning. Lieut Oyler RFA Orderly Officer	7/MS
	2/5/16	11 pm	Two cable detachments doing field work today. 93rd Bde came for instruction.	7/MS
	3/5/16	11 pm	The other two detachments on field work. Lt Oyler RFA went with them	
	4/5/16	11 pm	Day chiefly spent in overhauling equipment and wagons	
	5/5/16	11 pm	Major 77th H.Q. RS returned from Special leave 6 Lt. L/Cpl Hannen transferred on loan	7/MS
	6/5/16	10 pm	Musketry, revolver practice Gallaghers commenced on R.E. III ch hours	7/MS
	7/5/16	9.40 pm	Telegraph line 16C Chateau cable construction	7/MS
	8/5/16	9.0 pm	Lt E.E. Blamwell returned from Abbeville	7/MS
	9/5/16	9.0 pm	Cable wagons out	7/MS
	10/5/16	7.30 pm	Cable wagons out, musketry & revolver practice	7/MS
	11/5/16	9.0 pm	Lt Rainsford R.S. joining from 9th Div Signal Co. S.	7/MS
	12/5/16	9.0 pm	2/Lt Rainford RS left for 2nd Army Signal Co. R.E. 2/Lt Schule taken to replace him from Plan on board Lt/W.C.	7/MS
	13/5/16	9.0 pm	2Lt Brampton on leave to U.K. 55th Inf Bde moved from Callas at short notice, horse show at Daggon cancelled sections typical Co were marching to support Thursday	7/MS
			will learn 4/6 weeks, 13rd prize £2, horse without wagon	
	14/6/16	11.0 pm	2/Lt Hanne returned from leave. N° E.E. Harris TLE & E. Little W.O. 10 Cy ? S E	7/MS

WAR DIARY or INTELLIGENCE SUMMARY

Army Form C. 2118

Place	Date	Hour	Summary of Events and Information	Remarks and references to Appendices
C8 c 2.8 Sheet 77	15/5/16	11.0pm	Lt EPKE wounded, Lieut SELK [?] in waggon line at Reserve. 77/7/1 in the Rosary killed accidentally on road to huts. Mrs SELL wounded. Major Leitenmer & Mrs & daughter	77md
	16/5/16	11.0pm	wounded. Found as an advance party GDR H2a.6.3 sheet 28.	77md
		11.0pm	Party from forward camp/gas hands at WORMHOUDT. Coal waton huts. Embussed	77md
	17/5/16	11.0pm	Preparation for move	77md
	18/5/16	11.0pm	further party proceeded forward to GDR	77md
	19/5/16	11.0pm	Col hand & 2" detachment proceeded to GDR abandoned officer billets for 77 [?] C.R.	77md
	20/5/16	11.0pm	2 Relief of GD officer sent over to relieve in	77md
Sheet 21 G1d 9.5	21/5/16	11.30pm	N°3 detachment also proceeded to relieve. Officers letter one an 10am. Relief of General Sir	77md
		11.0pm	at 10pm. The rest returned for leave & posted VTR	
	22/5/16	11.0pm	Part of Company officers stop at VTR turned at VTR, to camp & report again his (A's cooks parade)	77md
			Support. Telege. Pot. & Memo bombs etc. all under command of VTR	
	23/5/16	11.0pm	Works are necessary & restoration of war prewar wants from the officer in C of VTR on to occur	77md
			his Hans worked at 130	
	24/5/16	11.0pm	The same continued	77md
	25/5/16	11.0pm	2 supernumerary turns on of A/F ammony toed into offices, odd heavy ammon in funeral attendant.	77md
	26/5/16	11.0pm	arrangements to meet R.A. Vets in the Rank has been discussed.	77md
	27/5/16	11.0pm	No further news from Town. Call at 3 Rue de Bruges. Capt Ramford reported from 2nd Army	77md

WAR DIARY
or
INTELLIGENCE SUMMARY

(Erase heading not required.)

Army Form C. 2118

Instructions regarding War Diaries and Intelligence Summaries are contained in F.S. Regs., Part II. and the Staff Manual respectively. Title Pages will be prepared in manuscript.

Place	Date	Hour	Summary of Events and Information	Remarks and references to Appendices
Sheet 28 G.14.d.5.5	28/5/16	11.4 pm	Telegraph killed many last night plus 25 wounded on leave to UK	73 mg
(Hoogle)	29/5/16	11.15 pm	Hindenburg & work on tunnel route continued	73 mg
Inn dHall	30/5/16	10.30 pm	as on 29. Newton's Bay near BA 30 & tunnels to ment Div HQ	73 mg
	31/5/16	11.5 pm	Hindenburg work continued	73 mg

[signature]
Major R.E.
O.C. 2nd Division ? P.N.C.

Y.T. CIRCUIT DIAGRAM 14/5/16

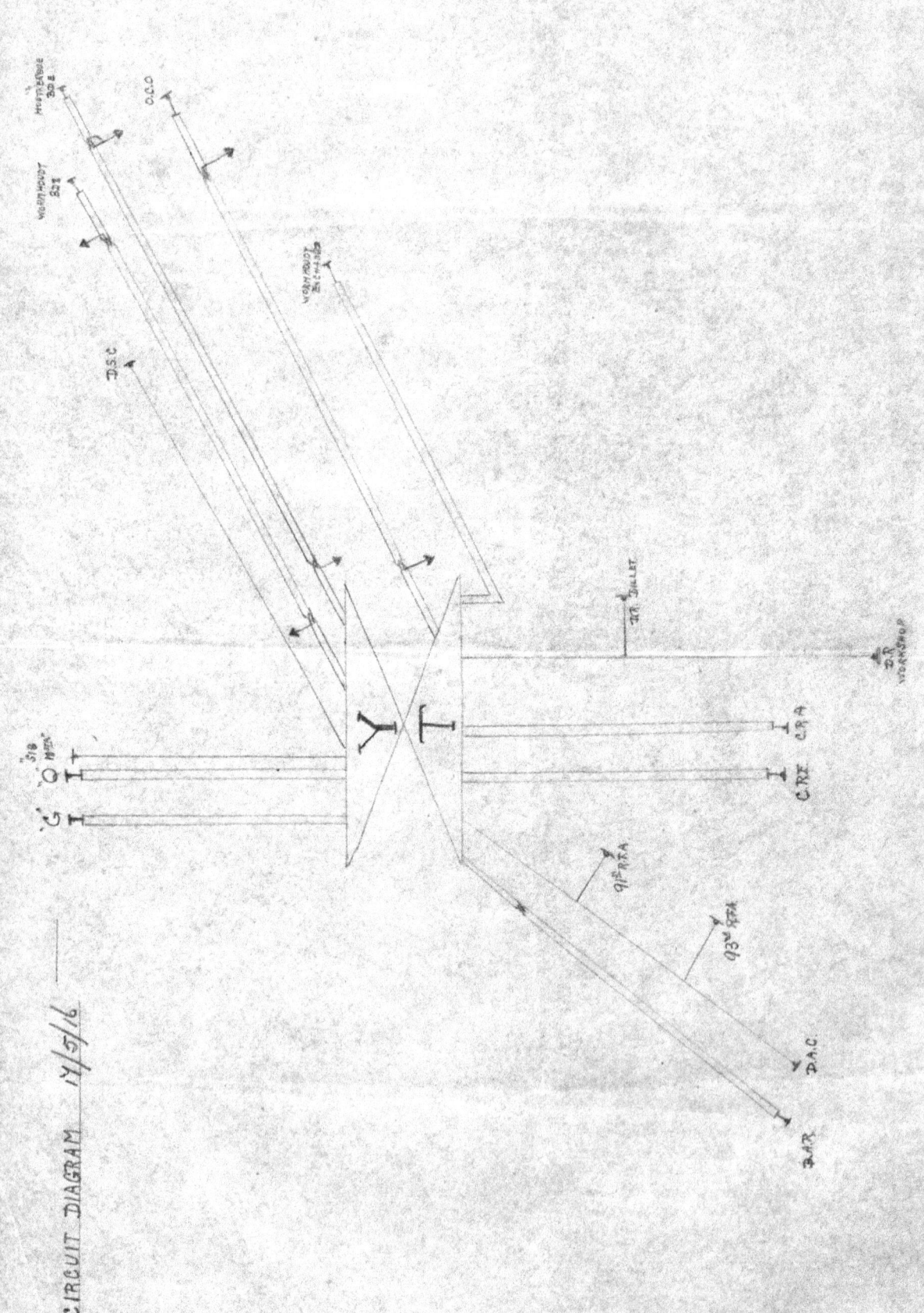

Y.T. CIRCUIT DIAGRAM 17/5/16

Army Form C. 2118.

WAR DIARY
or
INTELLIGENCE SUMMARY.
(Erase heading not required.)

Instructions regarding War Diaries and Intelligence
Summaries are contained in F. S. Regs., Part II.
and the Staff Manual respectively. Title pages
will be prepared in manuscript.

Place	Date	Hour	Summary of Events and Information	Remarks and references to Appendices
Sheet 24	1/6	11.0 pm	Preparation for new HQ at F30 continued. Observation instruments	
G.I.14,S.5	2/6	11.0 pm	Attack on Canadian front commenced. Rain was badly down. All lines to Ypres under a not	7 Jun
Voormezele Town Hall	3/6	11.0 pm	enemy interference from GC forward also suffered and down for some hours. Communication with front though apparent to a limit.	7 Jun
	4/6	11.0 pm	continued most strenuous. A 30 continued	7 Jun
	5/6	11.0 pm	6 OR joined in crew of establishment of tables etc. Worked new office at A 30 commenced	7 Jun
	6/6	11.0 pm	Spr Dalby & kelson awarded military medal in London Gazette.	7 Jun
	7/6	11.0 pm	Further fly wing on immediate front & night communication held throughout though all lines taken at one time or other. No cable laying party away to sept H. PROSSER.	7 Jun
	8/6	11.0 pm	Sit Rep cars made un all Mulks	7 Jun
	9/6	11.30 pm	Lt H. Granville returned from leave & Lt H. Snyder Cork reported. Strength of 2nd Bunny Signals	7 Jun
	10/6	11.30 pm	work on lines to new HQ at A 30 continued, also at MFs to forward units further.	7 Jun
	11/6	11.24 pm	Continued glaring and taking work in trench areas both parties sent up infantry. report from YR known with reports progress made by all original officers being other that sent on 131 and found wires continued.	7 Jun
	12/6	11.0 pm	all this fine to now PO to Battn. Being let down to shell fix these last words in the rear.	7 Jun

Army Form C. 2118.

WAR DIARY
or
INTELLIGENCE SUMMARY.
(Erase heading not required.)

Instructions regarding War Diaries and Intelligence Summaries are contained in F. S. Regs., Part II. and the Staff Manual respectively. Title pages will be prepared in manuscript.

Place	Date	Hour	Summary of Events and Information	Remarks and references to Appendices
Sheet 51	13/6	11.30p	At 1.30 am affected Canadian town to start on Sanctuary wood by gas demonstration and minor raids. Bns told to stand well to attention.	
G11 9 65	14/6	11.0p	Preparations for move to A.30 Battlefront as changed. Army orders Aug. Sep 14-15	77/4/1
	15/6	11.20p	Moved to new H.Q and 3rd bn. Commenced to dig out line in &c. Changes completed by night 15/16	
A 30 D.D.0			4th R.J. Reg. in reserve. Company changed to A company. Stood to in trenches Identifications taken of 6th Coy 10th Regt in reinforcements held 11pm. Dep 117 Transport in trenches BLR June 15-72	
	16/6	11.0p	Registered worked. During day fresh back by 5/4 to 5/9 H.Q. and F.B.N. also no heavy bombardment while burying dead Battalion suffered very heavy from enemy fire.	77/4/1
		11.20p	Moved back to Shtrenj in Town path during to bombardment for no change was of this kind	77/4/1
			Left till morning. Commenced change of battalion 6.30am. Change completed and situation returned to normal by 2.0pm	77/4/1
	18/6	11.20p	2nd R.F. Will took command of NPW (612-74th) sector Casualties week of 11th.	
			while 16/29 Select ordered flying scout on enemy Brenedle trench BLR return to dugout as ordered	77/4/4
	19/6	11.0pm	Tranches were and clearing up cable improved near A.30. Trenches could be held by continued.	77/4/1
	20/6	11.0pm	Trenches in dugouts reported to Officer in 4th Bde point for relief.	77/4/1

1577 Wt. W10791/1773 500,000 1/15 D. D. & L. A.D.S.S./Forms/C. 2118.

WAR DIARY
or
INTELLIGENCE SUMMARY.

Army Form C. 2118.

Place	Date	Hour	Summary of Events and Information	Remarks and references to Appendices
G.H.Q.5.	21/6	11.0pm	Heavy hour bard [in D.H.Q.] along horsemeat rate on POPERINGHE – VLAMERTINGHE road.	7.7M
	22/6	11.30pm	Maintenance, cleaning & burying continued	7.7M
	23/6	11.30pm	Ditto	7.7M
	24/6	11.30pm	The same	7.7M
	25/6	11.30pm	Raid on left of Bn front. Wires held up to battalions recently telephone line between further systems lost	7.7M
	26/6	11.45pm	The claim killed by shellfire during heavy enemy shell raid. Another heavy bombardment in afternoon all lines to left Bn front of battalion cut.	7.7M
	27/6	11.0pm	Very quiet day. Maintenance repairs	7.7M
	28/6	11.0pm	Ditto	7.7M
	29/6	11.0pm	Lt R.S. Clark left for 9th Corps Signals	7.7M
	30/6	11.0pm	Completed clearing up of H30 Camp	7.7M

F.J.M. Platten Major R.E.
O.C. 20th DIVISIONAL SIGNAL COY. R.E.

Confidential

20 Div Signals
Vol 12

War Diary for 20th Div Signal Coy.
from June 1st to 30th, 1916

F J M Foster
Major R.E.
O.C. 20th Divisional Signal Coy.

[stamp: 20th Divisional Signal Coy. R.E. 4/7/16]

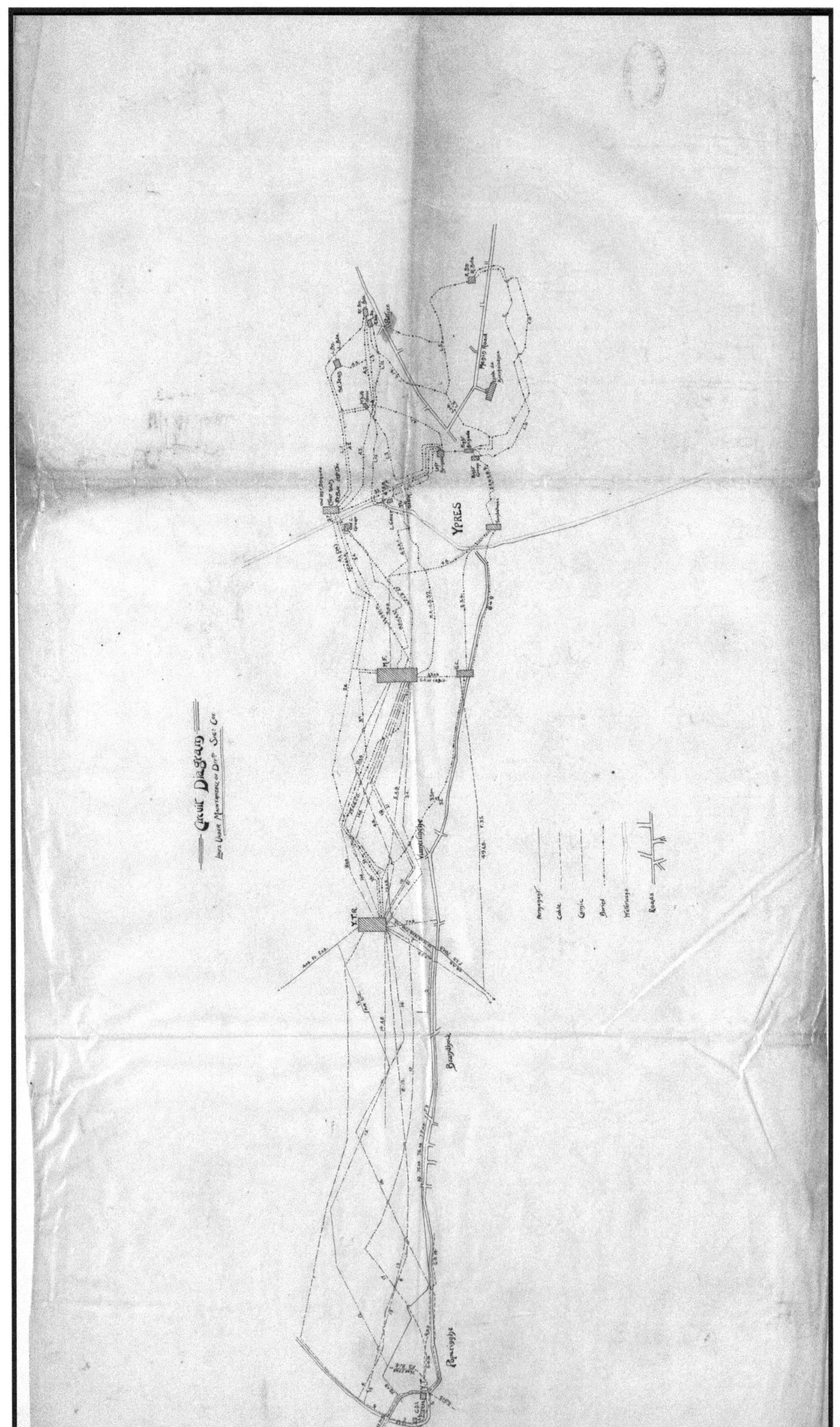

20th Divisional Engineers

20th DIVISIONAL SIGNAL COMPANY R. E.

J U L Y 1 9 1 6

July
Vol 13

Army Form C. 2118.

WAR DIARY
or
INTELLIGENCE SUMMARY.
(Erase heading not required.)

Instructions regarding War Diaries and Intelligence Summaries are contained in F. S. Regs., Part II. and the Staff Manual respectively. Title pages will be prepared in manuscript.

Place	Date	Hour	Summary of Events and Information	Remarks and references to Appendices
Sheet 28	1/7/16	11.30pm	Maintenance of lines. Duffy line fixed to 77R. Dugouts being commenced than by 96. KRRC.	77M
G.1495.5	2/7/16	11.30pm	Preparation for 91 demonstration ready for Role	77M
Potempe	3/7/16	11.30pm	In previous night lines held situations but Ypres now within 3 minutes of commencement of bombardment attempts. Considerable shell forward line, we still buried to Potyze. Lein Bridge & Railway wood front the line. Work of burying lines back to 77 completed and so dug out buried while amended to Potyze for work done on Tour 256 in rear area 19.9 bn. Shelter amended to Potyze wounded.	77M
	4/7/16	11.0pm		77M
	5/7/16	11.0pm	Maintenance & different work	77M
	6/7/16	11.30pm	Commenced dugouts line back from Wiltje. Capt Renford & 1 went	77M
	7/7/16	11.0pm	tonight line from left Brays to that the 6" railway line under switch to free 26 wild. the line from Ypres to Lt. Hamilton & Lt. Dyke (1st Lifeguard) to	77M
	8/7/16	11.0pm	Maintenance different work entered Wiltje. Ypres Potenge stelled to	77M
	9/7/16	11.30pm	Potenge stelled heavily many lines broken but not full action.	77M

Army Form C. 2118.

WAR DIARY
or
INTELLIGENCE SUMMARY.
(Erase heading not required.)

Instructions regarding War Diaries and Intelligence Summaries are contained in F. S. Regs., Part II. and the Staff Manual respectively. Title pages will be prepared in manuscript.

[Stamp: 20th DIVISIONAL SIGNAL COY.]

Place	Date	Hour	Summary of Events and Information	Remarks and references to Appendices
Sh.28	10/7/16	11.30pm	Digging work continued	F7 M4
G.11.9.0.5	11/7/16	11.0pm	Advanced posts of 6th Div Signals arrived and joined YTR	F7 M4
Poperinghe Town Hall	12/7/16	11.20pm	6 pm the afore shelled. Last night digging party Dickly. 60th Bde Hqs Flanders cooks ret'd morn (temporarily attached 62nd Amgne info) & digging party turned back.	F7 M4
	13/7/16	11.30pm	Enemy he shelled heavily in morning. Cooks under orders Div to move out to new camp of crossroads, move completed in afternoon.	F7 M4
A.25.d.1.6	14/7/16	11.0pm	Preparing for relief by YF	F7 M4
	15/7/16	11.0pm	Relieved by 6th Div. Returned to Poperinghe. R & R left in line	F7 M4
	16/7/16	11.0pm	Ordered to prepare for move to V Corps area at Observatoire	F7 M4
	17/7/16	11.0pm	Standby	F7 M4
	18/7/16	11.30pm	Orders received tonight for unit & unknown hour, to Kloosterhoek brought down to lorry in middle of staff arrangements 11.30pm	F7 M4
	19/7/16	11.0pm	Advance parts sent to Watou. Farm into S/S between	F7 M4
S.14.c.3.6 Watou	20/2/16	11.0pm	Hut & Baillul. lying at Rue du Muset. 24th Div relieved by us. Relief nearly completed in middle of afternoon. Installation completed	F7 M4
	21/7/16	11.30pm	Relief of this division by 30th Div & 31st Div is commenced	F7 M4

WAR DIARY
or
INTELLIGENCE SUMMARY.

Army Form C. 2118.

Place	Date	Hour	Summary of Events and Information	Remarks and references to Appendices
S.u.C 3.6	22.7.16	11.55pm	Relief of WM Bde by 108th Bde completed.	77 Inf
Bailleul sect 28	23.7.16	11.50pm	108th Bde relieved by 108th Bde, 36th Div.	77 Inf
	24.7.16	11.0pm	Company less motor cyclists cars & lorries proceeded by road to Hondeghem under Capt Crawford to bivouac there for the night, having marched by road, 28m 7/8c	77 Inf
Doullens sheet 57D A16	25.7.16	11.0pm	Company by train from Bainsdun to Doullens. Div Hq established there. Bdes at Halloy, Bouquemaison etc South	77 Inf
Bus les Artois sheet 57D	26.7.16	11.30pm	Division moved to Bus, Bus Antois, Bdes at Authie, Bus and Vauchelles	77 Inf
	27.7.16	11.30pm	Preparation for taking over line from 38th Div. advanced parties to Co1N	77 Inf
	28.7.16	11.0pm	59th Bde moved to Sailly au Bois &c.1 at to Mailly Mauillet taking over the sector opposite 60th Bde to Bus & 113th Bde to Bus. No notice of other move from brigade by GS. Some confusion in Bus - one Bde put into infantry camps, the other Bde put into huts.	77 Inf
Couin J.d.4.8 sheet 57D	29.7.16	11.0pm	Relieved 38th Div at COUIN.	77 Inf

20th Divisional Engineers.

20Th DIVISIONAL SIGNAL COMPAMY R. E.

AUGUST 1 9 1 6

SECRET & CONFIDENTIAL

20/

War Diary
of
20th Divn. Signal Coy R.E.

From
29. 7. 16.
to
30. 8. 16.

7? Whitton Ingall

O.O. 20th DIVISIONAL SIGNAL COY. R.E.

Vol. 14

[stamp: DIVISIONAL SIGNAL COY 30/8/16]

WAR DIARY
or
INTELLIGENCE SUMMARY.
(Erase heading not required.)

Army Form C. 2118.

Place	Date	Hour	Summary of Events and Information	Remarks and references to Appendices
CODIN	29/7	11.30pm	Setting hours new IPR	77My
9 b 4.0 Sheet 57D	30/7	11.0pm	Occupied in shouting out buried line system with exp.	77My
	31/7	11.30pm	Asdic trouble. Stuck to one use as air office	77My
	1/8	11.0pm	Went on line named Dell.	77My
	2/8	11.30pm	Infantry busy in office. 50 PA to Division security to units	77My
	3/8	11.30pm	Visited YCC and brought away IT set belonging to 2nd Army	27My
	4/8	10.0pm	Worked on buried lines, sorting them out and improving	47My
	5/8	11.0pm	as above	77My
	6/8	11.30pm	Preparing for new units in COIGNEUX	
	7/8	11.0pm	61 Bde lister morphine ad. delivered by 2 5th Div. Bde in reserve at COIGNEUX, motor to pass HC 57 and instructions expedition knot gears line.	77My
	8/8	11.0pm	Relief of 38 KRA by Seventh RA completed. St. Kruse of KDepril C will Enten brigand attacked	77My
	9/8	11.30pm	Lines buried from dugout at junction of NHPWE and 70 NE5 (become to trench in 30M COPSE and along front line to K23 d 3.5 - for army history ref. Capt Ranaport. Lt Pearce with Despatch or scouts wireless off work.	77My

WAR DIARY
or
INTELLIGENCE SUMMARY.

Army Form C. 2118.

Place	Date	Hour	Summary of Events and Information	Remarks and references to Appendices
COVIN TILHO (Hut57D)	10/8/16	11/40pm	Battalion signallers instructed in daylight lamps and IT sets with front trenches	77Ap
	11/8/16	11.30pm	IT set from 2KR taken up and installed in a dugout in Jones close to motor wire. Phone Flung & men to exchange by pulley system	77Ap
	12/8/16	11.30pm	Visited IT set with troops from 2KR. Failed to find IT set as it had moved a slight no address. Discovered it had been dug out by auxiliaries of 12 KRR about a few yards away. Seven connectors given away & relief overdue. 2nd Lt Appleford Staples brought equal reinforcements of B Sqn before Red Roy & Campion. Relt only out B Sqn	77Ap
	13/8/16	11.0pm	Preparations start by Guards Division. Inf Div wont on Bspn. Shell little found where lines had been standing in a RA Lieutenant filled in again.	77Ap
	14/8/16	11.30pm	Parties sent with 2KR and 60KRB de and Battr speakers. Very fair success Lamps, screens, wireless and hooters all used.	77Ap 77Ap 77Ap
	15/8/16	11.0pm	Two instr explts sent to 6 Div RA who were out until 20th Div.	77Ap
BEMVAt (Hut57D)	16/8/16	11.0pm	Headquarters moved to BEMVAt. Had Recent Army Signal Office.	77Ap
	17/8/16	11.0pm	We move except brigade complete moor from frontline	77Ap
	18/8/16	11.0pm	No change	77Ap

WAR DIARY
or
INTELLIGENCE SUMMARY.

(Erase heading not required.)

Army Form C. 2118.

Instructions regarding War Diaries and Intelligence Summaries are contained in F.S. Regs., Part II. and the Staff Manual respectively. Title pages will be prepared in manuscript.

Place	Date	Hour	Summary of Events and Information	Remarks and references to Appendices
Beauval Sheet 57D	19/8/16	11.0 pm	Company and wheeled transport of Div. moved to VICHERS BOCAGE by road.	77 Arg
TREUX 57D.LS	20/8/16	11.30 pm	Div HQ moved to TREUX. Bdes at MORLANCOURT, MESNILTE and VILLE-SUR-ANCRE	77 Arg
F.1.9	21/8/16	11.0 pm	Div HQ moved to F.2.b.d. Bdes at CITADEL F.2.1.b, Happy Valley etc and Sand Pits F.1.9	77 Arg
Sheet 57D.2.7.16		11.30 pm	Bdes moved into line. 6/2/16 at area NE corner of Bernafay Wood. 5/ at BRIQUETERIE	77 Arg
MINDEN POST F.16.c.5.3	23/8/16	11.0 pm	Relieved 2nd Div at MINDEN POST F.18.c.5.3 Sheet 57D. Line is bad condition and mostly cable laid out of place and forward. No steady possible. Staff Bdes all day.	77 Arg
			All 3 cables thro' for a short time in afternoon. Traffic possible during the time to the left Bde through 2.E.1 & by visual through aero test station at gun pits. Also all the travelling wireless lamps wireless ne Bde HQ, both bellsjouweless stations. 3rd Div & 3 attached. 6 Div RA at (2 new letters) 3 pr Bde. thro' from Corry exchange to Gun Pit for time to 5 am. by Bde.	
24/8/16		11.0 pm	2 armoured connection cables laid in it. Rain though about 5.0 pm for a short time but fed with intermittent trouble all day tall night. Signal traffic however at times.	77 Arg
25/8/16		11.0 pm	New line to L/F Bde at base tonight by Capt Rainsford & will be redone to a break heavy damaged wires and not noticed by liaison at night.	77 Arg
26/8/16		11.30 pm	Trench bay from TRONES WOOD Bdewards, left Bde to old trench German Cable in TRONES ALLEY. Capt Rainsford /c.	77 Arg

Army Form C. 2118.

WAR DIARY
or
INTELLIGENCE SUMMARY.
(Erase heading not required.)

Instructions regarding War Diaries and Intelligence Summaries are contained in F. S. Regs., Part II. and the Staff Manual respectively. Title pages will be prepared in manuscript.

Place	Date	Hour	Summary of Events and Information	Remarks and references to Appendices
MINDEN POST F18.C.5.3	27/6	11.30pm	Trench to left B4 finished. Hand work on maintenance.	F/M
	28/6	11 pm	New line along railway in Valley got up to BRIDGE TENIS Cable trench dug up from forward Rd to TENIS TRENCH & TRAM HEAD COPSE. New lateral YT2 completed from R.E telephone in dotted line. Cable trench a newly laid trench.	F/M
	29/6	11 pm	Cable party out from latural YT3 to forward trench but shallow cable trench to TRAM HEAD COPSE. Lorst Pion YT29, Oak line led to reserve Pole battery thinly wounded. Pioneer Pearson + Spr Tavener killed by Shell wood from LG. Spr Pearson bodily wounded. Spr Tavener working to place R.E men walked over Some from 3rd A.E. were near about the line.	F/M
	30/6	11.30pm	Telephone working new WESTHOFEN again South End Lanett	F/M

F/M Shalt
Major RE
O.C. 20th DIVISIONAL SIGNAL COY. R.E.

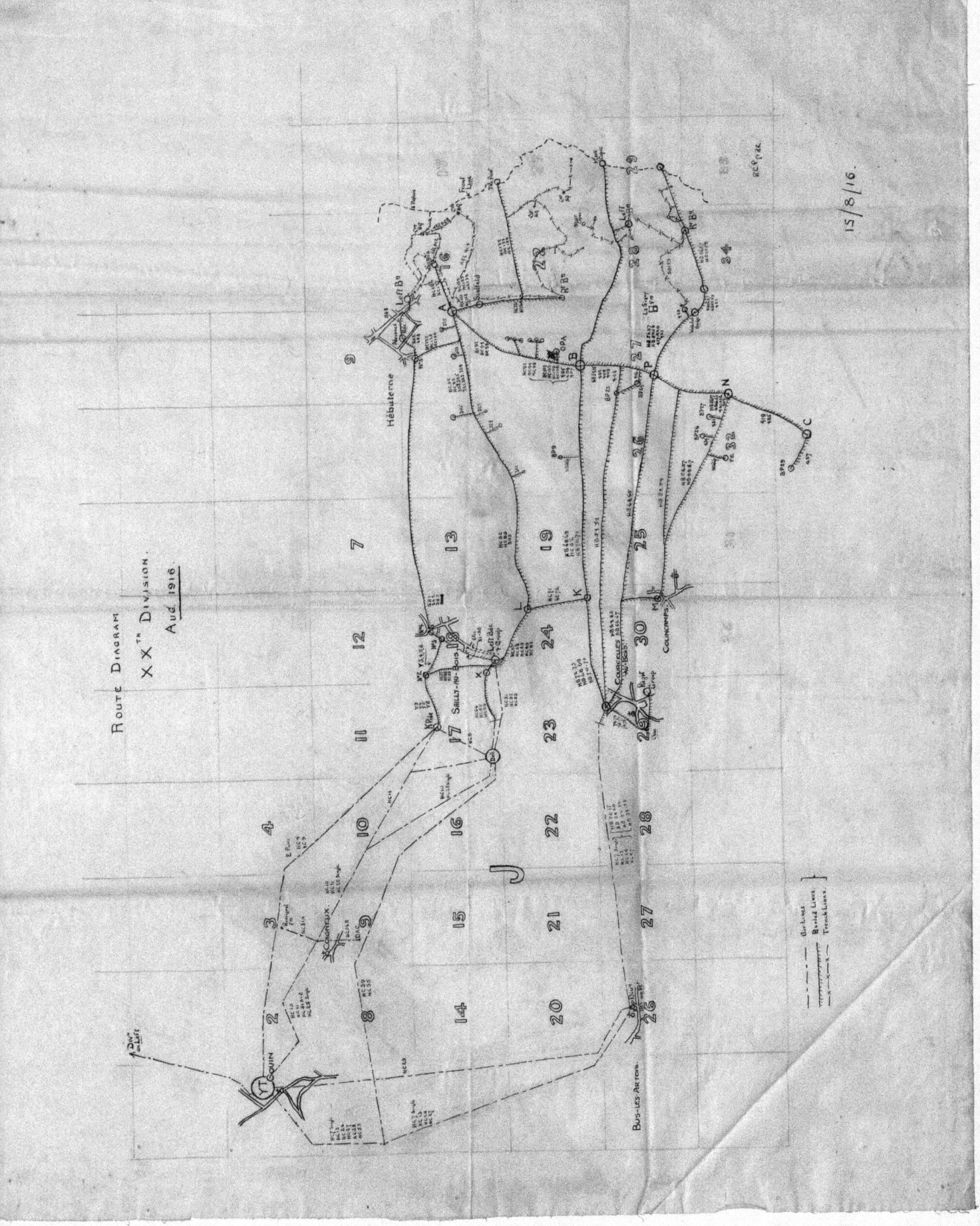

20th Divisional Engineers.

20th DIVISIONAL SIGNAL COMPANY R. E.

SEPTEMBER 1916

Confidential

War Diary of
O.C. Radio Signal W.R.E.
for Period 31/8 - 28/9/16

J J Hutton
Major R.E.

O.C. 2nd Divisional Signal Coy. R.E.

28/9/16

WAR DIARY or INTELLIGENCE SUMMARY

Army Form C. 2118.

20th Divisional Signal Coy

VOL/15

(Erase heading not required.)

Instructions regarding War Diaries and Intelligence Summaries are contained in F. S. Regs., Part II. and the Staff Manual respectively. Title pages will be prepared in manuscript.

Place	Date	Hour	Summary of Events and Information	Remarks and references to Appendices
MINDEN POST	31/8	11.30pm	Laid fwd loop on line YX2 to OAR. lagged	77M
FBC Sec 3 Delville Wood	1/9	11pm	Line to RIDGE gunny trench tonight. Fresh line laid up redans, line is aller heavens and began up QHR to Div. SERIQUETERIE by Cd Bde. Visual station on road between and	77M
	5/9	11.30pm	Fresh part laid on line to BRIQUSTERIE, right cell. New line laid forward from R/FBC. BUATERLOT FARM from RIDGE to ARROW HEAD COPSE.	77M
	3/9	11.0pm	Division attacked and captured GUILLEMONT and road from GINCHY to WEDGE WOOD. All wires held anyway between Bde in Beauty Wood which was frequently blown up. Lines of hand taken to or from afternoon Communication maintained by lateral line. Something to WATERLOT and ARROW HEAD held without very few short breakdowns. Good communication to signals and flares everywhere from frontline to forward wires near Flares.	77M
	4/9	11.30pm	Forward line still held very well. Attack passed in evening to LEUZE WOOD	77M

Army Form C. 2118.

WAR DIARY
or
INTELLIGENCE SUMMARY.
(Erase heading not required.)

Instructions regarding War Diaries and Intelligence Summaries are contained in F. S. Regs., Part II. and the Staff Manual respectively. Title pages will be prepared in manuscript.

Place	Date	Hour	Summary of Events and Information	Remarks and references to Appendices
MINDEN POST	5/9	11.30 pm	Relieved by 16th Div. H moved to Forked Tree 12.2.0. (Schurphtlu)	77 Inf
F.8.c 5.3 Albert ( ) Corbie	6/9	11.9 pm	Relieved by 58th Div. H moved to CORBIE, Divisional rest.	77 Inf
Corbie	7/9	11.0 pm	A Corbie. Company headed by Genl Fanshawe and many offrs & men,	77 Inf
	8/9	11.0 pm	Still at Corbie	
	9/9	11.0 pm	Still at Corbie	18 Inf
	10/9	11.0 pm	at Corbie	77 Inf
Industrie	11/9	11.0 pm	Div moved to Forked Tree. B.H at Meaulte, Hencourt, Bois de Taille	77 Inf
F.25.b (Albert m?)	12/9	11.0 pm	61st Bde from Hencourt to Bois de Taille	77 Inf
	13/9	11.50 pm	No move	77 Inf
	14/9	11.0 pm	No move	77 Inf
	15/9	11.0 pm	No move of Div HQ. 61st Bde joined GDS DIV	77 Inf
	16/9	11.30 pm	55th Bde & 60 Bde relieved GDS DIV in frontline. HQ move.	37 Inf
MINDEN POST F.8.c 5.3	17/9	11.30 pm	Div H.Q. moved to MINDEN POST. Advanced HQ at BERNAFAY WOOD at S.28.5.7. Rely on Staff & Col Rumfud at 77 TR, 12 Bde &c. Exchange at VT. Communication with Bde (55 & 66 in line) by two routes by buzzer and telephone. 2 Brigades in A.I.S.	77 Inf

Army Form C. 2118.

WAR DIARY
or
INTELLIGENCE SUMMARY.
(Erase heading not required.)

Instructions regarding War Diaries and Intelligence Summaries are contained in F. S. Regs., Part II. and the Staff Manual respectively. Title pages will be prepared in manuscript.

Place	Date	Hour	Summary of Events and Information	Remarks and references to Appendices
MINDEN POST	18/9/16	11.30pm	Very wet day. Div. troops most of day find the level to 15th Bde at WATERLOT FARM	77 Inf
BERNAFAY WOOD	19/9/16	11.0pm	Attempts made to work forward the Guards line from 1st Gt. Potion relieved & one have had outposts pushed through. Reachline have improved. Guards northern units partially doing it full.	77 Inf
	20/9/16	11.0pm	Two new lines built to left front. Lewis positions to TRONES WOOD	77 Inf
FORCED TREE	21/9/16	11.0pm	Relieved by Guards Div. Returned BTRENX to E Camp	77 Inf
P.S.C. (Abouts) TROUX J.S.G. (62 D)	22/9/16	11.0pm	Returned BTRENX. Bath at MEAULTE. MORLANCOURT. VILLE-SUR-ANCRE	77 Inf
	23/9/16	11.0pm	No change. Div troops on aeroplanes & Indiscriminate	77 Inf
	24/9/16	11.30pm	No change	77 Inf
	25/9/16	11.0pm	No change	77 Inf
	26/9/16	11.0pm	No change. Bdes moved forward into bivouac.	77 Inf
And the (Shipilled)	27/9/16	11.0pm	Relieved 5 Div. Relief carried straight by French & Div	77 Inf
Forked Tree	28/9/16	11.0pm	Moved last to forked Tree. Posh all. — Canny Valley. — Communicated by D.K.	77 Inf

20th Divisional Engineers.

20th DIVISIONAL ENGINE

20th Divisional Engineers

20th DIVISIONAL SIGNAL COMPANY R. E.

OCTOBER 1 9 1 6

Vol 16

OC/16

20th Divn
Signal Company

WAR DIARY or INTELLIGENCE SUMMARY

Army Form C. 2118.

Place	Date	Hour	Summary of Events and Information	Remarks and references to Appendices
FORKED TREE CAMP BERNAFAY WOOD Sq16 5.6	29/6	11.0pm	Recce: 161 moves to Bernafay Wood. 61st Bde relieved 62nd Bde in Trenches at LONGUEVAL. 55th Bde at CARNOY.	77A9
	30/6	11.30pm	Portions moved forward from 21st Div. Advanced T. Station GT. rode 1/48 in position near S12d9.2. Line to Bde when No5 from Delville Wood found once ends between Tank & Bn. Tank charged on front. Telephone to R.A. from battery.	77A9
	1/6	11.40pm	60th Bde moves forward to 728.35 on the west Edge. It moved to MINDEN POST. 61st Bde advanced to front middle south of heavy artillery demonstration to Etampes at MINDEN POST.	77A9
	2/6	11.30pm	60th Bde moved forward communication station by line from GT.	79A9
	3/6	11.0pm	Working on cable buried route. Car transport to Rainsford. Rained all day.	77A9
	4/6	11.25pm	55th Bde relieved 61st Bde.	79A9
	5/6	11.5pm	Inflexible telephone into ports on buried route forward 678.	79A9
	6/6	11.0pm	At Rainsford with Bn on infantry route. Spade - L.H. men working on side lines to Inf Bde and R.A. group. Artilleries with Infantry arranging wires from 16 Fd Bde. 61st Bde relieved. 65th Bd = Infantry.	77A9
	7/6	11.30pm	Attacked & obtained known line. Corps route collapsed half an hour before zero by enemy shell fire. Front of Bn to Division most shelled. English railway train, whole company up to front work though shrapnel all day most under shell fire. No heavy casualties so that communication ranks been to Divisional observers & 55th Bde maintained successfully. Front attempted Divisional analyst staff failed to fill trust.	77A9

WAR DIARY
or
INTELLIGENCE SUMMARY.

Army Form C. 2118.

Place	Date	Hour	Summary of Events and Information	Remarks and references to Appendices
Beaudoin Wood	8/10/16	11.15pm	Relieved on night by 1st Div into line. Cliff Trench + Salt 37th Bde BMBA & LTG	Trench
	9/10/16	11.30pm	Div. relieved by TREUX. also to Ville Ramparts + Mead LTG	Trench
	10/10/16	11.9pm	Rest. Car sent to Supply Column	
TREUX	11/10/16	10.30pm	A class for Battalion Signal Officers is being formed today. Will probably last whole time division is in rest.	Att.
	12/10/16	11pm	Nine Battalion officers have reported for instruction from all battalions except 10th KRR, 11th KRR, 12th RB, 6th Ox and Bucks LI, and 12th Kings — 2/Lt CARNEGIE to acting as Chief Instructor for the school.	Att.
	13/10/16	10.30pm	No change	Att.
	14/10/16	11pm	No change – Sgt Bullock and Sgt Crawley detailed as instructors for Signal officers school.	Att.
	15/10/16	11.30pm	Operation Orders have been issued for a move tomorrow to CORBIE.	Att.
CORBIE	16/10/16	10pm	Divisional Hqrs opened office at 12 noon in the school, Rue de Mercerie CORBIE, closing at TREUX at same hour. 60th and 61st Bdes have opened offices at CORBIE, 59th still at VILLE-SOUS-CORBIE.	Att.
	17/10/16	10.30pm	Signal Class re-opened.	
	18/10/16	11pm	Warning Order for Div to move tomorrow. 60th Brigade has moved from VILLE-SOUS-CORBIE to FRANVILLERS. 59th Brigade moved from CORBIE and opened office at ALLONVILLE. Communication to both places eventually obtained through 4th Army exchange at QUERRIEU	

Instructions regarding War Diaries and Intelligence Summaries are contained in F. S. Regs., Part II. and the Staff Manual respectively. Title pages will be prepared in manuscript.

WAR DIARY
or
INTELLIGENCE SUMMARY.
(Erase heading not required.)

Army Form C. 2118.

20th DIVISION SIGNAL COY.

Place	Date	Hour	Summary of Events and Information	Remarks and references to Appendices
CORBIE	18 10/16 Continued	11 pm	C.R.E. with 83rd, 84th, and 96th Field Companies RE and 11th D.L.I. (pioneers) moved to-day to the CITADEL, to work under CE XIV Corps.	AHB
VIGNACOURT	19 10/16	10 pm	Div Hqrs opened office at VIGNACOURT at 10am and closed at CORBIE at same hour. 60th Bde moved from ALLONVILLE to FLESSELLES and opened office in Chateau at latter place. 61st Bde moved from CORBIE to ALLONVILLE. All communication through 4th Army sub office at VIGNACOURT. 59th Bde remain at FRANVILLERS.	AHB.
"	20 10/16	11 pm	61st Bde moved from ALLONVILLE to Chateau at LA CHAUSSÉE-TIRANCOURT. 59th Bde from FRANVILLERS to ALLONVILLE. Division is to move tomorrow. C.R.E. has moved up to the CRATERS, and communication is maintained with him through 14th Corps Heavy Artillery.	AHB.
BELLOY-SUR-SOMME	21 10/16	10 pm	Div. Hqrs opened at 10 am at BELLOY-SUR-SOMME and closed at VIGNACOURT same hour. 59th Bde moved from ALLONVILLE to PICQUIGNY.	AHB.
"	22 10/16	11 pm.	Division is now apparently settled for a few days. Officers Signal School started again	AHB.
"	23 10/16	9.30 pm	Rest.	AHB.
"	24 10/16	10 pm	~~Ch~~ 10th Corps supplied 2 French Lamps & Folding Shutter discs for instructional purposes.	AHB.
"	25 10/16	11 pm	Car returned from Column. 2/Lt Carnegie has relieved Lt HANNEN with the Divl Arty. at Bernafay Wood. Sgt. McLaren's party was relieved yesterday.	AHB.
"	26 10/16	10 pm	LT PEACHE returned from 60th Bde where he has been relieving Lt BRACE, on leave	AHB
"	27 10/16	10 pm	~~The~~ The CRE and 84th Coy RE have moved from CRATERS to CONDÉ near FLIXECOURT	AHB.
"	28 10/16	10.30 pm.	Officers Signal Class examined and disbanded.	AHB.

1577 Wt. W10791/1773 500,000 1/15 D. D. & L. A.D.S.S./Forms/C. 2118.

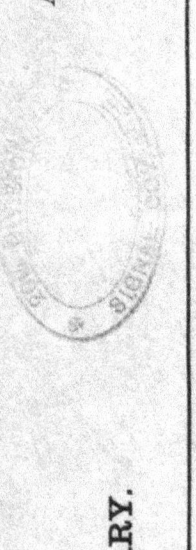

WAR DIARY or INTELLIGENCE SUMMARY.

Army Form C. 2118.

Place	Date	Hour	Summary of Events and Information	Remarks and references to Appendices
BELLOY-SUR-SOMME	29/9/16	11.30pm	No change	77 MP
	30/9/16	9 pm	Second class for officers started. Arrangements complete for large class for N.C.O. & men. have been sent to Boullenl for class of wet days work	77 MP

F.T.M.Clark
Major R.E.
OC 46th Signal Coy RE

Confidential

War Diary
of
OC 30th Div. Signal Co. R.E.
Sep 29. 1916 – Oct 30 1916

F.J. Falkiner Major RE
OC 30 Div Signals RE

20th Divisional Engineers

------- -----

20th DIVISIONAL SIGNAL COMPANY R. E.

NOVEMBER 1 9 1 6

SECRET

Army Form C. 2118.

WAR DIARY
or
INTELLIGENCE SUMMARY.
(Erase heading not required.)

Vol 17

Place	Date	Hour	Summary of Events and Information	Remarks and references to Appendices
BELLOY SUR SOMME	31/10/16	11.30pm	No change	77M
CAVILLON	1/11/16	10.00am	Div HQ moved to CAVILLON 10057. Company Kampford liaison with Capt Rainford & 2/Kochi Doussy. Officer relief of 91 to CAVILLON. Brigade HQ at PICQUIGNY, 60th at SOUES, 6/A.I. MOLLIEN-VIDAMES, Communication broken by wire	77M 2M
		11.00pm	Settling in. No change	7.7M
	2/11/16	11.30pm	No change	7.7M
	3/11/16	11.0pm	No change	22M
	4/11/16	12.0pm	Signal school started at CONDE. S/Chandler	3.7M
	5/11/16	11.30pm	2/Lt Hamilton R.E. T.C. joined for duty.	2.7M
	6/11/16		No change	3.2M
	7/11/16	11.45pm	No change. Capt A.J. Rainford left England on 7 days leave	1M
	8/11/16	10.45pm	No change. Little Brown Testkat during 3 increased	7.7M
	9/11/16	10.30pm	Signal school move to Fourdrinin reconde rides or 10 Div. School of Instruction. Officer to relieve Cartpeter	7.2M
	10/11/16	1.00p		7.2M
			No change. 2/Kociegie took over N° section L/Kochsn Renoweil.	7.0M
	11/11/16	10.30pm	Second officers candidates examination 6/5.D. infantry signallers at Hamilton	7.2M
	12/11/16	10.0pm	Ground attendis Gmd. 2/Lt Hamilton took command of N° section. No change	7M
	13/11/16	10.30pm	No change. O Attendings for have to proceed on. Inchely by 10.45am	7.7M
CAROIS	14/11/16	10.00pm	Div moved to CAROIS 51, RCB de to VILLE 51 en Bois to TAILLY remaining minutes 15th to 10th Division	7.0M

WAR DIARY
or
INTELLIGENCE SUMMARY

Army Form C. 2118.

(Erase heading not required.)

Place	Date	Hour	Summary of Events and Information	Remarks and references to Appendices
COMBLE	15/11/16	10.0 pm	60th Bde moved to COMBLE	F.S. my
	16/11/16	10.0 pm	No change	F.S. my
	17/11/16	10.30 pm	No change. Relief sent	F.S. my
	18/11/16	12.0 pm	61st Bde moved to AIRAINES	F.S. my
	19/11/16	10.0 pm	No change. Wheeler (still in 15th Corps HQrs) over via 33rd Divn. returned from wireless course	F.S. my
	20/11/16	10.0 pm	Pigeon course for 60th Bde & aeroplane course for 60th Bde also	F.S. my
	21/11/16	10.0 pm	No change	F.S. my
	22/11/16	10.30 pm	59th Bde aeroplane course for two days.	F.S. my
	23/11/16	7.0 pm	No change	F.S. my
	24/11/16	10.0 pm	Examination of signal class at promotion to LCorpls. 2Lt Hamlin 1/Beale returned from leave	F.S.M.S.
	25/11/16	10.0 pm	Divisional school moved HQurs. Advanced section joined with 20 Div Hqs opened from Sernafays Wood	F.S. my
	26/11/16	10.0 pm	Lt Hamer rejoined from Sernafays Wood	F.S. my
	27/11/16	9.40 pm	2/Lt Hamlin left f 5 days leave to Paris. Capt assume LT command	RSB
	28/11/16	9.30 pm	No change	RSB

R.S. Rose Capt R.E.
O.C. 20th Divisional Signal Coy.

20th Divisional Engineers.

20th DIVISIONAL SIGNAL COMPANY R. E.

DECEMBER 1 9 1 6

WAR DIARY
or
INTELLIGENCE SUMMARY

(Erase heading not required.)

Army Form C. 2118.

Signal Coy
20th Division
Vol 18

Place	Date	Hour	Summary of Events and Information	Remarks and references to Appendices
CORBIE	29/2/18	11 pm	No change	7 JMY
	30/2/18	10 pm	No change. 61st Bde returned to Corbie	7 JMY
	1/3/18	10 pm	Inter-Batten Signal competition finished 11 K.R.R., 5 K.S.L.I., 11 D.L.I. and 12 K. Rif.	7 JMY
	2/3/18	10 pm	No change	7 JMY
	3/3/18	10 pm	No change	7 JMY
	4/3/18	10 pm	No change	7 JMY
	5/3/18	10 pm	No change. Battn competition finished 11 K.R.R., 1st at End	7 JMY
	6/3/18	10 pm	No change	7 JMY
	7/3/18	10 pm	No change	7 JMY
	8/3/18	10 pm	No change	7 JMY
	9/3/18	10 pm	Advanced party of linemen under 2/Lt A to HQ 29 R Divn advance by to Citadel	7 JMY
	10/3/18	12 pm	Stores being unpacked. Company at Néove under Sch Bonne 2 Lt Marsden	7 JMY
	11/3/18	10 pm	Capt Bennet & Lt Marsden to new H.Q. 20 Div R A relieved 29 Div R A	7 JMY
Hed. 4-8 Sentelle Plat	12/3/18	10.30 pm	Divn relieved 29 Divn in line 10 am. Headquarters manned by Divn personnel in sept for our wrs Lts Baker & two signlrs. Lt Atkins Government S.D.N (L.D. 46) 750 +Bde wart of supply and at G VILLEMONT WEARES advd dispatch at 78 and establised there	7 JMY
	13/3/18	10 am	Settled in to telephone & Linemen further up Rd to B to 78 detachments & into busy bay	7 JMY

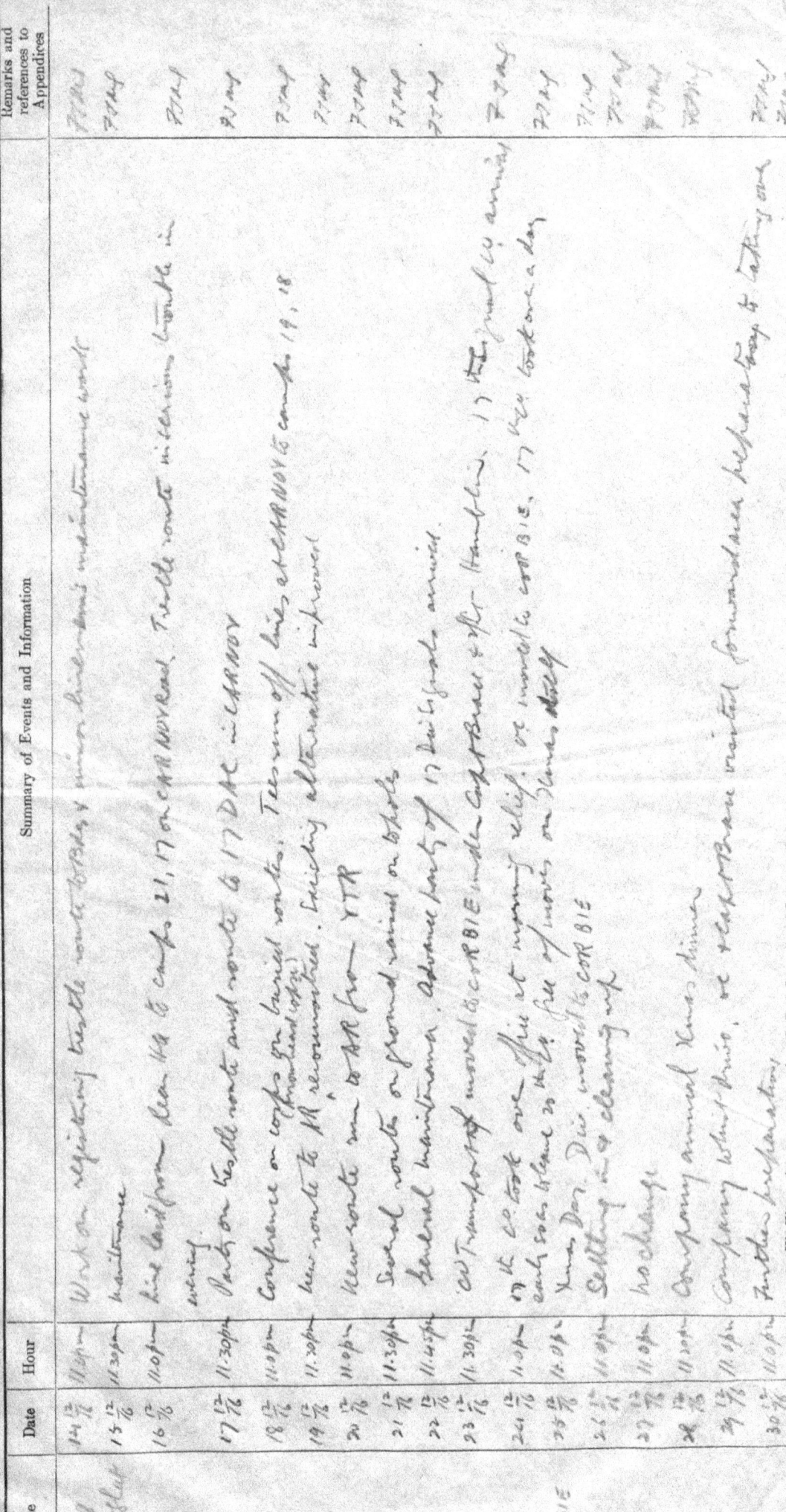

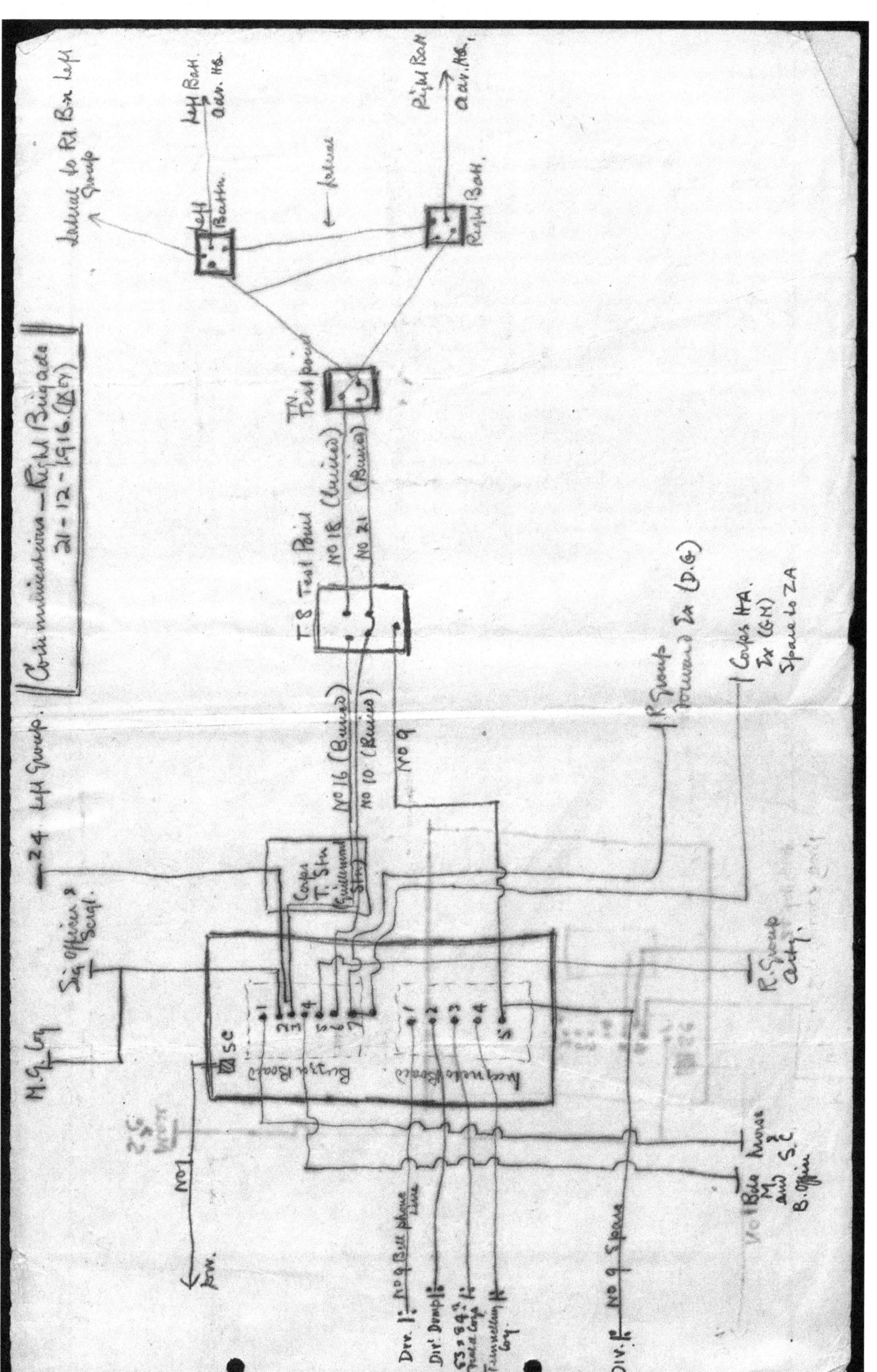

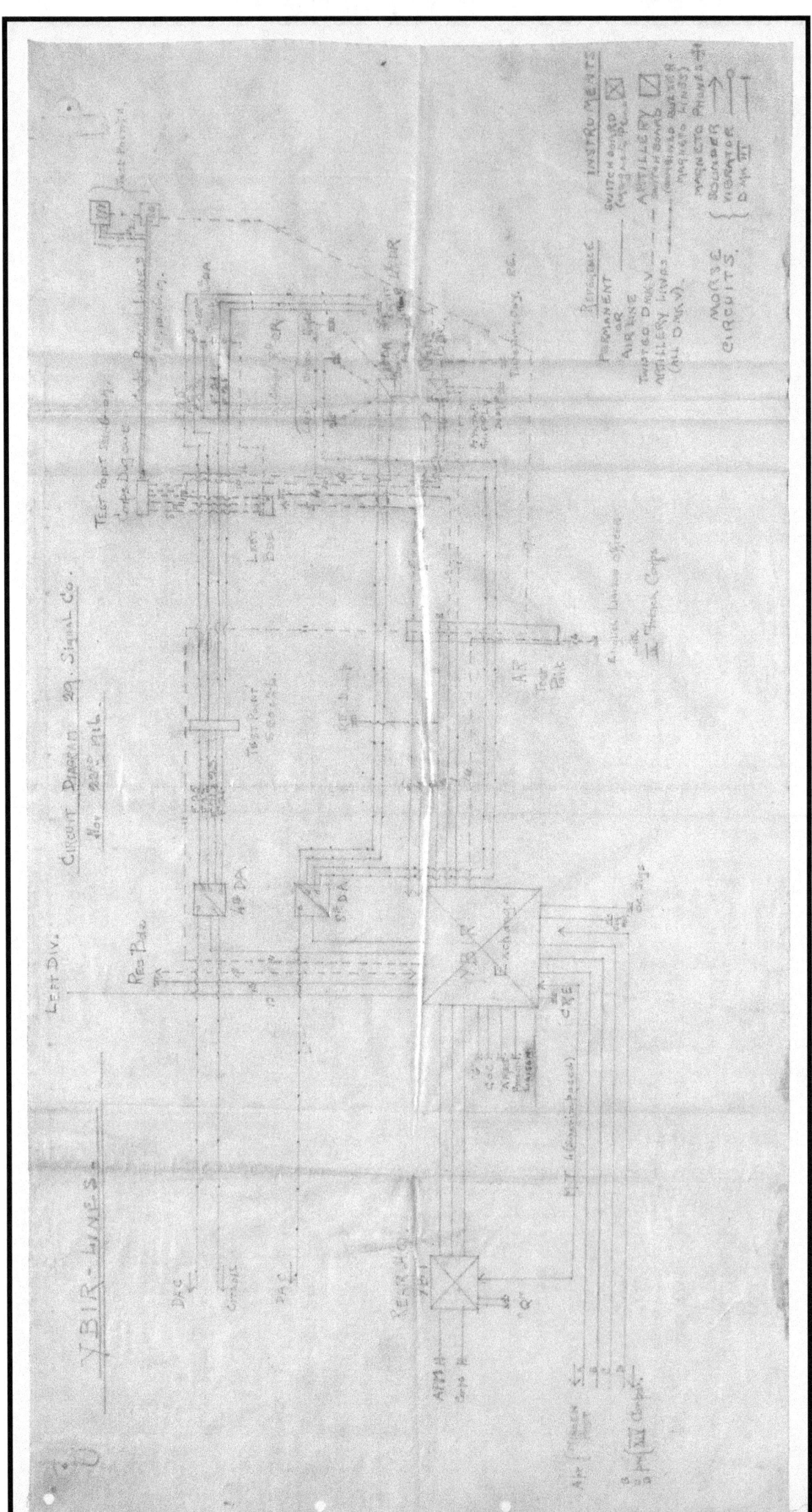

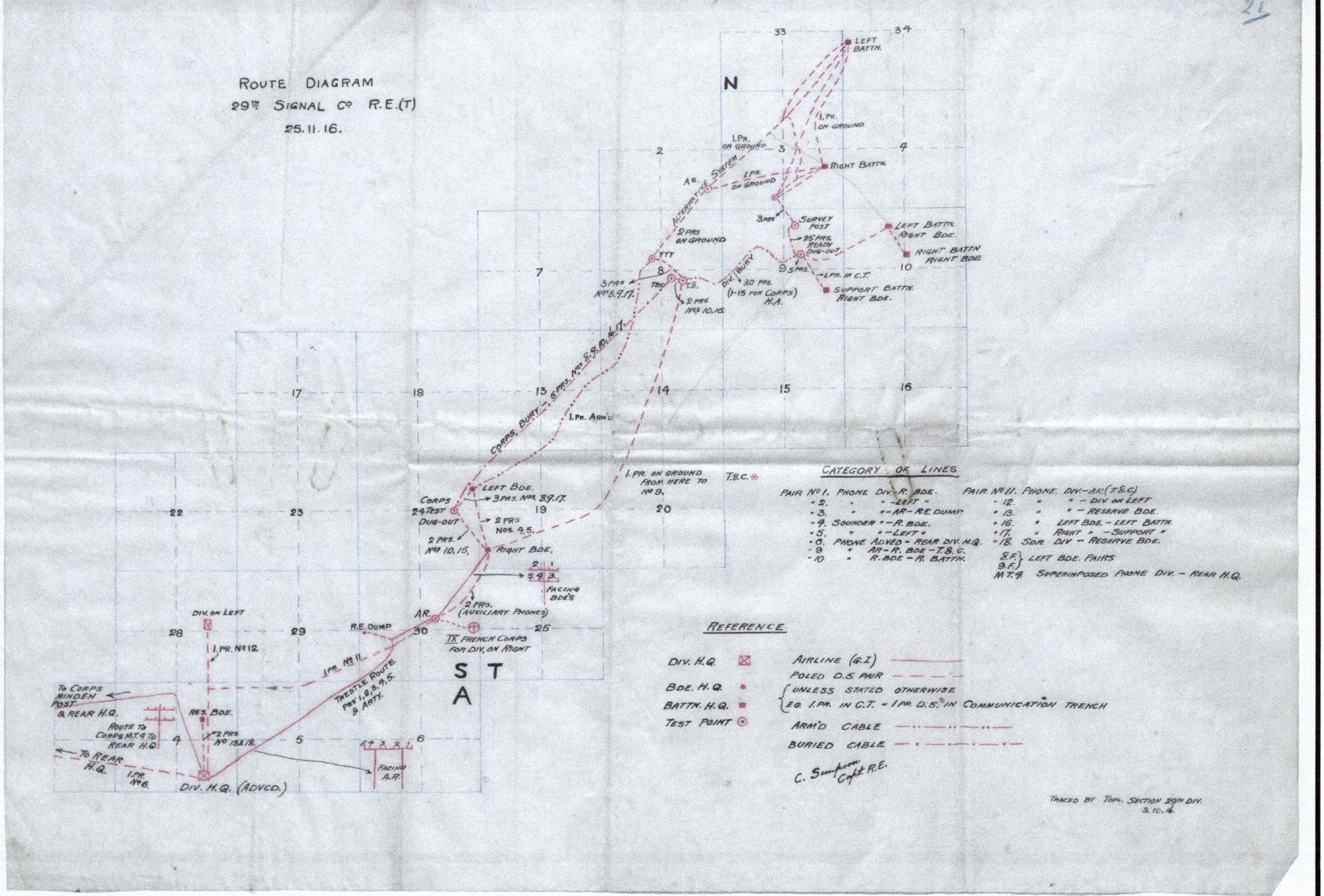

21
ROUTE DIAGRAM
29TH SIGNAL Co R.E.(T)
25.11.16.
N
S T
A
LEFT BATTN.
RIGHT BATTN.
1.PR. ON GROUND
ALTERNATIVE SYSTEM
AR.
2 PRS ON GROUND
SURVEY POST
3PRS
25 PRS. READY DUG-OUT
LEFT BATTN. RIGHT BDE.
RIGHT BATTN RIGHT BDE
5 PRS.
1.PR. IN C.T.
SUPPORT BATTN. RIGHT BDE.
YYY
3 PRS Nos 8.9.17.
T.8.
2 PRS Nos 10.16.
DIV. BURY
30 PRS. (1-15 FOR CORPS) H.A.
CORPS BURY - 5 PRS. Nos 8.9.10.16.17.
1.PR. ARM'D
1.PR. ON GROUND FROM HERE TO No 9.
T.S.C.
LEFT BDE.
3 PRS. Nos 8.9.17.
CORPS 24 TEST DUG-OUT
2 PRS Nos 4.5.
2 PRS. Nos 10.15.
RIGHT BDE.
FACING BDE'S
2 PRS. (AUXILIARY PHONES)
IX FRENCH CORPS FOR DIV. ON RIGHT
DIV. ON LEFT
1.PR. No 12
R.E. DUMP
1.PR. No 11
TRESTLE ROUTE PRS 1,2,3,4,5. & ARTY.
TO CORPS MINDEN POST & REAR H.Q.
ROUTE TO CORPS M.T.4 TO REAR H.Q.
RES. BDE.
2 PRS No 13 & 18.
TO REAR H.Q.
1.PR. No 6.
DIV. H.Q. (ADVCD.)
FACING A.R.
CATEGORY OF LINES
PAIR No 1. PHONE DIV.-R. BDE.
" 2. " " -LEFT "
" 3. " " -AR - R.E. DUMP
" 4. SOUNDER " -R. BDE.
" 5. " " -LEFT "
" 8. PHONE ADVCD - REAR DIV. H.Q.
" 9 " AR - R. BDE - T.S.C.
" 10 " R. BDE - R. BATTN.
PAIR No 11. PHONE. DIV.-AR. (T.S.C.)
" 12. " " - DIV ON LEFT
" 13. " " - RESERVE BDE.
" 16. " LEFT BDE. - LEFT BATTN.
" 17. " RIGHT " - SUPPORT "
" 18. SDR. DIV - RESERVE BDE.
8.F. 9.F. LEFT BDE. PAIRS
M.T.4 SUPERIMPOSED PHONE DIV. - REAR H.Q.
REFERENCE
DIV. H.Q.
BDE. H.Q.
BATTN. H.Q.
TEST POINT
AIRLINE (G.I.)
POLED D.S. PAIR
UNLESS STATED OTHERWISE
E.G. 1.PR. IN C.T. = 1 PR. D.S. IN COMMUNICATION TRENCH
ARM'D CABLE
BURIED CABLE
C. Simpson Capt. R.E.
TRACED BY TOPL. SECTION 29TH DIV. 3.12.16.

95C19

War Diary.
of the
20th Divisional Signal Company.

January 1917

SECRET

Army Form C. 2118.

WAR DIARY
or
INTELLIGENCE SUMMARY.
(Erase heading not required.)

Instructions regarding War Diaries and Intelligence Summaries are contained in F.S. Regs., Part II. and the Staff Manual respectively. Title pages will be prepared in manuscript.

Place	Date	Hour	Summary of Events and Information	Remarks and references to Appendices
CORBIE	31/7/16	11.55pm	Further preparations for move to forward area	Army
	1/7	11.30pm	Advanced parts of Division under Lt. Nilsen reported to Guards Div HQ near Arrowhead	Army
			Copse. Staff gun teams & transport left Station	
			Capt Ram - Esqpt transport left Station in Horse Transport of Company to Citadel	
	2/7	11.20pm	Offenville moved up with transport of Company to Citadel DHQRs	Army
	3/7	11.10pm	Offer Ram and party moved into new HQ Office; relief not known to arrive next close.	Army
			Cars and remaining transport to middle Post. Batt transport at CITADEL	
ARROW HEAD	4/7	11.0pm	Relieved Guards Div Signals. Battned BOISDALE, CORBLE & BOISDAY FARM	Army
COPSE	5/7	10.30pm	New Yard Despatch - Despatch Rider Station & MG & Caprence & Stations mentioned in	Army
S. 20d 3.8 (Whenflat) 			despatches. Trade routes to BOISDALE played. Line BDR & BOISDAY FARM put into working order	
	6/7	11.0pm	Further route on BRUNFAY FARM routes, routine to DCO laid	Army
	7/7	11.0pm	New line to DADO3 at MARICOURT, N.R.C Parcles left for Midid Survey Co RE	Army
			Lt Hammond from 7th Div DADS to report relief of Gueracd RA by 20 Div RA	
	8/7	11.45pm	Burial hd. to 59 Bn in trenches all day. Defective lines between BDow& B Company	Army
	9/7	11.30am	New line laid emergency from BD & TB to replace lastbury	Army
	10/7	11.0pm	Temp 25th Division in line BUK. Capt Ag Brace commanding the Company	Army
	11/7	1.00	Work on Pont Sub at Maple Copy.	Army
	12/7	11am	RE Transport line used to end office	App B
			This morning Brigs signallers	App B
	13/7	11am	"Skin orderlies" details to Boisdale office	
			DC moved on Equit school. 2 Lt F Campbell (Jeenry) joined Coy -	App B

1577 Wt. W10791/7773 500,000 1/15 D.D.&L. A.D.S.S./Forms/C. 2118.

Army Form C. 2118.

WAR DIARY
or
INTELLIGENCE SUMMARY.
(Erase heading not required.)

Instructions regarding War Diaries and Intelligence Summaries are contained in F. S. Regs., Part II. and the Staff Manual respectively. Title pages will be prepared in manuscript.

Place	Date	Hour	Summary of Events and Information	Remarks and references to Appendices
ARROWHEAD COPSE S.30 d.3.5 Albert Sheet	14/9	10 PM	Route to BnS DORE badly shelled during night - several members in morning	AgB
	15/9	11 PM	Party by day laying cable from Corps Sig Office - 2 wires attempted - working party Zero Corps Subordinate from 4pm to 10:30 - 3 pairs wire laid from GD of Corps Bgy to new Brigade wire (L/R)	AgB
	16/9	11 PM	Left Section B.H. Wr. party from BnS DORE (S7C S.41 T17 89.4) Corps Bury found not fit for soundel. Work on Corps buried cable at night. Bn Subordinate area.	AgB
	17/9	11 PM	Line laid from COMBLES Test Box to MOEUVRE Tun Bay on Top of Bury for Southern to Left Side.	AgB
	18/9	11 PM	Work on Corps Bury at night - Work on Permanent line to BnSDOTE - 3 spans Shelled Dug night	AgB
	19/9	11 PM	Work on Corps Bury at night	AgB
	20/9	11 PM	Cable Drawn from Corps Bury 2 night Dig laid out	AgB
	21/9	11 PM	Heavy Party Group work from TRONES to COMBLES recovery lines etc (W.J)	AgB
	22/9	11 PM	Normal	AgB
	23/9	11 PM	Test Box in Corps Bury. Working Party working on Corps Bury laid first in Eperon in to work	AgB
	24/9	11 PM	Office in MAMETZ WOOD CAMP informed	AgB
	25/9	11 PM	Normal	AgB
	26/9	11 PM	Advance Party from 17 SigS arrive proceed to stations	AgB
	27/9	11 PM	Main Body 17th arrive Main Body 20th man to CITADEL	AgB
HEILLY	28/9	11 PM	By move to HEILLY - MZMC Corps nav out at Noon we take an office	PgB
	29/9	11 PM	Major STRATTON return from leave, Lieutenant G. Hatfield. Bn rel. - 24 hours	Ag B
	30/9	7 PM	Setting improvements made in billets	33 rd

F J Milkletle Major RE
O i/c Dros Signal L of C

WAR DIARY
or
INTELLIGENCE SUMMARY.

(Erase heading not required.)

Army Form C. 2118.

20 D Signal Vol 20

Place	Date	Hour	Summary of Events and Information	Remarks and references to Appendices
HENLY	31/7	11.0pm	Division rest in HENLY. No reports.	77 appx
	1/8	11 pm	No change. 2Lt Campbell to the school at D.H.Q.R.S. Lt Hannen called in temporarily from R.A.	77 appx
	2/8	11.0pm	Still in rest, no change	77 appx
	3/8	11.0pm	No change	77 appx
	4/8	11.0pm	No change	77 appx
	5/8	11.0pm	No change	77 appx
	6/8	10.30pm	Advanced party of Divisione to Brigadiers under OC Sect.	77 appx
	7/8	11.0pm	Company moved forward to Citadel Camp under Lt Hannen relief Hamblin.	77 appx
	8/8	11.0pm	Company to Brigadiers, OC to Brigadiers	77 appx
Brigadiers Aus Div	9/8	11.0pm	Took over from 25th Div at 10.0am. A 5th Australian Div in left, 17 Div in right	77 appx
	10/8	10.30pm	Capt Brace to school. 2Lt Campbell up to Brigadiers. Work on camp maintenance work on lines.	77 appx
	11/8	11.0pm	Maintenance work on lines.	77 appx
	12/8	11.30pm	Maintenance work on MH front lines to Brigade, rear contr from Brigade to adv melange at T9.b.23 via forward lead lines. Dugh works safely long to roads Brigade arranged by 2Lt Campbell.	77 appx
	13/8	11.0pm	Work on overhead between etc.	77 appx
	14/8	11.0pm	New line from T9.b.3.3.6 m dugout had going on we need alternative route from H.Q. R.A. to adv H.Q.	77 appx

WAR DIARY or INTELLIGENCE SUMMARY

Army Form C. 2118.

Place	Date	Hour	Summary of Events and Information	Remarks and references to Appendices
R.R.1 V DETRE Aug 4.2 (Installed)	15/7/17	11.0pm	Clearing wire and maintenance	77 Inf
	16/7/17	11.0pm	Several back lines destroyed by blowing up of ammunition dump or Pelham	77 Inf
	17/7/17	11.0pm	Clearing wire and work on 17th Div line	77 Inf
	18/7/17	11.0pm	Clearing wire and pulling hoops in line forward to 79. Transport of same forward hostilly. New precautions	77 Inf
	19/7/17	11.0pm	Maintenance & work in camp	77 Inf
	20/7/17	11.0pm	New precautions still on. Work as on 19th. Reconnoitring offensive went	77 Inf
	21/7/17	11.0pm	Clearing cable & other local work	77 Inf
	22/7/17	11.0pm	Work as in last few days. New precautions still keeping back necessary stores for forward work	77 Inf
	23/7/17	11.30pm	Local work. New precautions still on	77 Inf
	24/7/17	11.0pm	New hut to 24th Field Co R.E.	77 Inf
	25/7/17	11.0pm	Preparation for advanced Bde HQ or left for minor operation, new mud slay & made for carrying cable in forward area	77 Inf
	26/7/17	11.30pm	Further work for minor offensive. Preparations also for move forward. Parade to Ros Villa at 7.17 & 8.37. No news came to from ct town level by slip.	77 Inf
	27/7/17	6.0pm	Practice happen as Div HQ with contact patrol. DR arrangements, pigeons completed for minor operation	77 Inf

F J Matcalfe Major RE
or 2nd Div Signal Coy

WAR DIARY
or
INTELLIGENCE SUMMARY.

(Erase heading not required.)

Army Form C. 2118.

20 Div Sigs. Co.
Vol 21

Place	Date	Hour	Summary of Events and Information	Remarks and references to Appendices
BRIQUETERIE AMBR (Sheet Allen)	28/3/17	11.0 pm	Small attack massacre for statedroute to transport lines held up to battalions. Forward communications by hour Bn 58. Line maintained, one cable to but not met. Left Bde forwarded Ty k 3.3	
	1/4/17	11.0 pm	Bnd (B'Normal)	
	2/4/17	11.0 pm	New line to emported at middle line Highground R.A. forward line maintenance met	
	3/4/17	11.30 pm	Preparation for move of R Group R.O.A. to middle case	
	4/4/17	11.30 am		
	5/4/17	11.0 pm	R Div moved away Arty divisions ends front. We beyond maintd appx/alln took over a test station in line & Arty in change. All Bde moral rpts to Rev Bde in front of assault took over lighter tel par. 2	
	6/4/17	11.0 pm	Amplifiers of lines & circuits constructed and replaced always	
	7/4/17	12.0 pm	New line 8 BRIDGES	
	8/4/17	12.30 pm	Relief of maintenance. Such work of army	
	9/4/17	11.0 pm	Maintenance work. Rly troubles obtained from Hopshop Stations	
	10/4/17	10.30 pm	Line to 60th Bde not the best work	
	11/4/17	11.00 pm	Preparations at Guillemot to move left Bde forward to T 160	
	12/4/17	11.0 pm	new line from left joint & Bde Dump to new Hd of left Bde	
	13/4/17	11.0 pm	Further line extended for new M.H.O of left Bde	

Army Form C. 2118.

WAR DIARY
or
INTELLIGENCE SUMMARY.
(Erase heading not required.)

Instructions regarding War Diaries and Intelligence Summaries are contained in F. S. Regs., Part II. and the Staff Manual respectively. Title pages will be prepared in manuscript.

Place	Date	Hour	Summary of Events and Information	Remarks and references to Appendices
BRIQUETERIE T.2 d B.4 Stores Officer	14/3/17	11.0 pm	Preparation for hospital move of Divl HQ. Extra lines run to Guillemont from Divne Head Qtrs.	73 mg
	15/3/17	11.30 pm	Enemy strenuous bombing general near our arty front. Extra lines suppressed from left group. Left Brigade moves to dugouts in rear of Maurepas.	73 mg
	16/3/17	11.0 pm	First lodging obtained in enemy line. These did not long be retained.	73 mg
	17/3/17	11.30 pm	Advance becomes general along front. Retransfers + road to Guillemont overhauled and advance posts thrown forward up to area ROCQUIGNY. Visual back to Translay ridge gained and wires laid to Bois of Blds.	97 mg
Guillemont T.25.A 5.8	18/3/17	11.0 pm	Divl HQ moved. ROCQUIGNY fell into our hands. Cavalry moved forward. Communication by wire established up to ROCQUIGNY. 3rd Australian Div in BARASTRE. Corps cavalry forward HQRS	73 mg
	19/3/17	10.0 pm	Work on permanent route from M.E. to ROCQUIGNY commenced (mile set campaign with assistance from SOMME. Store taken up	73 mg
	20/3/17	11.0 pm	Civil Labour available. Working on route to ROCQUIGNY. Very heavy ground lines run forward to village together then felt into our hands.	73 mg
	21/3/17	11.0 pm	Ditto with Wrtel work to lines developed by Lieut Lort. BOIS DOTTE	73 mg
	22/3/17	11.10 pm	Reinstatement forward + gleaning dead work at Guillemont.	73 mg
	23/3/17	11.0 pm	As on 22nd	83 mg
	24/3/17	11.0 pm	Enemy 6.8 north of line. We look into utter lines at COMBLES	82 mg

Army Form C. 2118.

WAR DIARY
or
INTELLIGENCE SUMMARY.
(Erase heading not required.)

Instructions regarding War Diaries and Intelligence Summaries are contained in F. S. Regs., Part II. and the Staff Manual respectively. Title pages will be prepared in manuscript.

Place	Date	Hour	Summary of Events and Information	Remarks and references to Appendices
			[handwritten entries, largely illegible]	

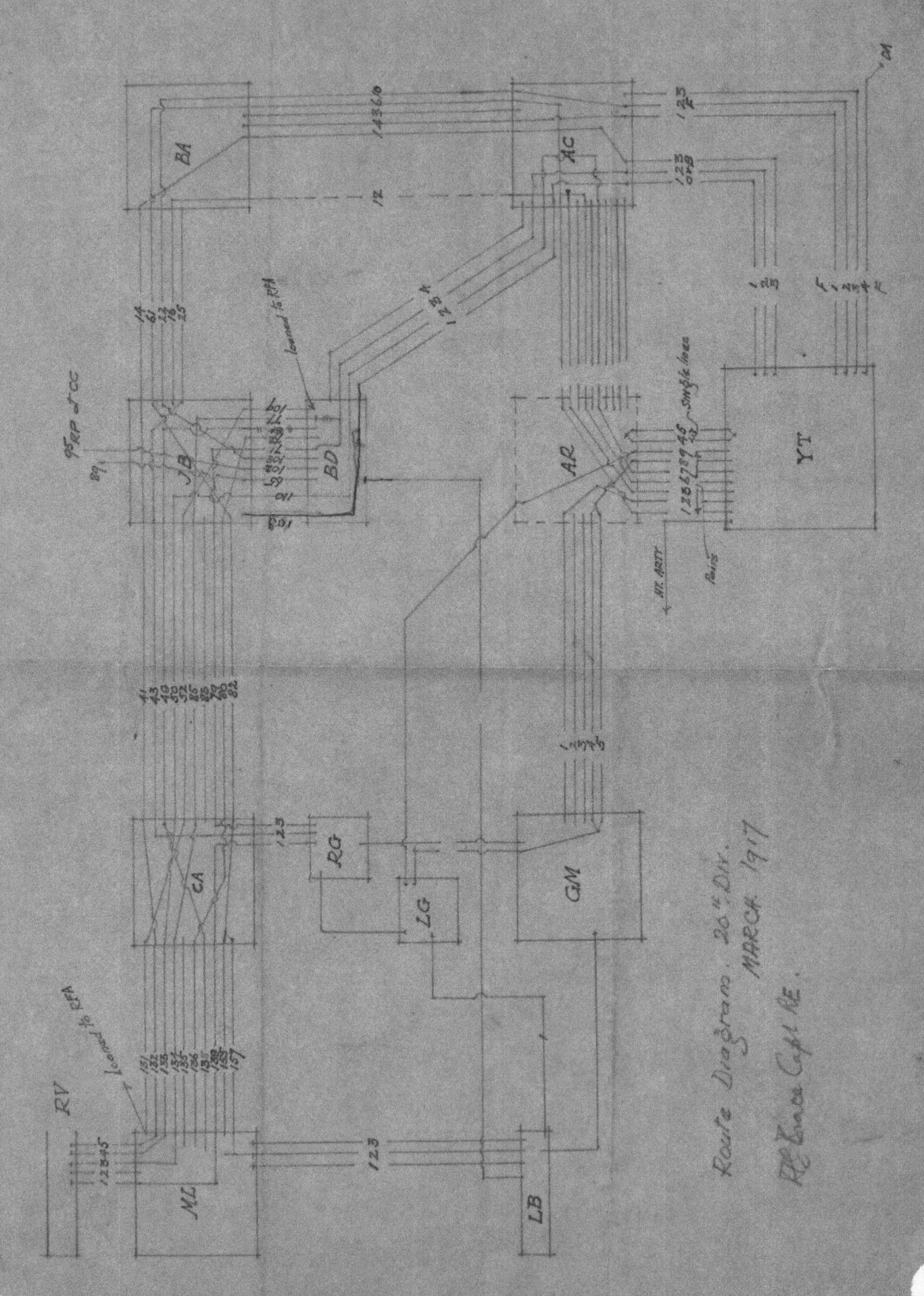

Army Form C. 2118.

WAR DIARY
or
INTELLIGENCE SUMMARY.
(Erase heading not required.)

2nd D.V. Signals Vol 22

Instructions regarding War Diaries and Intelligence Summaries are contained in F.S. Regs., Part II. and the Staff Manual respectively. Title pages will be prepared in manuscript.

Place	Date	Hour	Summary of Events and Information	Remarks and references to Appendices
GUILLEMONT TRENCH PLOEGS'C	31/7/17	11.0 pm	Enemy 'ph' communication broken up by shellfire. Heavy rain & several unauthorised [illegible] 225 Mallett shocked	77 ms
	1/8/17	11.0 pm	Final preparations for move to RADINGHEM. Wet [illegible] weather.	77 ms
RADINGHEM 027.a.7.5 Sheet 57c	2/8/17	11.0 pm	Headquarters moved 11 am. Through several convoys [illegible] before change. Corps lines in trouble all day. Heavy [illegible]	77 ms
	3/8/17	11.30 pm	Reconnoitred forward signalling in [illegible]. Difficult work. New accommodation made run to Le Traxeloy	77 ms
	4/8/17	11.0 pm	Castle latch. Division relieved Metz and Mill[?]am Visual stations both [illegible]. New visibility, but through by enemy from B to M.D in foreward [illegible] of places named	77 ms
	5/8/17	11.30 pm	Bringing down upfrom buillement & Castle. Fetch cattle route off roads safe from road repairing parties and house-breakers. Pilot route cattle/plaited from Koseziring & 4 No.	77 ms
	6/8/17	11.0 pm	Pilot route continued	77 ms
	7/8/17	11.0 pm	line to you relaid for move forward of left Bde. Pilot route continued	77 ms
	8/8/17	11.0 pm	New lateral laid between brigades. Pilot route continued	77 ms

WARDIARY
INTELLIGENCE SUMMARY
(Erase heading not required.)

Army Form C. 2118

Instructions regarding War Diaries and Intelligence Summaries are contained in F.S. Regs., Part II. and the Staff Manual respectively. Title Pages will be prepared in manuscript.

Place	Date	Hour	Summary of Events and Information	Remarks and references to Appendices
REQUIEM	9/17	11.5pm	Work on plant system continued. Maintenance of existing works. Bn. Hd reported peaceful	7 May
02707 5 Sheets 7C	10/17	11.30pm	Reg. Heavle on route the evening receities. Pilgrim's work continued	7 May
	11/17	11.0pm	Continued work on plank route	8 May
	12/17	11.30pm	Pilgrim's have plans of reinforcement again moved forward	7 May
	13/17	11.0pm	Left 1st Bde. followed up front to new gpz	7 May
	14/17	11.0pm	Maintenance. Pilgrim's route continued	7 May
	15/17	11.30pm	Rained all day. Continued todd route. Picked up old route	7 May
	16/17	11.0pm	Offered a Het station at wireless station in gpz	7 May
	17/17	11.30pm	Work commenced in preparation for move Hd at Little Wood gpz	7 May
	18/17	11.0pm	Above continued	7 May
	19/17	11.0pm	General maintenance. Putting up routes	7 May
	20/17	11.30pm	Route forward from Little Wood to Reymolents in preparation for move		
			w/d Left 13th Bn.	
	21/17	11.0pm	Infrd to Auzor Bries-Beaumetz	8 May
	22/17	11.0pm	New route to projected Rozett. From Little Wood to Hamincourt wood. Francourt fell into our hands	7 May

WAR DIARY
or
INTELLIGENCE SUMMARY
(Erase heading not required.)

Army Form C. 2118

Place	Date	Hour	Summary of Events and Information	Remarks and references to Appendices
RACOURT	23/5/17	10.0 pm	Work at new Div Hdr. & new forward lines for new Rt Bde HQ in HARGICOURT WOOD	Appx
RUYERE	24/5/17	10.0 pm	Drafts for him for new billets HAVRINCOURT	Appx
Litchwood	25/5/17	11.0 pm	Div HQ moved to little wood. 4th Rt Bde moved to HAVRINCOURT WOOD, P. Bol 4.4.	Appx
"	26/5/17	11.30 pm	Settling in. Relief line from Rt Bde Staff Bde which moved to Ruyaulcourt	Appx
Metz	27/5/17	11.15 pm	Commencement of back route	Appx
8hors 7C	28/5/17	11.15 pm	Work on back route continued. Adjustments of unit lines for new HQ	Appx
"	29/5/17	11.0 pm	New line drawn ready for 92nd Bde moving over for relief tomorrow	Appx

FJM Stratton
Major RE
OC RE Div Signal Coy RE

Army Form C. 2118

WAR DIARY
or
INTELLIGENCE SUMMARY
(Erase heading not required.)

Vol 23

Place	Date	Hour	Summary of Events and Information	Remarks and references to Appendices
YPRES Little Wood Pop 6.2.3 Sheet 27C	30/4/17	11.0pm	Line laid to new HQ of 92nd Bn RFA (Q15 c 5.2). Bde detached to cover area of division on night for a raid on La Vacquerie. Gleaning round Bns.	77M/S
	1/5/17	11.0pm	Maintenance. Gleaning. Running through cable station.	77M/S
	2/5/17	11.0pm	New air line route from YMCA to where = A36 ends ran ato 11A of 11.00 Bn. New line through BROQUEVILLE for DADSS testified and cable route.	77M/S
	3/5/17	10.30pm	11 Div continued. Last laid from 104 Bde to 92nd Bn. No alarm apparatus to hand. D1 Div continued. Routes for alarm apparatus.	77M/S
	4/5/17	10.0pm	D1 Div continued. Routes for alarm apparatus 10.0pm.	77M/S
	5/5/17	11.0pm	Patrolling & maintenance. Routes to 104 Bde finished.	77M/S
	6/5/17	10.0pm	The new establishment of cable n. RSA interesting completed so for personnel concerned. New punctually maintained and instructional work carried out.	77M/S
	7/5/17	10.30pm	detachment regularly on daily programme, while contracted light duties kept off casualties. MG detms. Polis brought in. 27 KB Compn RE left MG cable pit for temporary duty.	77M/S
	8/5/17	11.0pm	Weather doubtful, maintenance & instructional work. Further line laid.	77M/S
	9/5/17	11.0pm	All ranks picked up twice in through Beam.	7M/S
	10/5/17	11.0pm	New RE 2nd sections formed. Sgt Boots placed i/c 91st 2nd detachment 2Cpl Fowler i/c 92nd Bn detachment.	77M/S

Army Form C. 2118

WAR DIARY
or
INTELLIGENCE SUMMARY
(Erase heading not required.)

Instructions regarding War Diaries and Intelligence Summaries are contained in F.S. Regs., Part II. and the Staff Manual respectively. Title Pages will be prepared in manuscript.

Place	Date	Hour	Summary of Events and Information	Remarks and references to Appendices
YPRES with Wood Pts 1,2,3 Shelks 7c	11/5/17	11.0pm	New 2pr airline route started. Observation Wood for a thrice RA Bde & Inf/Bde in line	9 May
	12/5/17	11.0pm	New route finished. Other old routes picked up.	9 May
	13/5/17	11.0pm	66th Bde moved from reserve at Ypres into line at Sleepers Wood W16.1.5. RSn Sub. Spur formed for 3 weeks. Heavy hostile shelling in Inundation road at R27c	7 May
	14/5/17	11.0pm	Maintenance started work. Local lines for subaltern of reserve Bde on to Divl Exchange	7 May
	15/5/17	11.0pm	Glassy huts suffer by wind of reserve Bde	7 May
	16/5/17	11.0pm	None of enemy	7 May
	17/5/17	11.30am	2nd Lt J. HADDEN, R.E. joined from England for duty	7 May
	18/5/17	11.0pm	New ROC instructions issued. R.K.personnel attached. Sgt Beam to 91st Bde A/Sgt	7 May
			Route B92 at Bde HQ	7 May
	19/5/17	11.0pm	Preparations for relief of the Div by 42nd Div. Divison backline 5th Australian Div in front between Queen's & Battlevonde. School closed down. Temporarily + Kandolone to 42nd Div Signal O/RS. 107th Bde in Ypres	7 May
	20/5/17	11.0pm	61st Bde moved BSpt Asyen cross - H24 central. 128th Bde in Ypres	7 May
	21/5/17	11.0pm	Preparations for move	7 May

WAR DIARY or INTELLIGENCE SUMMARY

Army Form C. 2118

(Erase heading not required.)

Instructions regarding War Diaries and Intelligence Summaries are contained in F.S. Regs., Part II. and the Staff Manual respectively. Title Pages will be prepared in manuscript.

Place	Date	Hour	Summary of Events and Information	Remarks and references to Appendices
Y.C. Little Wood	22.5.17	11.0pm	Further nothstanding Adamy from to town H.Q. Bie brickworks from Wancs Balance Rent	22 may
P28 A9.3 sheet 57C	23.5.17	11.30pm	(H15 C 3.6 Sheet 57C) underlap B.mst. During moved to tremout, being relieved by 42 who are being relieved	23 may
Dreanwary M15C3+6 sheet 57C	24.5.17	11.0pm	of 60 Bon by Div — camp be J't Aadjar etc Scotty's down in rear lift	24 may
	25.5.17	11.30pm	59 D. Bde moved to offensive flank in night 24-25	25 may
	26.5.17	11.30pm	60 Bde moved to left - reserve of twee by 25-26. DO Div took over the front from 5 cents. Div — buttress to stayed to 190 at 14 DX. Troops the George there under Corps where stayed in lept	26 may
	27.5.17	11.30pm	Apible (65th) shelled out returned to ath. his H9 at 14DX. Signal office closed unoded.	27 may
			We are busied up to hound later to telll fire + disconnected extension lines left 7t of front between 92 + Bde RSG	
	28.5.17	11.0pm	Div. RA tost over from 2nd Australian Div. # Artillery.	28 may
	29.5.17	11.0pm	Retgrent moved back to Hotkije	29 may
	30.5.17	11.0pm	Road work round Zandud. Work on straightening of buy continued	30 may

F J Nikitski Mayor QS

O.C. 20th DIVISIONAL SIGNAL COY. R.E.

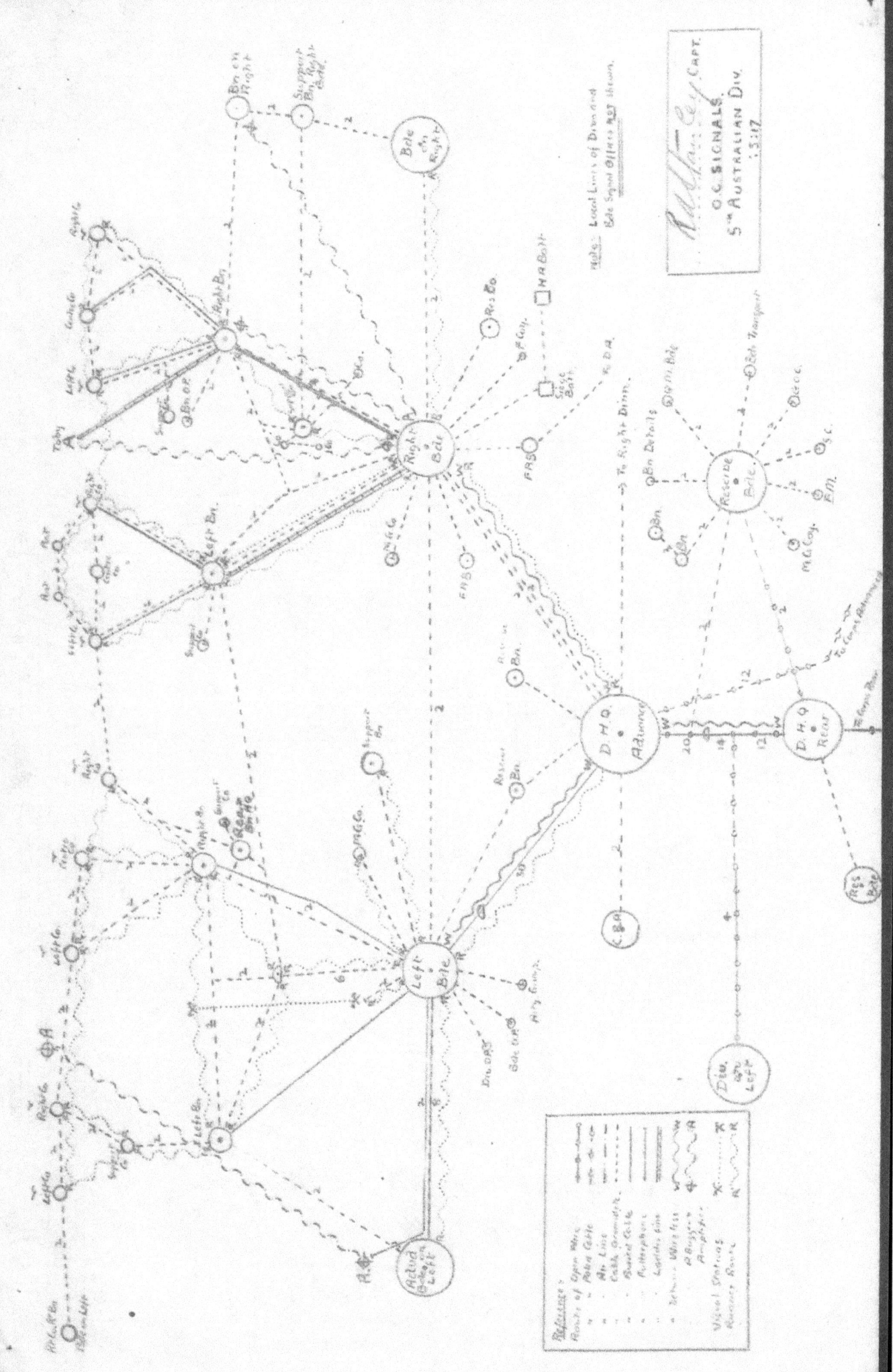

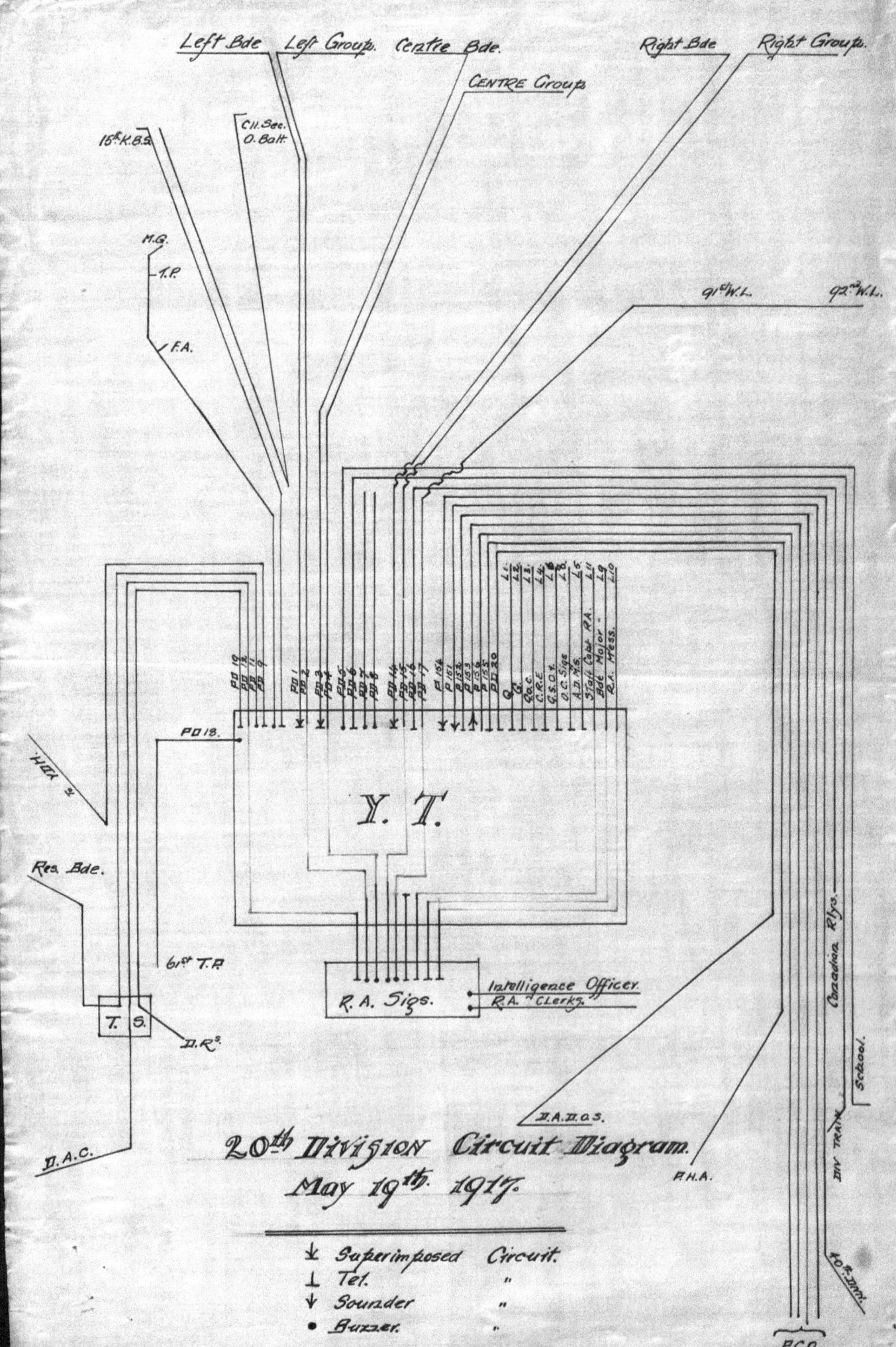

WAR DIARY
or
INTELLIGENCE SUMMARY

Army Form C. 2118

Place	Date	Hour	Summary of Events and Information	Remarks and references to Appendices
BHQ Pot Movement	31/5	11.0 p.m	Transferred from 5th Army to 3rd Army	77 M-g
	1/6	11.0 p.m	Rums to Rt. Bn allowed delayed rec. broken.	77 M-g
WSC 3.6 Plat 57E	2/7	11.0 p.m	Maintenance of cable overhead.	77 M-g
	3/7	11.30 pm	Shelling round about 14A lines cut but communication maintained	77 M-g
	4/7	11.0 pm	Further trouble on lines broken at BHQ. Transfer of RA instruction to 77 M-g	77 M-g
	5/7	11.0 p	Personnel under OB 1046 completed.	77 M-g
	6/7	11.0 p	Line patrolling. D.R. Sent papers. Cpl. overhead	77 M-g
		11.30 p	Major O.M. Sheather on leave to U.K. Capt. A.G. Bruce in command. Capt. B. Hammer	77 pt
	7/7	10 am	returned from leave to U.K.	APPB
	8/6	10 am	Work on buried route completely fortive - clearing up lines in FAREUIL. Sgt. Saywest awarded ΛΤCM.	APPB
	9/7/17	9.30 pm	Ballon mate onto buried route behind new Test bht.	APPB
	10/7	12 mn	New Test bht between adv. Bn. + Present Test place started.	APPB
	11/6	11. pm	Main route to VAUX & Saffery onto broken communication maintained by adv. DU HQ as exchange for RA + Bof Bdewark. Party of 7 to Seaside. + Took on Test bht completion.	APPB
	12/7	11.15	Loops laid to birl miles to adv. HQ 1½ mile back. Camp improvements - Shown details of same.	APPB
	13	12 mn	Sgt. Maclure + detachment continue work behind lines - fits last line in SYDNEY TRENCH. - line laid from Sgt. Maclure's Bn. direct to CIOCEST. 15.	APPB
	14	3. pm	advanced Sgt. Saywest and detachment return. Sgt. Maclure: Loft Pole went to another - considerable trouble on attack by Bn. on left during night 14-15. Fwd. Coys to Bn.Q spoken	APPB
	15	10 m	New lines - Gas alarm at 6. pm. Enterlon Bng. lines Changed. - Cable cut out for instructional purposes.	APPB
	16		line (air) from BGposs to Bn. Tm. battery at H.7674.	

WAR DIARY
or
INTELLIGENCE SUMMARY

Army Form C. 2118

Place	Date	Hour	Summary of Events and Information	Remarks and references to Appendices
Pot Monument HQSC3.6 Sheet 57K	17.6.17	11.0 pm	Major J Walbank RE returned from leave. Resumed command	77M7
	18.6.17	11.0 pm	Maintenance & cable overhead. Reptable moved up to adv. HQ. 7 Pet Walker returned to take charge	77M7 77M7
	19.6.17	11.0 pm	Work on overhead cable forward of NOREUIL	77M7
	20.6.17	11.30 pm	Further work on bury forward of NOREUIL	77M7
	21.6.17	11.30 pm	General maintenance & cable overhead	77M7
	22.6.17	11.0 pm	2/Lt Midlett on leave to UK. 2/Lt Hadler (1.2.1. Capt Brace to UK	77M7
	23.6.17	11.15 pm	Work on party of bury W/of NOREUIL where new test house formed + stations + party have been installed. Carried of other advanced party of 62nd Divn	77M7
	24	10.30 A	Work on forward stns of bury. Rescuers for 62nd Divn Fs to set stations	77B
	25	11.55	Major Shutton ordered to 19th Corps. Capt. Brace return from Avancille. Party of 62nd Divn	77B
	26	10. A	Major JP M Shutton to 19th Corps Capt Robins take over as GC Command. Training hand over to 62nd	77B
	27	10.30	Communications as usual	77B
	28	10.35	Ammunition transport leave for the LUCHEUX. 82nd Divn Sigs arrive. Taken over office at 5pm	77B
Bonneville	29	11. 0.	Closed at Monument opened at Bonneville at 11 am. Coy by train + transport from LUCHEUX & to Bonneville. RE H. WOs return to. A6 Corps Montes Troops	77B
	30	10. A	Arrangements for moving Div HQ to DOMART commenced. 2 lorries from Corps HQ allotted	77B

R.S. Trace Capt RE
CMDG. 20th DIVISIONAL SIGNAL CO.

WAR DIARY
or
INTELLIGENCE SUMMARY
(Erase heading not required.)

Army Form C. 2118

Place	Date	Hour	Summary of Events and Information	Remarks and references to Appendices
DOMART	1/7/17	10 A	Division H.Q. move BERNAVILLE to DOMART — Railway Signal office at BERNAVILLE closed	A/S.B
"	2	10	Ammunition to BERNAVILLE. Railway arranges 2 p.m. to close B Cable Wagon	A/S.B
	3	9	Bugle line laid to Bd. at FIENVILLERS for Bde. at AUTHIEUX. Arrangements for open signal school commenced.	A/S.D.
	4	7.30	Div Signal School opens at FRANQUEVILLE. "2/Lt Brenton takes charge of this line."	A/S.D.
	5	11.15	Preparing for Inspection by G.O.C.	A/S.B.
	6	11.0	Physical Trg. under Army Instructor. Inspection by G.O.C. 20 Div.	A/S.B.
	7	11.0	Reorganisation of Coy commenced	A/S.B.
	8	10.0	nil	A/S.B.
	9	10	With own art. Trng.	A/S.B.
	10	11	Normal. Trng. Continued	A/S.B.
	11	10	Trng. Permanent. lie and tent	A/S.B.
	12	11	Arrangements for Visual Scheme. Capt. E.P. Reynolds from Coy 2nd in Command	A/S.B.
	13	10.30	Div. Horse Show. O.C. visits 19th Corps at Poperinghe.	A/S.B.
	14	11.0	Visual Scheme. Communication by lamp to Bdes. Causes all manner of trouble	A/S.D.
	15	10.0	Div. Signal school take over Visual Scheme. At mid difficulties for trucks of School	A/S.B.
	16	11.0	Visual Stations close down at noon. — Cable line in connection with scheme reels in	A/S.B.

WAR DIARY
or
INTELLIGENCE SUMMARY

(Erase heading not required.)

Army Form C. 2118

Place	Date	Hour	Summary of Events and Information	Remarks and references to Appendices
DOMART	17/7/17	AM.	Cable wagon of Field Cay Pontoon bridges in DOMART Square. - Signal School dispersed.	APB.
	18	10	W/T Set to 4th Corps for repairs & use, returns same 8th. Cay. Spark at DOMART.	APB.
	19	10	Loads of Sigs Stores prepared to move.	APP.
	20	10	Sig - Cable wire laid by Cos to Bernaville, Fienvillers (Cr poles) in - A drawn	APP.
			Brt leaves for PROVEN.	
PROVEN	21	11.	Coy proceed by train to CANDAS to PROVEN. - Div HQ open at PROVEN at 10 and	APB.
	22	12	Sully into Billets. - OC Sigs to Poperinghe and into OC 38th	APB.
			- Conference at 14th Corps.	ASA
	23	13	Stores unloaded	APB
	24	14	Lawnel	APB
	25	11.0	Relle Section Commanders PB Squad Instruction on DmH	APP
	26	11.0	Trans. Field Section PB Squad Continued	APB
	27	10.0	ADMS inspects Coy Horses. - Loads of Rely parties to speakers to Co	APB.
	28	11.0-	Lawnel. found dump at EMERGENCY instruct (1 km)	APB.
	29	10 A.	hostel. found area. arranging Relif	
	30	11 A.	Preparation for operation. 59 Fld hvs to Canada Ties area. - Visit 36" Div in Elverdinghe. - Visit with 3 Bdes. - Lt. Hadden to Canal Bank "A" cup dugout.	APB
	31	G.R.	Bn under orders to move at 3 hours notice. - advanced Gps to DRAGON Camp. - attack on 5th Corps front. at 3.50 am.	APB.

WAR DIARY or INTELLIGENCE SUMMARY

Army Form C. 2118

Place	Date	Hour	Summary of Events and Information	Remarks and references to Appendices
PROVEN	Aug 1	10£	Coy in readiness to move at Shows notice.	E.PR
	2	10A	Normal.	E.PR
	3	10A	Normal. Horse lines flooded out + moved to stables in POPERINGHE	E.PR
	4	10 P	Preparations for relief of 38th Div. Signal Coy.	E.PR
	5	11 A	Advance Party, hales men 38th Div. adv HQ and Remounted at DRAGON Camp. - 20th Div. Signal Section when 38 - 50. N. Hastler proceed to Adjunct + Tournebout with party of learners.	E.PR
DRAGON CAMP	6	12 N	Coy. moves to DRAGON Camp. - Relief of 38th Div. completed.	E.PR
	7	1 AM	Communication as required.	E.PR
	8	12 M	Cable buries to PILKEM. to Barnets Ho.	E.PR
	9	12 N	Cable burying continued.	E.PR
	10	10 AM	57th Bde attack on hrie STEENBEEK.	E.PR
	11	12 N	Cable burying STRAY FARM to MARSOUIN Farm begins 10/11. Preparing line intelligible	E.PR
	12	10 A	" continues	E.PR
	13	10 A	Further action by 57th Bde. - Work preparing adv. H.Q offices at Steentryes	E.PR
	14	10 A	Cable carry + trenches preparation for attack.	E.PR
FEUERDANME	15	10 A	Old Signal preparations completed. - Div HQ moves to Elverdinghe. Chau. for Staff Camps	E.PR
	16	10 A	Attack by Div on LANGEMARCK - Signal communication into Bde. maintained. - Work in	E.PR
	17	10 A	Forward areas some difficult.	E.PR
	18	10 A	Situation still sufficient - lines - forward area broken to repair. Cable lines out	E.PR
PROVEN	19	10 A	Arrangements for relief by 38th Div. Relief by 38th Div. Coy. moves to PROVEN	E.PR

WAR DIARY
or
INTELLIGENCE SUMMARY

Army Form C. 2118.

Place	Date	Hour	Summary of Events and Information	Remarks and references to Appendices
PROVEN	Aug 20	10 P	Cells to B.hks - changing up.	S.P.R
	21	6 P	Arrangements for Signal School commenced.	S.P.R
	22	10 A	"	S.P.R
	23	4 P	Div Signal School assembled.	S.P.R
	24	10 A	Normal	S.P.R
	25	10 PM	MAJ. G. BRACE proceeded on leave to U.K. Capt E.P. REYNOLDS assumed command of Company.	S.P.R
	26	10 PM	Normal	S.P.R
	27	10 PM	Normal	S.P.R
	28	10 PM	Buzzer Class for linesmen commenced.	S.P.R
	29	10 PM	Map Reading Class commenced.	S.P.R
	30	10 PM	Normal	S.P.R
	31	10 PM	CRE inspected C.y presented cards of congratulation from GOC 20th Div to following NCOs & men in recognition of their gallant conduct during recent operations. 46121 CpC EMMERSON I.W. 53270 SpR BORER J.H. 48636 Pur BLOXHAM A.H. 148726 Pur REYNOLDS F.H.	S.P.R

E.P. Reynolds Capt R.E.
for Major
Commanding 20 Dn Sig Co.
RE

Army Form C. 2118.

20 D Signals
Nov 27

WAR DIARY
INTELLIGENCE SUMMARY

Instructions regarding War Diaries and Intelligence Summaries are contained in F.S. Regs., Part II. and the Staff Manual respectively. Title pages will be prepared in manuscript.

(Erase heading not required.)

Place	Date	Hour	Summary of Events and Information	Remarks and references to Appendices
PROVEN	1. 9/1/17		Training – Despatch Riding Scheme	
	2		Normal	
	3		Preliminary visit of O.C. to 38th Div Area	
	4		Training – Despatch Riding Scheme	
	5		Asst. Signals returning from leave. Normal	
	6		Major R.C. Bruce returns from leave	App 8
	7		Normal	App 13
	8		Normal	
	9		"Whelp" return from leave. – 61st Div. move up to line	App 8
	10		Arrangements for return distribution of 38th Div. for 38 Div	App 2
			Div. HQ. taken over 38 Div to the line	App 1B
HELSHAMS	11		Buried Cable continued from ADELPHI to AYRINGATE – works Party 300	App B
Cheveljen	12		Work on forward lines continued – Buried cable attempt continued works Party 300	
	13		2nd Li Dunlop attacked for duty. – Buried cable continued attempt completion to M.B. ENGINE	App B
	14		Buried Cable from MARSOUIN Pont to STRAY & from MATSOUIN Ave to CRAB APPLE	App B
	15		2nd Li Whigham return from N/T course GHQ. – works Party "Buried" cable below BUTT 15	App B
	16		to MARSOUIN Ave. Capt. Harrisen Superior.	App B
	17		Test cut buried mates. 2nd Li Whigham return to OK.	App 5
	18		"U. Carnegie" posted to Signals Co Signally. Relief of 61st Bde by 58th Nov to battle station	App 5
	19		Preparations for Signal Communication for battle completed. 11th Bde attacked for Wireless station	App B

R.F. Mackay Lt.

1577 Wt.W10791/1773 500,000 1/15 D.D.& L. A.D.S.S./Forms/C. 2118.

WAR DIARY
or
INTELLIGENCE SUMMARY.
(Erase heading not required.)

Army Form C. 2118.

Place	Date	Hour	Summary of Events and Information	Remarks and references to Appendices
NEUVE FSE	Sep 1918 20		attack of 25th Div. Communications & maintained	APB
	21		Minor operations continued by 62nd Reg't Bdes. Handing back in but no serious interruption of communication	APB
	22		Special School "Pack Horse" class complete - Further trouble on forward trunk lines	APB
	23		Corps horse taken over. Relief of 57th by Poles of 61st	APB
	24		Buried cable forward of MARCOING East. To H.Q. Div Divisionnes 6 pairs at Fins.	APB
	25		Main buried cable on Canal Bank. Work at S.S. ready, no alterations made via LEMCOURT	APB APB
	26		for EPEHY etc Div Sigl School closed - at 3 hour bris on forward buried rote 6 to & of S.S.Detacht to artly	APB APB APB
	27		Preliminary arrangements for Relief by 3rd & 4th Div Reg'ts Div settled. L/Cpl ___ wounds to Duke	APB APB
	28		arrangements for handing over completed - L/Cpl ___ to Hospital	APB
	29		A. Relief at 10 am. Hand to PROVEN - H/Corporal ___ returned from leave	APB
	30		L/___ to H.Q. Division via L/___	APB
			Normal	

R.P.[signature]
MAJOR R.E.
COMMANDING DIVISIONAL SIGNAL COY.

WAR DIARY

INTELLIGENCE SUMMARY
(Erase heading not required.)

Army Form C. 2118.

20 D Signals Vol 26

Place	Date	Hour	Summary of Events and Information	Remarks and references to Appendices
PROVEN	1/1/17	10 AM	O.C. proceeded to new area of HAPLINCOURT	APB
		3 PM	1st Advance Party entrained at PROVEN for new area at HAPLINCOURT	APB
	2/1/17		2nd Do Do Do Do Do Do	APB
			Main body of IV Corps to XIV Corps proceeded by road to near HAPLINCOURT attached to III Corps	APB
		5 PM	Main body of 20 Div Signal Co entrained at PROVEN for BAPAUME thence by road to HAPLINCOURT	APB
			Under IV Corps to administration	
HAPLINCOURT	3/1/17	10 AM	20 Div H.Q. took over from 55 Div at HAPLINCOURT	APB
PERONNE	4/1/17	8 AM	20 Div H.Q. moved to PERONNE. Comn under III Corps. Signal Coy Transport moved to Sorel & Grand under Lt Reynolds	APB
			E HADDEN proceeded on leave to U.K.	APB
	5/1/17		61 Bde moved from BARASTRE to HAUT ALLAINES	APB
			60 Bde moved into line from SOREL - relieved 120th Bde	APB
	6/1/17		59 Bde moved from BARASTRE to SOREL	APB
	7/1/17	1 AM	Time change at midnight	APB
			E ADDEN moved into right of SOREL relieves 119th R. Lec	APB
			Mallet from hospital returned to duty to 59 Bde Section. Lt Wenham returned to Div H.Q from 59th Adv section	APB
	8/1/17	9 AM	Wireless Station taken over by 40th Div - Responsibility of station from 40 Div Lig. lectures ? operators	APB
		5 PM	20 Div Artillery lines over to take over responsibility of station from 40 Div Lig. lectures ? operators	APB
			61 Bde Signals take over from HQ Bn lign at SOREL	APB
	9/1/17	8 AM	20 Div Signals take over from HQ Bn lign at SOREL	APB
			61st Bde troops into line from SOREL relieved 121st Bas	APB
SOREL-le-GRAND	10/1/17	10 AM	Relief of 40 Div complete by 20 Div at SOREL-le-GRAND.	APB
	11/1/17	5 PM	Div Signal School opened at NURLU	APB
			Patrols of lines. Camp improvements	APB
	12/1/17		Normal Camp improvements	APB
	13/1/17		Normal Camp improvements	APB
	14/1/17		Normal Maintenance of lines	APB
	15/1/17		Normal Maintenance of lines Camp improvements	APB
	16/1/17		Normal. Camp improvements	APB

WAR DIARY

INTELLIGENCE SUMMARY

(Erase heading not required.)

Army Form C. 2118.

Place	Date	Hour	Summary of Events and Information	Remarks and references to Appendices
SOREL-le-GRAND	17/10/17		Lt Baldwin returned from leave.	APB
	18/10/17	10 Noon	3rd Corps relieved by 7th Corps. Maintenance of lines	APB
	19/10/17	3 PM	Officers Class at Div Signal School NYRLU assembled. Capt E.T Reynolds proceeded on leave to U.K.	APB
	20/10/17		Normal - Maintenance of lines	APB
	21/10/17		Normal. Capt: Hannan + personnel 20 Div R.A Signals arrived in Camp at SOREL	APB
	22/10/17		Normal - Work on Camp Continued	APB
	23/10/17		Adv Div R.Q Signals moved quarters + offices to make room for 60th Div R.A.	APB
	24/10/17		Lt Moore DLI attached for duty at Div Signal School.	APB
	25/10/17	10 AM	20 DIV R.A Signals returned 40th Div R.A degs + took over office at SOREL	APB
	26/10/17	9 AM	Lt Wenham proceeded on leave to U.K. Lt Moore D.L.I O the Div Sig School Newton work of trading in Permanent Route commenced	APB
	27/10/17	9 AM	Pole Cable laid from QUEEN'S CROSS to Left Group R.A.	APB
	28/10/17	10 AM	Line Officer + from Corps went over forward area with O.C.	APB
	29/10/17		III Corps to reorganise as a N VII Corps T. 2 Party Div Eng. Railway Pole 20th CR E at Rau Camp Division Railway Pole to Road Running Pole S.G Route.	APB
	30/10/17		Work on Route continued A.R.P. Line overhauled.	APB

R.S. Orme
MAJOR, R.E.
CMDG. 20th DIVISIONAL SIGNAL CO.

WAR DIARY

INTELLIGENCE SUMMARY

(Erase heading not required)

Army Form C. 2118.

20 D S Co Sept
Vol 29

Place	Date	Hour	Summary of Events and Information	Remarks and references to Appendices
SORELLE-GRAND	31/10/17	10 a.m.	Captain E.P. Reynolds returned from leave to U.K. Maintenance of Lines & Work on Route continued. Work on Lines at HEUDECOURT under Lt Hadden.	RB
	1/11/17	9 a.m.	Lt Halsall & 30% Area Detachment reported for duty attached from III Corps Signals & assist in preparation work. Work on Lines in forward area under Lt HADDEN.	RB
	2/11/17	10 a.m.	Lt Jeffkes & 10 men 29 DIV Signals reported for work in forward area. Preparation work in forward area continued under Lt Hadden	RB
	3/11/17	10 a.m.	Capt Jack & 10 men 6th DIV Signals attached for work in forward area.	RB
	4/11/17	9 a.m.	Capt Reynolds attended Demonstration by Heavy Machine Gun Corps near BAPAUME. Lt Dodd reported to M 40th DIV for attachment (on month-) -finding in Permanent Route commenced.	RB
	5/11/17	8 a.m.	Forward Bury tested out Binding in of Permanent Route completed	RB
		8.30 a.m.	O.C. went one of forward area.	RB
	6/11/17	9 a.m.	Capt Rice Jones & 10 men 2/5 DIV Signals reported for work in forward area. Trench wiring work in Right Wireless Station withdrawn & sent to School for special instructional purposes	RB
	7/11/17	8 a.m.	Working Party forward under Lt Hadden.	RB
	8/11/17	7 a.m.	Working Party forward under Capt Hannan - preparation work. Working party forward under Lt Hadden	RB
		6 a.m.	Special ground assembled at Sig School for Officers in Trench Wireless Set. (Course A)	RB
	9/11/17	7 a.m.	Working Party forward under Capt Hannan. Working Party forward under Lt Hadden preparation work	RB
		10 a.m.	2/Lt Wenham returned from leave to U.K.	RB
	10/11/17	7 a.m.	Working Party forward under Capt Hannan preparation work	RB
		8 a.m.	Lt Jeffkes proceeded to A Bug out Bay on return of 29 Div Sig Coy to Div Sig tin work.	RB
		8 a.m.	Working parties forward, preparation work under Capt Hannan & Lt Hadden. O.C. went over forward area.	RB
	11/11/17		Instruction for Communication for forth coming operations sent in to G. Bourse A Wireless Set completed.	RB
	12/11/17	9 a.m.	Working parties forward under Capt Hannan & Lt Hadden - Arty Visual Course opened at DIV SIG SCHOOL (7 days) Special Course (B) assembled at DIV Sig School for Officers in Trench Wireless Set (3 days).	RB
	13/11/17	8 a.m.	Working parties forward under Capt Hannan & Lt Hadden preparation work Lt Rodd 29 DIV Sigs returned to Yorks.	RB
	14/11/17	8 a.m.	Working parties forward under Capt Hannan, Lt Hadden, preparation work Advanced Class DIV Sig School completed Signal Officers Course completed.	RB
	15/11/17	8 a.m.	Working parties forward under Lt Hadden preparation work.	RB

R.M. ——
MAJOR, R.E.
C.M.D.G. 20th DIVISIONAL SIGNAL CO.

WAR DIARY

~~INTELLIGENCE~~ SUMMARY

(Erase heading not required.)

Army Form C. 2118.

Place	Date	Hour	Summary of Events and Information	Remarks and references to Appendices
SOREL-LE-GRAND	16/11/17	9am	Working parties forward. Preparation works.	APB
			Source B Officers Trench Wireless Sets at Div. Sig. School completed.	APB
	17/11/17	8am	Working parties forward. Preparation works. Artillery Visual Signalling Lamps at Div. Sig. School completed. Lt MOORE forward to A Dugout. Wireless for 60th Bde established at left Cable Head.	APB
			DIV. Sig. School moved to HEUDECOURT. 60 Bde moved to HEUDECOURT.	APB
	18/11/17		Working parties forward. Preparation work.	APB
Nr HEUDECOURT	19/11/17	10am	Advance DIV HQ moved to Battle Head quarters near HEUDECOURT – Rear HQ remaining at SOREL-LE-GRAND. Lt WEIR to Battle HQ advanced office obtained 3p.m. 60 Bde moved to Battle H.Q. VILLERS PLUICH 3p.m. 161 & 59 F. Bdes. also moved.	APB
		3pm		APB
		6am	Attack commenced 6:20am. 59rd Div HQ moved forward to VILLERS PLUICH 4pm. O.C. moved forward to 60th Bde HQ. VILLERS PLUICH 6pm. Lt Sig Office at HEUDECOURT. Lt LOVETT i/c. Great difficulty keeping communications owing to retiring TANKS.	APB
VILLERS PLUICH	20/11/17	6pm	Attack continued	APB
	21/11/17		Situation unchanged. Permanent poled Cable line laid from Rt Cable Head to Rt Bde under Lt Hallett. Working parties on lines. Troop of Northumberland Hussars attached for D.R. work.	APB
	22/11/17		Situation unchanged. Work constructing new communication system continued.	APB
	23/11/17		Situation unchanged. New work continued.	APB
	24/11/17		Situation unchanged. New work on lines continued. Lines laid from left Battle Head to Lt Rbde under Capt Hannan. 60 Bde moved to Right Sector 3pm. 61 Bde moved to left Sector 3pm. 59 Bde in Reserve.	APB
	25/11/17	3pm		APB
	26/11/17		Situation unchanged. Patrol of lines.	APB
	27/11/17	10am	Permanent Visual Stations established. Situation unchanged. Working parties laying LATERAL lines under Lt Hallett.	APB
	28/11/17	8am	Situation unchanged.	APB
	29/11/17		59 Bde relieved 60 Bde in Right Sector. Twins to Mr Otz +APS Conzeacourt. Lt Hallett. Lt Mallett proceeded on leave to U.K. 2/Lt Wenham to 59 Bde of 1/p of Signal Section.	APB
	30/11/17		Capt Hannan proceeded on leave to U.K.	APB

R.B.Hau
MAJOR, R.E.,
CMDG. 20th DIVISIONAL SIGNAL CO

20 D Signals
W 30

WAR DIARY
~~INTELLIGENCE~~ SUMMARY
(Erase heading not required.)

Army Form C. 2118.

Instructions regarding War Diaries and Intelligence Summaries are contained in F. S. Regs., Part II. and the Staff Manual respectively. Title pages will be prepared in manuscript.

Place	Date	Hour	Summary of Events and Information	Remarks and references to Appendices
VILLERS-PLUICH	30/11	7am	Adv Div HQ at VILLERS PLUICH. Rear Div HQ + Sigs Transport at SOREL-LE-GRAND. Enemy attacked on the Right. 60 Bde moved to FARM RAVINE, 61 Bde to HINDENBURG SUPPORT, 59 Bde to SURREY RAVINE. Communication very difficult. 10AM Lines laid under Lt HARDEEN	7B5
		10 am	between REVELON RIDGE and SOREL.	7B
		11 am	Advance Party under Capt Reynolds moved to QUEEN'S CROSS. Party proceeded by road under the O.C.	7B8
		MIDNIGHT	Div HQ at VILLERS PLUICH deserted, office opened at "B" dugout (Q 21 c).	7B
B. Dugout QUEEN'S CROSS	1/12/17	7am	15th Area Detachmt Sigs attached to 12th Div. Adv Div HQ at B Dugout. 36 + 37 Fifty 13des under 20 Div + 59 and 60 Bdes of VILLERS PLUICH. 184 Bde in Reserve.	7B8
	2/12		Sqn and 60 Bde relieved by 183 Bde (6 Div). NORTHUMBERLAND HUSSARS attached to 20 Div Sigs transferred to 6th Div Sigs.	7B3
SOREL-LE-GRAND	3/12/17	MIDNIGHT Nov 2/3	15th Area Detachmt Sigs complete midnight 2/3 by 61 DIV Sigs Signal Coy relieved at 12.700 2nd Lt LOVETT R.E. 3 Army Sigs transferred to 9th Div Sigs. 2 Lt C.C. STRICK joined from 3 Army Sigs. Lt MARSHALL + men of 30 Area Detachment returned to 3rd Corps Sigs. R.A. HQ Sigs at NETZ.	7B8
		3PM	15th Area Detach transferred to 30th Area Detachment Sigs 3rd Co. H.Q. O.C. remaining party of Adv Div HQ arrives at SOREL from B Dugout. R.A. HQ Sigs at NETZ	7B3
BIAZIEUX	4/12/17	10am	Div moved to BIAZIEUX by road + train. Transport by road under Capt REYNOLDS came under 3 Corps 3 Army.	7B8
	5/12		Lt SKAIFE W.F., 91 Bde RFA Sig Sub section to U.K. resigned communicn Auty 15.G.HQ. 1920 11/12/17	7B3
HUCQUELIERS	6/12		2Lt C.C. STRICK returned to 3 Army Sigs. Div HQ moved to HUCQUELIERS. 10th Corps 2 Army. Transport proceeded by road under Capt Reynolds. Train party under Lt MOORE II DLI attached Sigs)	7B3
	7/12		Normal	7B3
	8/12		Normal	7B3
	9/12		Normal	7B3
	10/12		Normal	7B3
	11/12		Adv Party proceeded to new Div HQ BLARINGHEM.	7B3
BLARINGHEM	12/12		Div HQ moved from HUCQUELIERS to BLARINGHEM under IX Corps 2nd Army. Transport proceeded to Blaringhem by road. Stayed night at 13 CCS	7B3
	13/12		Lt MOORE II DLI attached to 20 Div Sigs returned to his unit. Transport arrived at BLARINGHEM.	7B8

CMDG. 20th DIVISIONAL SIGNAL CO

MAJOR, R.E.,

D. D. & L., London, E.C.
(A2839) Wt. W809/M1672 359,000 4/17 Sch. 52a Forms/C/2118/14

WAR DIARY
or
INTELLIGENCE SUMMARY.

Army Form C. 2118.

Place	Date	Hour	Summary of Events and Information	Remarks and references to Appendices
BLARINGHEM	14/12/17		T/Lt DODD E.C. returned to 40 Div Sig. Co. Lt MALLETT, O.C. No 3 Section returned from leave to U.K.	PPB
	15/12/17		normal	PPB
	16/12/17		MAJOR A.G. BRACE proceeded to ABBEVILLE Wireless GHQ Course. Capt. E.P. Reynolds assumed command of Company	PPB
	17/12/17		normal	PPB
	18/12/17		Capt E.P. Reynolds went over forward Area 30 Div. 2/Lt WENHAM G posted to No 3 Section vice Lt LEDINGHAM	PPB
	19/12/17		Capt L.C.D. HANNEN returned from extended leave to UK. Div Sig School opened at BELLE CROIX for Officers & Beginners.	PPB
	20/12/17		normal	PPB
	21/12/17		normal	PPB
	22/12/17		2/Lt WEBB.O.S. No 4 Section proceeded to UK on leave. From 2nd Army to 4th Army	PPB
	23/12/17		O.C. returned from Wireless GHQ Course ABBEVILLE	PPB
	24/12/17	7 AM	O.C. & Capt Reynolds visited forward Area 30th Div. 2/Lt R.L HOLMES joined from Army Sig Co as supernumerary	PPB
	25/12/17	1 PM	Company Xmas dinner held in Village School BLARINGHEM. Concert in evening.	PPB
	26/12/17	2.30 PM	N.C.O's dinner.	PPB
	27/12/17		Capt Reynolds proceeded to PARIS on leave.	PPB
	28/12/17		Cable Detachment from RA Sig regiment. Riding School held.	PPB
	29/12/17		Officers & 74 O.R from Div Sig School proceeded to IX Corps Sig School - 26 O.R. remaining at Div School	PPB
	30/12/17	2.30 PM	RA moved to 51 JAN CAPEL. Riding School. Tests held	PPB

MAJOR, R.E.
C.M.D.G. 20th DIVISIONAL SIGNAL Co

Army Form C. 2118.

WAR DIARY
or
INTELLIGENCE SUMMARY.
(Erase heading not required.)

20th Division Signal Co RE

Place	Date	Hour	Summary of Events and Information	Remarks and references to Appendices
BLARINGHEM	31/7	8.30 pm	1× Corps Lt & Army Capt Reynolds returned from Paris leave. Working parties on replacing cable on	MB
	1/8	9 pm	Local lines with permanent route. D.R. service. Work on local lines & on airline route to WARDREQUES.	RB
	2/8	8.30 pm	Work continued on Air Line Route to WARDREQUES. Flying Practice at LE CROQUET. Cleaning up cable in village.	RB
	3/8	8.30 pm	Work on Clearing up Cable continued. Div. Signal School closed. Lt J.R. Parker leave to UK.	RB
	4/8	8.30 pm	Advance Party to Lt Kaddies proceeded to forward area to commence relief of 30th Div.	RB
	5/8	"	30th Div line men in Temp? Advance relieved by 20th Div linemen. W.T. Station of 30th Div taken over by 20th Div W.T.	RB
	6/8	"	20th Div Trench Light provided & carried away. Capt Reynolds staying night 6/7 at GODEWAERSVELDE from 30th Div on 7/8. Lt Milt from leave UK.	RB
		"	2nd Advance Party proceeded to forward area to relieve 30th Div.	RB
WESTOUTRE	7/8	"	20th Div H.Q. took over from H.Q. at WESTOUTRE relieving the 30th Div. Signal Co. taken over at same. Transport parked in street at WESTOUTRE.	RB
	8/8	"	Visited Div. W.T. station + TORTOP + CHINDA Tunnels observing stations with Corps W.T. officer.	RB
	9/8	"	Minor operation by 37 Div on right. Other German raid on our left Battn.	RB
	10/8	"	Saw Signals Co rep communication preceding recent at JACKDAW Tunnel, arranged detail re PBx Amb hr Stables.	RB
	11/8	"	Lt Holmes posted to 20 Div Sigs from Sidcup re-mng.	RB
	12/8	"	Court Enquiry re motor cyclist. O.C. not forward	RB
	13/8		Normal	RB
	14/8		Capt E.P. Reynolds to 37th Div as O.C. Lt Pla & posted to 20th Div Sigs an Movable Officer & from Sigs Reinfry in Corps.	RB
	15/8		Lt (Mafr) Porter H E L posted as 2nd in Command (vice Capt Reynolds) from 16th Div Sig Co	RB

B Turco
MAJOR, R.E.
CMDG. 20th DIVISIONAL SIGNAL CO

Army Form C. 2118.

WAR DIARY
or
~~INTELLIGENCE~~ SUMMARY.
(Erase heading not required.)

20th Division Signal Coy RE

Place	Date	Hour	Summary of Events and Information	Remarks and references to Appendices
WESTOUTRE	16/9	9.0PM	Normal	App B
	17/8	"	Normal	App B
	18/8	"	Normal	App B
	19/8	"	Visited Left Section Bath Stations W/T Amplifiers	App B
	20/8	"	Reconnoitred a route of proposed bury with Lt Haddon.	App B
	21/8	"	Visited Rt Sect. Lt Platt returned from 10 Corps - working Rt Corps Schools with Corps-Div. S. services. Commenced bury from V.R. to R.R. (I.39.c 3.9 to I.39.d 4.1) Lt Haddon i/c. Rear 2/5th 98 & 20th A/B commenced.	App B
	22/8	"	24 Platn to Abbeville on Musketeers Course. Buried cable party continued work. Radio 27 + 274 + 28 complete.	App B
	23/8	"	Lines officer from 22nd Corps collected Rel/ Change over. Capt Parker arrived from 16 Div. Buried cable work continued.	App B
	24/8	"	Moth on New Div. H.Q. Camp DICKEBUSCH	App B
	25/8	"	Capt Hannon proceeded on Marshall Course BAIZIEUX. Buried cable work continued. Extent 595 & 596 + Sub Sect + A6mm left 3mm. Relieved Rt Sect Visual Trenching Station work in shell by H.Q Camp DICKEBUSCH. 24/1/25 595 Bde relieved 60th Bde	App B
	26/8	"	Buried cable work continued. Wireless Horse Lines near root to Divers Bde HQ continued.	App B
	27/8	"	Buried cable work continued.	App B
	28/8	"	Visited W/T Sta Phone CLAPHAM JUNCTION EXCHANGE. New arrangement for starting Arranged with Sigs for Divnal Artillery Liaison Lines. Cable to Rt Flank to MENIN TUNNEL. P86 & Rd Div hospital + W.D.W.N Fr Rd Harbour.	App B
	29/8	"	Capt Hannen returned. The bury work is down. Bury & F.B carrying party & Buff Ambulance complete. 21 attached t work at FORK. Still no light however flew on casualty's.	App B
	30/8	"	Saw 22 Corps Artillery Liaison. Offer of Bedford House. Arranged Bury & Amonbd of Bedford tree & arranged buried cable N + S + Rail routes. Due locals - arranged details for laying lines N + E + routes buried R.G.A. Exmt W.Z. 50 a Lge# Bn Regt Bde 9.10AM C.R. Sec cancelled.	App B
			23rd Cofs tube cover & 21 amm lines but through O.K. & W.CO. + Corps Duck Station tube over & 21 9k L6, L6.	App B

A.J. Inow
MAJOR R.E.
O/C 20th DIVISIONAL SIGNAL COY.

Army Form C. 2118.

WAR DIARY
INTELLIGENCE SUMMARY.
(Erase heading not required.)

Instructions regarding War Diaries and Intelligence Summaries are contained in F. S. Regs., Part II. and the Staff Manual respectively. Title pages will be prepared in manuscript.

20th Division Signal Coy RE

VM32

Place	Date	Hour	Summary of Events and Information	Remarks and references to Appendices
WESTOUTRE	31/10/18	5 PM	22nd CORPS, 4TH ARMY. OC went forward to inspect w/r. 60th Bde relieved by 59th Bde in left sector	1429
"	1/2/18	8.15 AM	Terminal Pole and two bays of wire brought down by weight of ice on wires. Serious trouble at HPS pits. Breakdown party out. Line through at 11.45 AM. 12 PM Both lines to Corps down. Worked through NZ Div	112LP
"	2/2/18	10 PM	Many contacts on open routes. Line troubles continued all day. Traffic not held up. All lines OK 10 PM. Put stops on 6 pair WHP route	112LP
"	3/2/18		Propose change of Right Bde HQ. New bearer on buried route arranged with Corps.	112LP
"	4/2/18		Lt. T.H.B. HOARE leave to UK. Normal	112LP
"	5/2/18		Normal	112LP
"	6/2/18	8 PM	Armoured cable laid by 59 Bde to new Battalion HQ taken over from Division on left Bde relief. New Office for 91st Bde wired up to Task Bay.	112LP
"	7/2/18		Lines on busy but through to new Battalion HQ. Trouble on open routes due to contact. 91st Bde RFA to JACKDAW TUNNELS. Wiring of new office at HALFWAY HOUSE	112LP
"	8/2/18		Change of Bde HQ cancelled. Reserve Bde DORMY HOUSE. Work on buried route where Traffic. OC visited W/T stations charging set at BEDFORD HOUSE near NZ Div. Direct line for through to NZ Div. RE dump.	RAP
"	9/2/18		Line laid from BEDFORD HOUSE to Pub Ca near NZ Div. Direct line for through to NZ Div. RE dump connected to Rt Bde exchange. Bomb scare. Otherwise normal.	112LP
"	10/2/18		Wind screen put up at station. Otherwise normal.	112LP
"	11/2/18		Lt F.D. TACKSON reports for duty from 4th Army. O.C. went forward with OC 37 Div Sig Co	112LP
"	12/2/18		Stable subject gying. Refuse not covered. Bomb screen for stables continued.	112LP
"	13/2/18	10 AM	O.C. went forward with O.C. 37 Div Sig Co. Refuse at stables continues to	112LP
"	14/2/18		Normal	112 S
"	15/2/18		Advance party of w/r personnel and linesmen for forward stations arrive from 37 Div with Lt KNIGHT	112LP

112LP Capts

D.D. & L., London, E.C.
Wt. W809/M1072 250,000 4/17 Sch. 50A. Forms/C/2118/14

Army Form C. 2118.

WAR DIARY
INTELLIGENCE SUMMARY

(Erase heading not required.)

20th Div Signal Coy.

Place	Date	Hour	Summary of Events and Information	Remarks and references to Appendices
WESTOUTRE	16/2/18		Advance party by lorry to BLARINGHEM. Transport started by road staying at STRAZEELE. W/T personnel and forward linesmen relieved by 39th Div.	W.I.P
BLARINGHEM	17/2/18	10 AM / 1 PM	Div HQ closed at WESTOUTRE & opened at BLARINGHEM. Transport arrived at BLARINGHEM. Lt JACKSON to Sig Bde.	W.I.P
"	18/2/18		Battled at Signal Stores. Lt PLATT returned from wireless course. Div RA moved to MORBECQUE.	W.I.P
"	19/2/18		O.C. proceeded on leave to U.K. Capt PORTER in command of Coy. Overhaul of stores.	W.I.P
"	20/2/18	5 PM	Normal. Advance party with stores proceeded to new area by rail. Lt HADDEN in charge.	W.I.P
"	21/2/18	11 AM	Lorry by road to new area with office staff and technical stores, staying in PREVENT area.	W.I.P
On the Road	22/2/18	10 AM / 12 Noon	Transport by road to STEENBECQUE Station under 2/Lt HOLMES. Div HQ closed at BLARINGHEM.	W.I.P
ERCHEU	23/2/18	10 AM	15th CORPS. 5th ARMY. Signal office opened at ERCHEU.	W.I.P
"	24/2/18		Lt F.T. MALLETT starts preliminary course of instruction in staff duties. Lt F.D. JACKSON assumes command of No 2 Section. Div RA arrive at ERCHEU. Abbuhm she built.	W.I.P
"	25/2/18	9 AM	Linesmens course of instruction in Trak Station work begins under Lt HADDEN. Riding school finds. Line laid by cable wagon from LIBERMONT to ESMERY-HALLON. RA signal office opened.	W.I.P
"	26/2/18	9 AM	Course for Brigade Power Buzzer Squad commences at Div HQ under Lt B. PLATT. 2/Lt MOORE attached as O/C SIGNAL SCHOOL. 2/Lt E. BURTON RE from 5th ARMY as Instructor musketry.	W.I.P
"	27/2/18		Latrine built for HQ Co and Sig School.	W.I.P

20th Divisional engineers

20th DIVISIONAL SIGNAL COMPANY R. E.

MARCH 1 9 1 8

Army Form C. 2118.

WAR DIARY
or
INTELLIGENCE SUMMARY.
(Erase heading not required.)

20 DIV SIGNAL Co RE

9 D 33

Instructions regarding War Diaries and Intelligence Summaries are contained in F. S. Regs., Part II. and the Staff Manual respectively. Title pages will be prepared in manuscript.

Place	Date	Hour	Summary of Events and Information	Remarks and references to Appendices
ERCHEU	28/2/18	Noon	Lt HADDEN proceeded to U.K. on leave 14 days	1819
"	1/3/18		Div Standing by under 24 hours notice to move	1819
"	2/3/18	9am	Opening of Div Signal School (Lt MOORE "DLI") postponed until W.K. in at Work on camp, ablution tables etc	1819
"	3/3/18		Capt FORSTER visited forward area accompanied by CAPT HANNEN	1819
"	3/3/18		Parsing out as a wholikew linemen's course commenced. Buyer Pa/Bdt Class Bde sections Bombshell course. Examination held. HQ Div under 1 hours notice to move	1819
"	4/3/18		No.5 WB/S proceeded to 5 Army Sig School. 2/Lt BUZBY Wireless course. 2/Lt HOLMES RE resumed command of No.1 Section. Div Signal Bd School opened 2/Lt C.K. MOORE "DLI" i/c. Wiring Work at	1819
"	5/3/18		Proposed new Div HQ HAM carried out under 2/Lt BURTON. 1 hour notice to move cancelled + Div cars under 12 hours notice to move	1819
"	6/3/18		Bdts Perm Pa/Bdt Class commenced under Lt G. PRATT. Leaving out examination to Linemen course completed. All ranks passed through Div Gas Chamber	1823
"	6/3/18		60 BDE HQ moved to HAM MAJOR A.G. BRACE, MC, returned from leave to U.K. and took over command of Company	1823
"	7/3/18	9am	Re reconnoitred forward and battle areas	PCB
"	8/3/18		Firing practice at LIBERMONT motor 2/Lt ENDON	PCB
"	9/3/18		2/Lt WENHAM on leave to U.K. 14 days. Summer hours commenced 11pm. Wireless scheme at Div HQ	PCB
"	10/3/18		Div at 12 hours notice to move	PCB
"	11/3/18		Visited & tested Visual Stations from HAM to Brigade Positions	PCB
"	12/3/18		Testing of M.C. personnel and DLI signallers etc. for formation of No 6 Section	PCB
"	13/3/18		B.O.C. inspecting transport. Visual Stations sited and tested in Battle Zone	PCB
"	14/3/18		Firing practice at LIBERMONT. O.C. visited Mt Coy[?] Battalion PB Class closed, Re establishment of No 5 Section. Examination held	PCB

R.F. Knox MAJOR
CMDG 20th DIVISIONAL SIG

WAR DIARY
or
INTELLIGENCE SUMMARY.

(Erase heading not required.)

Army Form C. 2118.

Instructions regarding War Diaries and Intelligence Summaries are contained in F.S. Regs., Part II. and the Staff Manual respectively. Title pages will be prepared in manuscript.

Place	Date	Hour	Summary of Events and Information	Remarks and references to Appendices
ERCHEU	15/3/18	—	Visit by Bdes and Div Sigs.	PPB
"	16/3/18		Normal	PPB
"	17/3/18		Lt HADDEN returned from leave. Walk in lines at ESMERY/HALLON.	PPB
"	18/3/18		O.C. recommended forward area with Capt. PORTER.	PPB
"	19/3/18		Normal.	PPB
"	20/3/18	8PM	O.C. visited at 5:30 pm with Lt PLATT. 2pm Div area under orders to move at one hour's notice. Practice move returned to Buba at 8:30 pm.	PPB
ERCHEU and HAM.	21/3/18		15th Corps Memo Battery Standard message received. Bde ordered to move at once with scheme D at 9 pm. Moves to HAM immediately under Lt HADDEN. 9/W BURTON with beam & office staff left & Capt PORTER in car and all lines as previously arranged & working again to old Bde Rear details by about 8 am. 6th Bde moved to ST SIMON and not to DURY. In consequence Lt W. HOLMES attempted to lay cable from DURY via AUBIGNY Line to ST SIMON failed no success. Visual Station established. Working from DIV H.Q. to 59 & 60 Bdes fully. No communicating stations. Quickly 59 & 60 Bde drawn from Army Bump at AUBIGNY and distributed to Brigades. 61st Bde handed over to 36 DIV.	PPB
HAM.	22/3/18		61st Bde at OLLEZY. Visual still to exale. Cpl RAWLINGS takes lead in Mailbag cart at dawn to relieve OK Pujmielow in New Bde headline exactly as ordered. 50 & 61 Bde in SANCOURT. 60 & HAM. Cct of Infantinov to 8w HQ impossible. Mailing to EPPEVILLE. That station established & line at connected to Brigade Hunt. HAM-EPPEVILLE 3 pairs laid Lt HADDEN in charge. 183 Cable leave HAM in NESLE during afternoon ARMY from NESLE to ROYE. Command moved to EPPEVILLE during afternoon. Bde move to ESMERY/HALLON. 9 pm DIV H.Q. move from HAM to EPPEVILLE at 9 pm. Bde lines OK. In touch with CORPS thru' Bde HAM & EPPEVILLE. Office closes at 11:0 pm Bde do not move to Sequeseged lending but to ST SULPICE. BW Bde Station & W/T station which had been joined Behind Bdes. Lt wanting in this aim. W/T for army reason failed to get through. Bde sent orderlies and eventually found the Stadium who turned bat Bde Stations. At MIDNIGHT Capt PORTER returned and advances further passed to NESLE Lines through to all Bdes until Stadium vacated and Bdes closing down during the 1st Bdes to DIV HQ. made of Bde sends word in the Bde Lt HOMBLEUX & WEBB returned from MESNIL inseparable yesterday. 20 ARE spotted in the evening all lines held well. Capt HANKEN with one-cart and line to 14 H.A.G. and 232 Q. F.A Bde.	
NESLE.	23/3/18		Lt HADDEN laid lateral from ROVY to HOMBLEUX.	PPP

PPMoon

MAJOR, R.E.
CMDG. 20th DIVISIONAL SIGNAL CO.

Army Form C. 2118.

WAR DIARY
or
INTELLIGENCE SUMMARY.
(Erase heading not required.)

Instructions regarding War Diaries and Intelligence Summaries are contained in F. S. Regs., Part II. and the Staff Manual respectively. Title pages will be prepared in manuscript.

Place	Date	Hour	Summary of Events and Information	Remarks and references to Appendices
NESLE	24/3/18		Bdes of 81st Bn come under Dft Div. and move to NESLE. May come in to evening CRA Bn line in Bn H.Q. Mons. Sgt Bde move to ROAD JUNCTION on main ANVIL S.E. of ROUY on main NESLE-HAM road. 50t Bn (and Div) move to BACQUENCOURT. Communications maintained by Sgt WOLFE and Sgt BILL at TOMBLEUX. New HOMBLEUX but do not relieve Lt JACKSON until Capt WOLFE 2/Lt BURTON kept cable to BREUIL in anticipation of 60th Bde moving the cables in to BACQUENCOURT.	PPB
		2pm	Div moves to RETHONVILLERS taking new line at Div HQ and remains. Lt WEBB in charge estabg. Invited HQ Station at NESLE until 12 midnight. 183 and 50 Bdes at HAM, 60th Bde at CRESSY. 81st DV leaving a cable detachment 2/Lt. BURTON leaves Ham all mg with his detachment arrives to HAM and remains overnight. Lt MOORE & HADDEN and all heavy handcart move to CRESSY. FRENCH begin to send on the others during night 24/25. 50th M Bde relief to RETHONVILLERS. Line laid to them. Div still at RETHONVILLERS. 3pm BROWNING & Lt KENDALL take cable to CRESSY.	
RETHONVILLERS and CARREPUIS	25/3/18		Div moves to CARREPUIS at 3pm. Always has been diverted through RETHONVILLERS after Bde near CARREPUIS. Halted immediately on arrival battle laid to Tythorn Bdes at WAUCOURT - BALATRE. Artillery at BALATRE and GRUNT. Orders to move to ROYE recd. 25/5/26 received at 4pm- reconnoitred office with Lt MOORE.	PPB
		10pm	Lt MOORE remains to fix office you etc in advance CARREPUIS remaining as Div stations. Capt PORTER and others still having you in no change. HADDEN to fix WEBB and HADDEN	
ROYE and LE QUESNEL	26/3/18		Midnight 95/26 riding sidecar to meancele ROYE and march to LE QUESNEL received artillery to remain. Capt HANNEN with hts GS waggons and RA Section - on approach him thus much bdes laid down nr by on Column moves off at war of main road at 5.30 am. Autobiography marched. Found himself astride ROYE in early having been working all night. No warning of the move and fit to get head and now knocked no the rest in time. One had make our castle with them but to hunt a dismantel. Gunners balloons up. Some long range shrapnel our column. Porter- ROYE- VILLERS- ERCHES- ARVILLERS- QUESNEL - arrived QUESNEL 1.30pm. Orders to be ready move again at 4.30 received HQ in QUESNEL CHATEAU. Bdes 59 & 60 at QUESNEL 61st at BEAUFORT. 50th move to FOLIE 60th ARVILLERS- lines laid to 59 & 61 Bdes. WT detachment to ARVILLERS- WT to Corps lines to MEZIERES with Lt MOORE. Coin HQ in MOREUIL	PPB
LE QUESNEL	27/3/18		Div HQ still at LE QUESNEL. Bdes at BEAUFORT, FOLIES and ARVILLERS. 60 came to station at R.29.C. Capt PORTER in car to MEZIERES in returns and change. 2/Lt BURTON laid line from DR3 very hard worked. Aeroplane messages left in to church June 29. 81st Bde to 50t Bde SHERWOOD received it after carrying communcations by him. Gunners. O.P. in church opens contracted by him from all day but gunners of out looking at 10th had no Bdr. has new OVILLERS Monk many (ARVILLERS) Officer. Lt HADDEN WEBB & MOORE at R.29 H.Q. OC Capt PORTER, Lt BURTON & PLATT forward leave to CORPS drawn all morning. Hessinally	PPB
DOMART	27/28/3/18		After that him through about 2pm. Relief by FRENCH arranged.	

P. Hines MAJOR, R.E.
OMDG. 20th DIVISIONAL SIGNAL CO

WAR DIARY
or
INTELLIGENCE SUMMARY.
(Erase heading not required.)

Army Form C. 2118.

Place	Date	Hour	Summary of Events and Information	Remarks and references to Appendices
	28/3/18		Relief proceeded. B/W at QUESNEL. B/dres b/t col BEAUFORT. 59th on FOLIES. 60th on road W of ARVILLERS through to 59 Bde by wire - to bt by W/T. Early lovely morning. Village getting a good deal of shelling. Transport moved out from behind in to undergrowth in north. DOMART ROAD - 12 mtrs S.E. of DOMART (B.10.b) 59 Bde & 61 Bde relay new wireless instrument but W/T station on action till last minute. Enemy away but W/T station on Quesnel TRR area. W/T station heavily in action till last minute. Enemy went great W/T station on Quesnel TRR (Capt PARK & Lt WHITBREAD) Capt PORTER & SELF. Broad daw 9 a.m. Rode away under considerable enemy shelling activity caused by ? transport on mule and road exposure in considerable shelling. 1 newly half halt all CROSS ROADS and office fixed in mule nut shelter and ? through to CORPS - 60 battalion same area 59 Bde on road C.I.K.b. 61st Bde in DEMUIN C.I.K.b. 61st Bde HQ located after great difficulty in barn outside tucked up on old communal route to SAINS AMIENOIS - at 8pm. Advance guide in C.10.b. close at 8 pm. DEMUIN 6 pm. Principal moves back to DOMART. Signals office at DOMART in debut ? with shrapnel and wounded.	P.18
	29/3/18		59 Bde moves through to MEZIERES. tried to get through in old route but no success. J. WEBB leaves him to 61 Bde at DEMUIN successfully with cable wagon. 12.10pm 60 Bde return to establish wire through 50th Div. must muster 60s B/W all Bde HQ arrd at 9.10.b. 2.30. all wire to establish through. Moved line DOMART to 149 Bde (50 Div.) at CROSS ROADS. Cable wagon cut to establish through station at 9.10.b. Lt BURTON remains ? with line to 61 Bde direct to this station from 9.10 to all Bdes through Tech station 8.20 pm.	P/8
	30/3/18		B/W HQ still at DOMART preparing to move to BOYES. Bde HQs 60 & 59 Bdes HORGES. Shelling in DOMART. Col of hospital at BOYES. Lt WEBB with 3 hr lorry to reconnoitre office at BOYES. Only through line to 60 Bde 61 HANGARD CHATEAU artillery in uncertain quantity but sent to 84 D.A. in DOMART,CHATEAU office switch W/T behind (Lt DENTON Sp.) (Lt RIMINGTON). Went 2 pm Div. HQ moved to null in DOMART-AMIENS road new land rail along road to ruined house. And HQ which in BOYES about 8 pm. Signal office switched - all B/W HQ in line at out of DOMART about 11pm. Cable easy in use. Line to 60 Bde 1 to CORPS ? Repr.Siv. Lt HADDEN laid alternative line across groundway to 61 Bde at HANGARD cunning to 60 Bde. Three crumps attack by S.W. on afternoon of 30th, reduced line of the morning a bit about 50 prisoners.	P/8
	31/3/18		B/W. HQ moved up. 7.30 am. Communication first. All about 12 noon. Then Mitchell kind of ? pigeon in here and road to AMIENS. B/W HQ admit to HILL. Lcpl THOMPSON killed in early attack developed from enemy too. All lines out and naked on CORPS line. Many casualties in cont. Grand advance continued. B/W. HQ. wire to X stachon on BOYES GENTILLES road. Picked up CORPS laid lines to GENTILLES viz. to 59th at DOMART both in BERTAUCOURT out of reach. New HQ in BOYES. Lt. WEBB & BURTON out to replace O.C. & Capt PORTER.	P/8

P/P.Reeves
MAJOR, R.E.
HQ, 20th DIVISIONAL SIGNAL CO

WAR DIARY
INTELLIGENCE SUMMARY

WD 34 Army Form C. 2118.

20 Div Signal Co. R.E.

Place	Date	Hour	Summary of Events and Information	Remarks and references to Appendices
CROSS ROADS BOVES-GENTILLES AND BOVES.	1/7/18		Adv Div H.Q. at CROSS ROADS on BOVES – GENTILLES Roads. Div HQ at BOVES. Quiet day. Relieved by 14th Div impending. Cable Detachment Sgts to D.S. 14th Div Signal Coy on arrival. 3.30 pm Relief taken over. Break Down in Transport. By Road via AMIENS. Rendezvous NAMPS-AU-MONT.	WB
NAMPS-AU-MONT	2/7/18	6.20 am	Met advance Rear Party rejoining coy at NAMPS-AU-MONT in a Field. Slept. Rest.	WB
NAMPS-AU-MONT QUEVAUVILLERS	3/7/18	2.30 pm	Move to QUEVAUVILLERS 6 m. Div HQ opened at QUEVAUVILLERS 3 pm. Near Cath. of Probable further move. Lent a gun & strengthen up Transport.	WB
QUEVAUVILLERS	4/7/18		Clearing up or overhauling Stores.	WB
Do	5/7/18		Ditto. Wireless Stations established at 59th & 61st Bdes.	WB
Do	6/7/18		Normal	WB
Do	7/7/18		Normal	WB
Do	8/7/18		Normal	WB
Do	9/7/18	9 am	advance party proceeded to new Div H.Q. HUPPY under Lt HADDEN	WB
Do	"	12 Noon	Office opened HUPPY noon	
Do	"	9 am	Remainder marched by Road under Capt PORTER sta. gn & night for ½ night at ALLERY.	
Do	10/7/18	11.30 am	Office at QUEVAUVILLERS closed at noon. Telephone exchange QUEVAUVILLERS taken over by XIX Corps. Dismounted party arrived by Bus at 11.30 am & one & to Breakdown in Bus the other did not arrive until 6.30 am on 11th y/k.	WB
HUPPY GAMACHES	11/7/18	10.0 am	Div H.Q. closed HUPPY 10 AM & opened at GAMACHES same hour. Transport moved at 10 from ALLERY to GAMACHES. Adiona Party left HUPPY for GAMACHES 7 am. Lt R. HOLMES 16. Dismounted Permanent Party marched from Huppy to GAMACHES, starting at 8.30 am	WB
GAMACHES	12/7/18		Unloaded & overhauling Stores. Stores dd to R. d. Section Workshop-deliveries at civil Exchange. Operators & linesmen to Sidewal (Civil Exchange WOINCOURT which is to take over now).	WB
GAMACHES	13/7/18		Direct Circuit through N to 59 Bde – 60th & 61st Bdes via WOINCOURT Exchange	WB

Army Form C. 2118.

WAR DIARY

(Erase heading not required.)

20 DIV SIGNAL Co R.E.

Instructions regarding War Diaries and Intelligence Summaries are contained in F. S. Regs., Part II. and the Staff Manual respectively. Title pages will be prepared in manuscript.

Place	Date	Hour	Summary of Events and Information	Remarks and references to Appendices
GAMACHES	14/7/18	9.0 AM	W/T Stations established at 59th + 6th Bdes	APB
Do	15/7/18		Normal	APB
Do	16/7/18		Technical Stores drawn to Corps + distributed to Bde Sections. W/T Station at Bdes closed down. Cable Detachment joined RA HQ at MAREUIL. War "O" Order issued for Div to move by rail to 1st Army Area. Advance party L/Hadden. Left for new Div HQ at R.E.L. lorry 10.30 AM. Transport less 8 Mules to move by Road under Capt Porter staying at EAUCOURT-SUR-SOMME arrived 3.30 AM. Left 10.15 AM 15th inst.	APB
Do	17/7/18			APB
VILLERS CHATEL	18/7/18	8.0 AM 8.30 AM	Train party proceeded from GAMACHES to new Div HQ under L/Holmes entraining at F.U. Demounted party from GAMACHES proceeded by Bus. Q.M. office relief party stationed at WOINCOURT proceeded by Car. party later to new Div HQ. 2/Q' founds allotted for Stores. Transport detached 8th & 12th Div at WILLENCOURT.	APB
		10.0 AM	Office closed GAMACHES 10 AM and opened VILLERS CHATEL 18th CORPS 1st ARMY W/T loaded + Stores from Coy + 12 Div Lottie J Reconnoitering lines for Bdes connections to DIV Bdes on Permanent Route. Transport staged night at TACHINCOURT.	APB
Do	19/7/18			APB
Do	20/7/18	2.45 PM 5.30 PM	Transport arrived at DIV HQ. Train party under Sgt McLaren (Basket lorries) arrived. Corps Commander's Conference TRAINING SCHEME commenced	APB
Do	21/7/18	9.10 AM	Church Parade.	APB
Do		10.0 AM	Lines but through to 20 Div M T Coy	APB
Do	22/7/18	9.0 AM	Training Cable Drill.	APB
Do	23/7/18	9.0 AM 11.0 AM	Training Continued - 2 Cable Detachments on E under L/Hadden & 2/Lt Holmes. Bath the officers bought opened at DIV HQ. Drew R.E. Stores from Corps for local Wt sets. Experimented with loads of WT Trench Sets on Pack Pony, found that complete Trench set can be carried on ordinary G.S. Wallets.	APB
Do	24/7/18	9.0 AM	WORK - Making up P.L. Stores for locals + Commencing Work. Training officers course (13 Sig officers) continues. Cpl Porter Visual in morning L/Moore. 2/Lt Holmes until afternoon. 2 Cable Detachments out - L/Holmes + Sgt McLaren 1/c Draft of 6 men arrived	APB
Do	25/7/18	9.0 AM	Work on new local lines on demi permanent Route continued Training 2 Cable Detachments out - L/Hadden + L/Holmes 1/c - officers class continued	APB

[signature] MAJOR, R.E.,
CMDG. 20th DIVISIONAL SIGNAL CO

WAR DIARY
INTELLIGENCE SUMMARY
(Erase heading not required.)

Army Form C. 2118.

20 Div Signal Co RE

Place	Date	Hour	Summary of Events and Information	Remarks and references to Appendices
VILLERS CHATEL	26/7/18	9.0 AM	Training. Cable Detachments out. Officers class continued. Lt. Olatt for Amplifiers. Local lines work at Div H.Q. on 2 mi. permanent Routes completed & Area cleared of old lines. Draw out another cable route made to Div Instructional bath house. 2 Horses (L.D.) broke loose & one ran & two new stables at night. Rifle Practice. Training Cable Detachments training on permanent line with R. D.L.I. Signallers. Classification test. Harness Inspection.	F/3
Do	27/7/18		Rifle Practice.	F/3
Do	28/7/18	9.10 AM	Church Parade. 3 days leave for Batt. Power Buzzer. Personnel commenced at Div.	F/3
Do	29/7/18	9.0 AM	Training (Instruction of linesmen under Gas). Officers class continued. 10 a.m. No. 61st B.D.S. move to VILLERS AU BOIS (Canadian Area). Orders received for Div H.Q. to prepare to move. Afterwards cancelled & ride to old Billets.	F/3

signature
MAJOR, R.E.,
CMDG. 20th DIVISIONAL SIGNAL CO

WAR DIARY

Army Form C. 2118.

20 DIV SIGNAL Co R.E.

Vol. 35

Place	Date	Hour	Summary of Events and Information	Remarks and references to Appendices
VILLERS CHATEL	30/9/18	9 am	XVIII Corps 1st Army. Training - cable carts out under Lt. HADDEN + 2/Lt HOLMES. Battn Signal Officers Course continued. Linesmen's Course continued. Firing Practice	APP B
VILLERS CHATEL	1/5/18	9 am	Training - cable Drill Linesmen's course continued. Battn Signal Officers Class closed. Firing Practice. Division under orders to move. Visited 4 & 3rd Canadian Div Area	APP B
VILLERS CHATEL VILLERS AU BOIS	2/5/18	9 am	Personnel of No 5 Section (under 2/Lt C.K. MOORE No. 1) joined 20th M.G. Battn for duty. 5pm 20 DIV HQ closed at VILLERS CHATEL + opened at VILLERS AU BOIS same as out. WIRELESS: Div Directn Stn established at VILLERS AU BOIS. Trench Set established at night in Red Trench for work with 60 Bde but was dismantled same night as trains were under observation of enemy. Trench Set established in ANGRES for work with "C" 61st BDE.	APP B
VILLERS AU BOIS	3/5/18	6 am	20th DIV Artillery commenced to relieve 8th + 9th C.R.A. Bdes — O.B with 2/Lt HADDEN visited forward area to inspect communications in Right Sector. WIRELESS - Trench Set erected near CRUMP'S CORNER communicating with 60 BDE to Power Buzzer + Amplifiers.	APP B
VILLERS AU BOIS	4/5/18		Disposition of linemen with No. 3 + 4 Area Detachments arranged.	APP B
VILLERS AU BOIS	5/5/18	6 am	Artillery Relief complete. 10 am CRA 20th Div assumed Command of Artillery Reconnaissance of Bury in HERONDELLE WT Station	APP B
VILLERS AU BOIS VILLERS AU BOIS CHATEAU de la HAIE	6/5/18	6 am 9 am 9/5/18	60th Bde relieved by 59th Bde. Div moved from VILLERS AU BOIS to CHATEAU de la HAIE. 5 pm Office close at VILLERS AU BOIS + opened CHATEAU DE LA HAIE same time. Transport moved 2.30 pm. Bde Sig School. Personnel moved under Division to CHATEAU DE LA HAIE. Advanced Station installed in ground behind CHATEAU de la HAIE	APP B
CHATEAU de la HAIE	6/5/18		Wireless Trench Set. Removed alt night from CRUMP'S CORNER + established in Dugout above SA Test Point. About 400 yards from 60 Bde HQ.	APP B
CHATEAU de la HAIE	9/5/18		Working Party to go to camp above + clear site of Trench. Iny New Bury line from MT Ca M V through HERONDELLE WOOD. Night Guard Tactics + Cable Working Parties under Capt PORTER + Lt HOLMES. Visual Station established in Big Lean-to VIMY RIDGE - Linked to XO. Post Bank + continued on Bury Road to the Visual Stn Telephonic Communication between Wagon Lines 59 & 61 B2 Bde. Also established on Bury Emergency + Divl Artillery Sig School under Sgt HADDEN 2 lines between Div Artillery Groups which ran to SLN. + Established at M27 b.6.7. Cable Cart under Sgt SARGENT. 61 Bdy HQ moved at 4.30 am + established at M27 b.6.7.	APP B
CHATEAU de la HAIE	10/5/18		Visual Station VIMY RIDGE. The area — STATION South M7 b. 83a Field Cy RE. 59 Bde relieved 61st Bde. Wireless. Trench Set with 61st Bde moved with 59 Bde to LIEVIN — a Station established there working to 59 R Bde. Division + Left Flank BDES.	APP B
do	11/5/18	9 am	Work continued all day on new Bury buried by personnel of Signal Coy under Capt PORTER + Lt HOLMES. Wireless equipment made up with dry cells as substitute for accumulators. Daylight Working Party of 50 hands carrying cable to required position. Battery for Bury of Bury tested, laid out + tried.	APP B
do	12/5/18	6 am	O.C. + Lt HADDEN visited 2/Lt Right Bde areas — also site of new Bury and VIMY RIDGE Visual Station.	APP B

R.G.Kerr MAJOR R.E.
CMDG 20th DIVISIONAL SIGNAL CO

Army Form C. 2118.

WAR DIARY

~~INTELLIGENCE SUMMARY~~

(Erase heading not required.)

Instructions regarding War Diaries and Intelligence Summaries are contained in F. S. Regs., Part II. and the Staff Manual respectively. Title pages will be prepared in manuscript.

20 DIV SIGNAL COY. R.E.

Place	Date	Hour	Summary of Events and Information	Remarks and references to Appendices
CHATEAU de la HAIE	13/5/18	8.30 a.m	Working Party of Div Sig. Coy continued work on New Buries under Capt PORTER. "Lt HOLMES" cable for 2nd half of Bur to be laid, laid out & roped. WIRELESS Special Aerial erected at 59 Bde to improve intercommunication with NI Sigs with Bde on left. Change of Wireless communication carried forward. P Buzzers, Amplifiers giving a 2 way service to Battalions with P. Buzzy giving one way service from Coy to Battalions. Infantry Working party of 90 joined Sig Coy party to work on Buries at Dusk. work continued until 3.30 am who lift	RKB
do	14/5/18		Infantry Working party of 400 working on New Burys under Capt PORTER, Lt HADDEN, Lt HOLMES assisted by Sig Coy personnel. Work proceeded from 8 pm until 2 am 15th instant.	RKB
do	15/5/18		Normal	RKB
do	16/5/18	7 a.m	Working Party consisting of 180 Infantry assisted by Div Sig Coy personnel continued work on Bury under Capt PORTER. Track completed except for 30 yds of Spur to old M.V. Test Cons. Cable Indoor laid & laid out.	RKB
do	17/5/18	9 a.m.	Working Party Sig Coy personnel continued work on Bury under Lt HADDEN & Lt HOLMES. To School personnel accompanied Wkg party in instruction in Buried Cable Work.	RKB
do	18/5/18	9 a.m	Working Party Sig Coy personnel continued work on Bury under Capt PORTER. O.C. Visited Visual Station & Buried Route.	RKB
do	19/5/18	9 a.m	Working Party Sig Coy personnel continued work on Bury Test Bxes. O.C. Visited Visual Stations. 59 Bde relieved by 61st Bde in LENS Section during night 19th/20th.	RKB
do	20/5/18		60 Bde relieved by 50K Bde in AVION Section (during night 20th/21st. 60th Bde off to rest & train in CORPS RESERVE	RKB
do	21/5/18		Normal	RKB
do	22/5/18		In conjunction with Sig officers C.H.F. arrangements for scheme to improve HQR S Exchange which had to below considered	RKB
do	23/5/18		Infantry Working Party assisted by Sig Coy personnel commenced work Digging in Bury Cable Trench under Lt HADDEN & "Lt HOLMES" (NO.5 Simple Nemin's Scheme b). Training Rudiment of Div Sig. also parent. Div GAS Chamber	RKB
do	24/5/18	1.30 am 8.00 am	9:00 am Attack on enemy by 1st bde of XVIII Corps too placed. Working Party assisted by Sig Coy personnel continued work on Digging in Bury in a tree (No. 5	RKB
do	25/5/18	8.0 am	Working Party Infantry assisted by Sig. personnel continued work on Bury Cable Trench Buried route. also wireless ton Rx etc a (No. 5 improvement Scheme) Training personnel of Signal Coy passed through Div Gas Chamber	RKB
do	26/5/18	9 a.m	Work on Bury carried by Div Sig Coy personnel continued & work on Bury to HOLMES continued. Herry completed, Lts IKENDELL Schemes) Lt 13 PLATT proceed to C.E. S Burly. Lt 13 HOLMES and 2/4 No 14 Section No 13 A/G stationed to C/O Sec 57 K DIV. 8 AM 24 hour duties commenced. Division Telephone Exchange Cape Work Sig nected to Div Signal for work.	RKB

RK[signature]
MAJOR, R.E.
CMDG. 20th DIVISIONAL SIGNAL Coy.

WAR DIARY

Army Form C. 2118.

20th DIV SIGNAL Co. R.E.

Place	Date	Hour	Summary of Events and Information	Remarks and references to Appendices
CHATEAU de la HAIE	27/5/18	1.50am 8.0am	Gas attack by enemy on left Bde front. Several battle casualties (Wounded Gas) including 2/Lt R.L. HOLMES. Working party (Signals) personnel continued work on Bury cable (Hop 5 Improvemt Scheme) Unit work had to cease. Party having to GAS in the nicknour Hood.	REB
	28/5/18	4.0pm Midnight 9.0am	Lt J. HADDEN ½c N°4 Section vice 2/Lt R.L. HOLMES (wounded GAS) Further Gas attack by enemy on left Bde front about midnight. Lt O.S. WEBB M.C. proceeded to 157th DIV. 9.0am Arrival of Box CAR as additional transport for Technical Stores - b/1 BDE have Office to Hop EXCHANGE. 8.0 am Working party of DIV Sigs personnel continued work on Hop 5 Improvemt Scheme - Jointing - Sgt McLAREN i/c.	REB
do	29/5/18	4bm 8.0am	O.C. visited left BDE Wag party, Signals personnel return to old position 2/Lt TAYLOR J.N.B. joined from 10th Corps Sig. Coy. in temporary duty (Wireless) - Lt LASSEN E.J. joined from 1st Army Sig: School for temporary duty. O.C. visited forward Stations with 2/Lt TAYLOR. During night 29/30 59 ROE relieved by 60 R.A.E.	REB
do	30/5/18		Final closing down of Old Hop 5 completed by wireless party. Div signals. A.D.Signals visited O.C. re Communications to HERONDELLE & BEAMONT SPURS.	REB

R.F.Knee.
MAJOR, R.E.
CMDG. 20th DIVISIONAL SIGNAL CO

Army Form C. 2118.

WAR DIARY

(Erase heading not required.)

20th Div Signal Coy. No. 26

WR 36

Place	Date	Hour	Summary of Events and Information	Remarks and references to Appendices
CHATEAU DE LA HAIE	31/5		XVIII CORPS FIRST ARMY	
			MOP 5 Improvement Scheme completed. All lines through on new routes.	RKB
do	1/6/18	9am	Signal Ground went through Divisional Gas Chamber	RKB
do	2/6/18	8am	Second Phonetics Day experiment. Corps Visual Station (LORETTE) manned. 16th Div Sig Co Signallers. Wireless communication tested by Power Buzzer and Amplifier between HIRONDELLE and VIMY – not satisfactory.	RKB
do	3/6/18	8am	Phonetics Experiment ends. Wireless communication again tested by Power Buzzer + Amplifier between HIRONDELLE & VIMY. Signals now satisfactory.	RKB
do	4/6/18		Wireless communication test'd by Power Buzzer & Amplifier between HIRONDELLE and RIAUMONT. Complete'd with good results.	RKB
do	5/6/18	5.15am 9.00am	Orders received "Test-Man Battle Station" LORETTE RIDGE Visual Stat'n manned by Sig Officer & 2 Infantry Dig Party of 128 men. Assist'd by Div Sig Officer in belle tree digging Power Buzzer holes. HIRONDELLE – RIAUMONT Sch'n & Power Buzzer buried at HIRONDELLE for Power Buzzer & Amplifier.	RKB
do	6/6/18		Normal	RKB
do	7/6/18		61st Rde relieved by 59th Rde. Bde Office closed 9.10am & opened same hour Bivvu RDE Preparations for Artillery Scheme Green R and Brown lines. Wireless Stat'n erected on VIMY	RKB
do	8/6/18	8am	Third Phonetics Experiment (48 hrs) commenced. LORETTE RIDGE Visual Stat'n manned by Div Signallers Digging Party & School personnel at RIAUMONT. At TAYLOR 10. Bdes buried at RIAUMONT. Power Buzzer & Amplifier Station erected at HIRONDELLE - VIMY and RIAUMONT	RKB
do	9/6/18		Normal	RKB
do	10/6/18	9am 8am	Signalling Class commenced at Div Signal School for R.F.A. Signallers. Phonetics experiment ends.	RKB
do	11/6/18		Wireless Station dismantled at RIGHT BDE & work taken over by Station at VIMY.	RKB
do	12/6/18		Normal	RKB
do	13/6/18		Normal	RKB
do	14/6/18		Bury Route from ST. to M.R. reconnoitred. Work done on Wireless, Visual Stn in BOIS d'HIRONDELLE 61st Bde Signallers attach'd during Div Sig School returned to their Units. Second Journey for R.F.A Signallers commenced at Div Signall School.	RKB

R.K. King
MAJOR, R.E.
O.M.D.G. 20th DIVISIONAL SIGNAL CO

WAR DIARY
INTELLIGENCE SUMMARY
(Erase heading not required.)

Army Form C. 2118.

20 Div Signal Co R.E.

Place	Date	Hour	Summary of Events and Information	Remarks and references to Appendices
CHATEAU de la HAIE	15/6/18		Normal	RSB
Do	16/6/18	8.50 pm	Lt TAYLOR IN B. Wireless Offr evacuated sick to C.C.S.	RSB
			61st Bde relieved 59 Bde in Left Sector	
Do	17/6/18	8.30 pm	59th Bde relieved 60 Bde in Right Sector	RSB
Do	18/6/18	8.0 am	Fourth Ploncken Bay experiment (24 hours) - 9.0 am Work commenced preparation for Newbury	RSB
		9.0 am	by Div Sig personnel assisted by Infantry working party Capt PORTER RE i/c change.	
		9.15 pm	Infantry working party of 100 on digging work for Cable Trench Lt MALLETT RE i/c	RSB
Do	19/6/18	9.0 am	Working party Signals personnel assisted by Infantry party continued laying out work on New Bury Capt PORTER i/c	RSB
		9.0 pm	Infantry Working party of 100 on digging work to Cable Trench Lt MALLETT i/c	
Do	20/6/18	9.0 am	Working party Signals personnel (Gable Trench) Infantry party continued laying out work on Newbury Capt PORTER i/c	RSB
		9.0 pm	Infantry working party of 2 Companies (125 men) continued digging Cable Trench Lt MALLETT i/c	
			2nd Lt HOLMES R.E. returned Hospital.	
Do	21/6/18	3.0 am	Working Party of Schools personnel proceeded with work on Cable Trench.	RSB
		8.0 am	Infantry Working party of 25 on laying out Cable 5T to MR part of New Bury. Sgt SARGENT i/c	
		8.0 am	Working party of Signal Personnel assisted assisted & Infantry on laying out Cable on New Bury Capt PORTER i/c	
		9.0 pm	Infantry Working both 10. th continued digging trench for Run Capt HANNEN R.E. i/charge	
Do	22/6/18	8.0 am	Infantry Working party assisted by Div Sig personnel continued work laying out cable under Capt PORTER	RSB
		8.0 am	as usual working party continued work on New Bury under 2/Lt HOLMES.	
		9.0 pm	Night working Infantry party continued digging trench under Lt LASSEN.	
Do	23/6/18	8.0 am	Infantry working party of 20 assists to Div Sig personnel on laying out Cable work Capt PORTER i/c	RSB
		9.0 pm	Night party of Infantry continued work Lt MALLETT i/c	
Do	24/6/18	8.0 am	Infantry working party with R.E. Signals personnel continued work laying out Cable under Capt PORTER	RSB
		9.0 pm	Night party of Infantry continued work Capt HANNEN i/c	
			Wireless Station at RIAUMONT dismantled at original location a re-erected at R.E. New Station being used also as a Power Buzzer & Amplifier Station for Right Batt in Left Bde.	
Do	25/6/18	8.0 am	Infantry Working Party assisted by Sig personnel continued work laying out Cable Capt PORTER i/c	RSB
		8.0 am	Fifth Ploncken Day experiment - 24 hours - Gas Masks worn by Divisional personnel whilst at their duties.	
		9.0 pm	Night working party Infantry continued work on Cable Trench Lt LASSEN i/c	

R.S. Brace
Major R.E.
CMDG. 20th DIVISIONAL SIGNAL CO.

Army Form C. 2118.

WAR DIARY

~~INTELLIGENCE~~ SUMMARY.

(Erase heading not required.)

20 Div Signal Co RE

Place	Date	Hour	Summary of Events and Information	Remarks and references to Appendices
CHATEAU de la HAIE	26/8	8.0 am	Infantry Working party assisted by Div Sig personnel worked on CANIVEAU TRENCH. LT MALLETT I/c.	283
		8.30 pm	60 Bde relieved 59 B'de in Right Sector.	
		9.0 pm	Infantry working party continued work on Bry Batte Trench CAPT HANNEN I/c.	7/B
			2/LT HOLMES R.L. proceeded on leave to U.K. 14 days	
Do.	27/8	8.0 am	Infantry Working party assisted by Div Sig personnel continued laying out cable work CAPT PORTER I/c.	8/B
		9.0 pm	Night Infantry Working party continued work on Trench. LT LASSEN I/c.	
Do.	28/8	8.0 am	Infantry Working party assisted by Div Sig personnel continued laying out cable work CAPT PORTER I/c.	8/B
		9.0 pm	Night Infantry Working party continued work on Trench CAPT HANNEN I/c.	
Do.	29/8	8.0 am	Infantry Working party assisted by Div Sig personnel continued laying out cable work CAPT PORTER I/c.	8/B
		8.0 am	Alread Infantry Working party did work on CANIVEAU TRENCH NOBLETTE to TM Bay LT MALLETT I/c.	8/B
		9.0 pm	Night Working party continued work on Trench. LT LASSEN I/c.	

MAJOR, R.E.,
CMDG. 20th DIVISIONAL SIGNAL CO

Army Form C. 2118.

WAR DIARY
INTELLIGENCE SUMMARY
(Erase heading not required.)

20 DIV SIG Co R.E.

Instructions regarding War Diaries and Intelligence Summaries are contained in F. S. Regs., Part II. and the Staff Manual respectively. Title pages will be prepared in manuscript.

Place	Date	Hour	Summary of Events and Information	Remarks and references to Appendices
Chateau de la Haie	30/8	8.0 am	18 Bde R/S 1st Army. Infantry Working Party assisted by Sigs personnel on work laying out cable for Bury	APB
		8.0 am	2nd Inf. Bty working Pty assisted by Sigs personnel on Canivea Trench work	
	1/18	8.30am	Infantry Working Party (2 companies) on work digging trench New Bury laying on cable & filling in. 2nd Inf. Bty working Pty proceeded with work on Canivea Trench from RV to Bde Hd Qts ABLAIN ST. NAZAIRE. 9 Div Signal personnel continued jointing work.	APB
		9.0 am	Visual Station moved from VIMY to LORETTE.	
	2/18	6.0 am	VIII Corps 1st Army.	
		8.0 am	Infantry working party continued work on Canivea W Working Party Div Signals personnel assisted by Infantry proceeded with work on GIVENCHY Bury. Capt HANNEN proceeded on leave to PARIS.	APB
	3/18	8.30am	Infantry Party (150 strong) assisted by Div Sigs personnel proceeded with work on Buried Cable. Party Div Signals personnel on jointing etc + N. Bury.	APB
	4/18	8.0 am	Party Div Sigs personnel proceeded with jointing work on New Bury Route. Party Div Sig personnel with men of RFA at Div Sig School laying cable in rear Canivea Trench. Wireless P.B + A Station at Left Bde moved to new position in LIEVIN. Lt. J.R. PATTEN 92 Bde RFA Sigs Sick to Hospital.	APB
	5/18	8.0 am	Work - Jointing new Buried Route. Left Bde Wireless P.B + A Stn changed position to N.33.d.8.8.	APB
		9.0 pm	59 Bde relieved 61 Bde	APB
	6/18	8.0 am	Infantry Working Party proceeded with work on MW. T.Q Route. No. 4 Area Officer I/C	APB
	7/18	8.0 am	Work Party ABLAIN CANINEAU	APB
		5.0 am	Phoneless Day 24 hours	APB
	8/18	8.0 am	Work Signals personnel jointing on New Buried Route	APB
	9/18	8.0 am	Work - Jointing new Buried Route - completed. Right Bde Wireless Stn on VIMY moved to A.7.9. P.B + A Stn moved to 516 1810.15.	APB
	10/18		Normal	APB
	11/18		Normal	APB
			Capt HANNEN returned from PARIS leave.	

R.B. Rowell

Army Form C. 2118.

WAR DIARY

~~INTELLIGENCE SUMMARY.~~
(Erase heading not required.)

20. DIV. SIG. Co. R.E.

Place	Date	Hour	Summary of Events and Information	Remarks and references to Appendices
Chateau de la Haie	12/7/18	6.0 AM	Infantry Working Party (450 strong) on digging trench for Buried Cable REDMILL to M.27.c.6.4 Nr Bde Hd Qrs.	PRS
		8.0 AM	Work commenced on new Wireless Station & Signal Office for Left Batte near Hd Qrs. 2 Lt HOLMES returned from leave to U.K.	
	13/7/18	6.30 AM	Infantry Working Party (50) continued work on REDMILL BURY for new Bde H.Q.	PRS
		2.15 AM	Gas Beam Attack for Div & Corps Fronts Signal arrangements to Discharge Points worked without hitch.	
		8.0 AM	Party Div Signals assisted by Artillery Sig School men proceeded with Laying Cable in new Bury Trench.	
		11.0 AM	Lt LASSEN, O.W. 60 BDE SIGS vice 2Lt NENHAM,G. on Wireless Course 1st Army Signal School.	
	14/7/18	6.0 AM	Infantry Working Party (90) filling in Cable Trench. Work continued making Test points on Newbury from REDMill	PRS
			P.B. & A. Sig Right Bde re-established on VIMY RIDGE.	
		9.0 PM	61st Bde relieved 59 Bde & occupied new Bde H.Q. position at M.26.d.8.3.	
			Lt PLATT rejoined from Sick Leave as Wireless Officer.	
	15/7/18	6.0 AM	Party Div Sigs personnel continued work on Test Points for Bury to new Bde H.Q.	PRS
		6.0 AM	Infantry Working Party (40) proceeded with work filling in Cable Trench.	
		9.0 PM	59 BDE relieved 60 BDE	
	16/7/18		Normal.	PRS
	17/7/18	11 AM	Signal instructions re Defence Scheme prepared & issued to Powl, Bu, & Res at Support Corps Res Bde dismantled. Battle Station at HIRONDELLE but into action for P.B + A Statn Left Battn Rt Bde. P.B + A Statn at V.S. but into action as Bde P.B + A Station.	PRS
	18/7/18	6.0 AM	Working Party Signal personnel proceeded on Cable Work in forward area	PRS
		9.0 AM	Artillery Signallers Class opened at Div Signal School	
	19/7/18	9.0 AM	Working Party Signals personnel on lines at Reserve Bde.	PRS
			2Lt HOLMES sick to hospital.	
			Power Buzzer & Amplifier class assembled at Div Signal School.	
	20/7/18		Normal.	PRS

R.P.Parker
MAJOR, R.E.
CMDG. 20th DIVISIONAL SIGNAL Co.

Army Form C. 2118.

WAR DIARY
INTELLIGENCE SUMMARY.
(Erase heading not required.)

20 DIV SIG COY R.E.

Place	Date	Hour	Summary of Events and Information	Remarks and references to Appendices
Chateau de la Haie	21/7/18		Normal	A/B
"	22/7/18		Normal	A/B
"	23/7/18		Normal. Power Buzzer + A class closed Div Sig School	A/B
"	24/7/18	9.0 AM	Working Party. Div Signals personnel on Cameron Trench X U 6 ABLAIN.	A/B
		9.0 PM	60 Bde relieved 59 Bde	
"	25/7/18	8.0 AM	Signals personnel proceeded with work at Bowie Bat H.Q. Bombing Raid on Camp	A/B
"	26/7/18	9.0 AM	Visited Forward Area with A.D. Sigs 6th Corps. Thanksgiving Day 24 hours (B.O.A.N.) Arrangements made to occupy dugouts during bombing attacks. Work continued at Reserve Bde H.Q. Lt PARKIN G.R. proceeded on duty from 1st Army Sigs. Power Buzzer Amplifier class for Bdes Signallers opened at Div Signal School.	A/B
"	27/7/18		Normal	A/B
"	28/7/18		3 K.W. Lister Set received (3 ton lorry) to replace 1 K.W. Set. Messenger dogs posted to both Bdes	A/D
"	29/7/18	10 PM	Left Rd moved to new H.Qrs at M 26 d 7.3.	A/B
"	30/7/18		Lt C.K. MOORE O I/c SIGS No 5 Section proceeded on leave to TROUVILLE.	A/B

R.P.Rice
MAJOR, R.E.,
CMDG. 20th Div Sig Coy

Army Form C. 2118.

WAR DIARY

INTELLIGENCE SUMMARY
(Erase heading not required.)

Instructions regarding War Diaries and Intelligence Summaries are contained in F. S. Regs., Part II. and the Staff Manual respectively. Title pages will be prepared in manuscript.

20th DIV SIGNAL Coy R.E.   Vol 38

Place	Date	Hour	Summary of Events and Information	Remarks and references to Appendices
Chateau de la Haie	31/7/18	8.0am	8th Corps 1st Army Works:- Salving Derelict cable in vicinity of Chateau de la Haie. Your cable relaid from G.T. to Div Visual Stn from 1 KW P.E.L. Set where is to 1st Army Workshops.	PPB
		10.50pm	Signal Office transferred to Deep Dugout owing to Enemy Bombing Raid. Re-opened in Visitors Office 4.20 a.m. 1/8/18.	
	1/8/18	8.0am	Work:- Maintenance of Corps Cariveau Trench. Salving Cable in vicinity of Div H.Q. (continued). Rewiring of Stables. Improvements on Div Rodolph Centre LORETTE RIDGE.	PPB
			Lieut MALLETT F.T. proceeded on leave U.K. 14 days	
	2/8/18	8.0am	Work:- Salving cable (continued):- Maintenance of Corps Cariveau in Digging out Trench X.D. - Chaton de la Haie Route.	PPB
			59 Rd[?] relieved 61st Bde in left sector	
	3/8/18	8.0am	Work:- Salving Cable + Maintenance of Corps Cariveau in vicinity of Div H.Q (continued).	PPB
			"Test ACTION" } in connection with Corps Defence Scheme.	
		8.30pm	"Test STATIONS" }	
	4/8/18	9.0am	Infantry Batt Signallers assembled at Div for Signal Course at Div Signal School. LIEUT WENHAM G. returned from Wireless Course at Army School.	PPB
	5/8/18	9.0am	Div Sig School Course commenced for Batt Signallers.	PPB
		5.0am	Poled Cable laid for new M.G. Group H.Q. at GIVENCHY.	
	6/8/18		Normal	PPB
	7/8/18		Normal	PPB
	8/8/18	2pm	Visit of H.M. THE KING to Div N.Q. - Work: Revetting etc in Camp. LIEUT MALLETT F.T. proceeded to S.W. Div Sigs at O/C Army Sigs.	MR
		8.0am	3 Officers + 14 O.R.s reported laid for preliminary Signalling Course at Div Signal School.	
			G.H. Vincent Capt R.E.	
			O.C. 20 Div Sig CO R.E.	

D. B. & L., London, E.C. W W3500/P713 750,000 2/18 Sch. 82 Forms/C2118/6.

Army Form C. 2118.

WAR DIARY

INTELLIGENCE SUMMARY
(Erase heading not required)

Instructions regarding War Diaries and Intelligence Summaries are contained in F.S. Regs., Part II. and the Staff Manual respectively. Title pages will be prepared in manuscript.

Place	Date	Hour	Summary of Events and Information	Remarks and references to Appendices
Chateau de la Haie	9/3/18	8.0 AM	Work: Revetting (continued) LIEUT PLATT. B. (Windlev Offr) ported to proceeded to 4th Army Sonals for duty.	APB
"	10/3/18	9.0 AM	Work. Revetting around Signal Office & Stables (continued)	APB
"	11/3/18	9.0 AM	Work. Revetting around Signal Office & Stables (continued). 10.30 Am Air Raid by Enemy - Signal Office opened in Deep Dug-Out; normal working resumed in upstairs office at 10.30am on 12/3. 91st Bde relieved 59th Bde (Lft Sector) Relief complete 1.50 a.m on 12/3 met.	APB
"	12/3/18		CAPT HANNEN. L.C.D. O/C R.A. Sigs proceeded on leave to U.K. (14 days). LIEUT MOORE C.K. returned from TROUVILLE leave. Conference at Chateau de la Haie I.G. Training. 59th Bde relieved 60th Bde (Right Sector)	APB
"	13/3/18		Work: Revetting at Stables & Signal Office (continued). Pool Shooting Competition.	APB
"	14/3/18	8.0 AM	Work: Signal party at FOSSE 6 testing out German Batty. Testing out XL-R route both Bdes. 34th Bde relieved 24th Bde MERICOURT (Sector) - 3 Bdes in line. Nuisance of Div Sig Office opened at ABN (ABLAIN) Late Reserve Bde H.Q - 20th M.G. Bn relieved 8th M.G. Bn.	APB
"	15/3/18		Normal.	APB
"	16/3/18		Work on Caviers & Trenches Div H.Q. vicinity	APB
"	17/3/18		LIEUT. C.K. MOORE posted O.C. Windev vice At PLATT. B. LIEUT G.R. PARKIN posted O/c Signals to 5 Section (M.G.R.N.) vice LIEUT MOORE C.K. Work. Div Signals prepared Road Crossing in sykes 14 pair Batty near MR. LAIN	APB
"	18/3/18	4.0 AM	Normal.	APB
"	19/3/18		LIEUT MALLETT. F.J. returned from leave to U.K. & proceeded to 8th Div as O/c Arty Sigs Work: Patrolling & clearing Banview Trenches.	APB
"	20/3/18	9.0 AM	Work: Patrolling & clearing Canview Trenches (continued). 8.15 AM Testing out German Batt'y forward to St JOHN'S Arty O.P. Arranged for G.W.P/G. Burg. for CRIN. O.P. in LENS. - LIEVIN ROAD.	APB

Copy Issued to O1. & O.C. Bn &c

Army Form C. 2118.

WAR DIARY
or
INTELLIGENCE SUMMARY.
(Erase heading not required.)

Instructions regarding War Diaries and Intelligence Summaries are contained in F. S. Regs., Part II. and the Staff Manual respectively. Title pages will be prepared in manuscript.

Place	Date	Hour	Summary of Events and Information	Remarks and references to Appendices
Chateau de la Haie	21/8/18		Work: Testing out German Army by Brit. Div. personnel continued under Lt. PATTEN. Party of Div. Signals assisted by A.O.C Wary works on clearing sigs for 7.5" Bty to CR.M.O.P.	APB
	22/8/18	8.0 a.m.	Phonelia Hay experiment (24 hours). Work: Testing out & putting through German Army continued. Party of Div. Sigs assisted by A.A. Sigs continued work clearing sigs for 7.5" Bty to CR.M.O.P.	APB
	23/8/18		Work: Putting through & testing German Army continued - Clearing sigs for 7.5" Bty. CR.M.O.P. continued. Work laid aside owing to enemy shelling. Inf. party on clearing out Dreveuil Div. HQ vicinity. Capt PORTER. H.E.L proceeded on leave to U.K.! (14 days). Lt HOARE T.R. 5th & 1st Army to school E.O. Curer.	APB
	24/8/18	5.0 a.m.	Work: Clearing gas pipe for 7 pair Bury CR.M.O.P continued assisted by Inf.y party. Infantry working party on clearing X.D. Canizeau. Revetting at Stables.	APB
	25/8/18	5.0 a.m.	Work: Revetting at Stables continued. Clearing gas pipe for 7 pair Bury CR.M.O.P (continued). Inf. Working party on clearing Barrieau Trenches.	APB
		2.0 p.m.	Test MERICOURT - in connection with Corps Defence Scheme.	
	26/8/18	5.0 a.m.	Work: Revetting at Stables continued. Clearing gas pipe for 7 pair Bury CR.M.O.P (continued)	APB
	27/8/18	5.0 a.m.	Work: Revetting at Stables continued. Clearing gas pipe for 7 pair Bury CR.M.O.P (continued). 2nd Cdn Divn took over ACHEVILLE SECTION from 8th Divn. Relief commenced 3.30 p.m. Capt HANNEN returned from leave to U.K. (14 days)	APB
	28/8/18	1.0 a.m.	61st Bde relieved by 93rd Inf. Bde & moved to THELUS CAVES (A,B,C,D,E) afterwards relieving 25th Bde of the 8th Div. 5.0 a.m Revetting at Stables continued. Lt PATTEN. J.R. proceeded on leave to U.K. (14 days)	APB
	29/8/18	5.0 a.m.	Work: Revetting at Stables (continued). Sign personnel on U.A.- M.V Cable testing on S.P. paths attempt	APB
		9.30 p.m.	TEST MERICOURT - in connection with Corps Defence Scheme.	
	30/8/18	5.0 a.m.	Work: Revetting at Stables (continued). Pool Shooting Competition.	APB

APRace. Maj RE
C in D 2nd Div. Co. R.E

Army Form C. 2118.

WAR DIARY
INTELLIGENCE SUMMARY

(Erase heading not required)

20th Div Signal Co. R.E.

Vol 39

Instructions regarding War Diaries and Intelligence Summaries are contained in F.S. Regs., Part II. and the Staff Manual respectively. Title pages will be prepared in manuscript.

Place	Date	Hour	Summary of Events and Information	Remarks and references to Appendices
Chateau de la Haie	31/7/18	8.0 am	8th Corps 1st Army. Duty of Signal Recruits from ABLAIN with view to improvement.	H.L.P
	1/8	9.0 am	Artillery Signallers Class (Div Sig School) closed & students returned to Units. Relief of Forward linesmen. Improvements of local Routes ABLAIN carried out.	H.L.P
	2/8/18	9.0 am	Work: Revetting at Stables and camp improvements.	H.L.P
	3/8/18	9.0 am	Work: Revetting at Stables and Camp improvements (continued). Extension of Services back from XO to Carr Field Ambulance (MRCY)	H.L.P
	4/8/18	9.0 am	Work: Revetting at Stables and Camp improvements (continued) - Improvements at "U.A" Test Bench. Div Visual Station LORETTE closed down.	H.L.P
	5/8/18	9.0 am	Work: Revetting at Stables (continued)	H.L.P
	6/8/18	9.0 am	Work: Revetting at Stables (continued). Reclassification test of Bn Signallers (in R.F.A) Tidying up Picking ground. Ressing R.L overland Route. Bgl Shooting Competition.	H.L.P
	7/8/18	9.0 am	Work: Revetting at Stables (continued). Work on R.L overland route (entrance). Captain PORTER H.E.B., M.C., returned from leave to U.K. 14 days.	H.L.P
	8/8		Normal.	H.L.P
	9/8/18	9.0 am	Work: Revetting at Stables (continued)	H.L.P
	10/8/18	9.0 am	Work: Revetting at Stables (continued) Filling up Road Crossing Rwy at ABLAIN. R.L. Robin Route.	H.L.P
	11/8/18	9.0 am	Reclassification Tests of Batt'n Signallers (R.H.A. Bde)	H.L.P
	12/8	9 am	Diggers Dump Holes for drainage of Cariveau Trench. Div H.Q. to Corps.	H.L.P
	12/8		Reclassification Tests of Batt'n Signallers (H.A.R.C) continued. Signal Dumpshelter (cont.)	H.L.P
	13/8/18	9.0 am	Digging Sump holes continued. Div H.Q. & Corps Cariveau. Lt PATTEN T.R. O/C Signals Subsection 92/3 Bde R.F.A returned from leave to U.K.	H.L.P
	14/8/18		Digging Dump holes for drainage of Cariveau Div H.Q. to R.T. Lt HOFFE T.H.B. D/C Signal Subsection 91st Bde RFA returned from 1st Army School of Course G.S 325.	H.L.P
	15/8/18		Infantry Signallers Course III Div Signal School completed. Classes/Clerks & personnel returned to Units. Commenced building Visual Station in HIRONDELLE WOOD, night work.	H.L.P

20th Div Sig Coy R.E.
MAJOR, R.E.

Army Form C. 2118.

WAR DIARY
~~INTELLIGENCE SUMMARY.~~
(Erase heading not required.)

Instructions regarding War Diaries and Intelligence Summaries are contained in F. S. Regs. Part II. and the Staff Manual respectively. Title pages will be prepared in manuscript.

20 Div SIGNAL Co. R.E.

Place	Date	Hour	Summary of Events and Information	Remarks and references to Appendices
Chateau de la Haie	16/9/18		2/Lt BURTON. C. proceeded on leave to U.K. in d.g.m. 2/Lt HOLMES. R.L. to 59 Bde sig Sion vice 2/Lt BURTON. C. Visual Station in HIRONDELLE WOOD completed	M.L.P
	17/9/18		1/Lt (A/Capt) PARSONS. T.S. D.S.O. RETF. reported for duty as O.K. Infy Sigs. 20 Div. Vice Capt HANNEN. L.C.D. posted to 39th Div SR. 2nd in command.	M.L.P
		9.0am	Lectures & Lectern Tests Baltn Signs M/Os at Div Sig Schools (3rd Rifle Brigade)	M.L.P
	18/9/18		Divisional Visual Stn built on VIMY RIDGE	M.L.P
	19/9/18		Reclassification Tests Batln signallers (Div signal School) 1/4 W.S.L.I.	M.L.P
	20/9/18		Capt. HANNEN. L.C.D. proceeded to 60. 30th Div as 2nd in Command. 2/Lt (A/Capt) PARSONS assumed duties as O.K. Inf Div. A/Lt. WEST. 2/o Div Vice Capt HANNEN. Lt SMITH. W.C. RETF. attached to 20th Div Signal Coy from 1st Army Sigs as supernumerary Offr. Cpl PODD I. Starting employment Death Collection of Reserve Cable from NOUVELLE and LORRETTE to DIV School	M.L.P
		8.0am	Preliminary tours assembled at Div Sig School for signallers proceeding to 5A Troop Signal School	M.L.P
	21/9/18		Conference at Div H.Q. Hos Police work on A.B.N. route	M.L.P
		11.30am	TEST ACHEVILLE in accordance with Corps Defence Scheme	M.L.P
	22/9/18	8.0am	Working party Infantry Excavating Buried Cable for repair. Renewing of Stables (continued)	M.L.P
	23/9/18	8.0am	Working party Infantry Excavating Buried Cable for repair (continued) at SOUCHEZ. Installing Switchboard (6 lines))	M.L.P
		8.0am	Working party Infantry Shed & improvements at Stables Buildings. R.O. Sig. 8th Corps Vacated. Ground area.	M.L.P
	24/9/18	8.0am	Working party Infantry Repairing Buried Cable for repair (continued) at SOUCHEZ. New Buy Fwd of M.U. Commenced (28 pairs) Relaying Cable on Cable Signallers (12 K.R.R.G.) of Div School of Int Uniform School. Reviewing Stables (continued) Building a Culvert. Shell & improvements to Rev Eng at Stables continued Working party Burning Cable from T.E. to new station H.Q	M.L.P
	25/9/18	9.0am	Resetting at Sta Div continued in accordance with Corps Defence Scheme	M.L.P
		11.19am	Test ACHEVILLE (continued)	
	26/9/18	9.0am	Renewing improvements at Stables (continued) New Buy connecting M.U. Sigs (6 end of LORRETTE RIDGE) combe Working party Burning Cable from T.E. to new station H.Q. MIDNIGHT-OSMA/Wire Sig & Int Bde with R.E. O.K.	M.L.P
	27/9/18	9.0am	Tests out new Buy from M.U. right working party to 6th Bde (compl Ed Bury from T.E. to new Batln H.Q	M.L.P
	28/9/18	10am	Lt CK MOORE proceeded for U.K. on leave (14 days)	M.L.P
		10am	S.O.S from 7th B.D.L.I. Re-numbering NT NV v SA route	M.L.P
	29/9/18		Normal	

W.L.R. von Guin
MAJOR
OC 20th DIVISIONAL SIGNALS

Army Form C. 2118.

WAR DIARY
or
INTELLIGENCE SUMMARY
(Erase heading not required.)

20 DIV SIGNAL COY. R.E.

Instructions regarding War Diaries and Intelligence Summaries are contained in F. S. Regs., Part II. and the Staff Manual respectively. Title pages will be prepared in manuscript.

Place	Date	Hour	Summary of Events and Information	Remarks and references to Appendices
Chateau de la Haie	30/9/18		VIII CORPS 1st ARMY. Major A.G. BRACE, M.C. proceeded on leave to U.K. (14 days) WORK - Drainage Improvements Div H.Q.	Init.
"	1/10	MIDNIGHT	30H/18t Contemplated time adopted. 2/Lt BURTON.C.J. returned from leave to U.K. (14 days)	M.L.P
"	2/10	18.00	61st Bde moved from Abbe 1.4 to B14 a.7.3. - O.K. for communication at 19.00. - Lt HORE.T.H.B. proceeded on leave to U.K. 14 days. Preparatory Orders received for Div H.Q. to open Advance H.Q. at S.T.	M.L.P
"	3/10	16.00	Order received to move forward to Advance H.Q. position (BERLIN 17.30) Order cancelled at 16.45.	M.L.P
"	4/10	11.59	P.P. Exchange closed. 21.00 Div Exchange opened at S.T. Left Bde H.Q. Left Bde moved to new position.	M.L.P
"	5/10/18		Preparations for Relief of Division.	M.L.P
"	6/10/18	11.00	S.T. Office closed & moved to DN Offs, also 13.00 Div H.Q. closed at CHATEAU DE LA HAIE & opened at VILLERS CHATEL Div was relieved by 12th Div. 1 Cable Sect Detachment remained with the Div with Signals	M.L.P
VILLERS CHATEL	7/10/18	13.30	Forward lines run to Div and M/T Stations relieved by 12th Div. Company complete at VILLERS CHATEL at 16.47.	M.L.P
VILLERS CHATEL	8/10/18	09.00	Training. Visual, and Cable Cart Drill. Recruiting Test held.	M.L.P
	9/10/18	09.00	Training. Cable Cart Drill. Visual Practice & lectures/instructions. 14/17 Sec. Pour Napes changes for R. de Point Bugget Pool. 15.00 Recreational Training continued	M.L.P
	10/10/18	09.00	Training and Lectures as on previous days above. Remustering Tests continued. Recreational Training in afternoon. Kit Inspection.	M.L.P
	11/10/18	09.00	Training continued as on the 8th, 9th, & 10th insts.	M.L.P
	12/10/18	09.00	Training continued as on previous days. Rifle practice. Lt. R.K. MOORE returned from leave to U.K.	M.L.P
	13/10/18	09.00	Training continued as on previous days. Rifle practice.	M.L.P
	14/10/18	09.00	Training continued. Buzzer instruction & practice. Rifle practice. Major BRACE returned from leave to U.K.	M.B
	15/10/18	09.00	Training. Cable Cart instruction, Visual practice. Visited ARTILLERY at CHERISY. Lt J. HARDEN proceeded on leave to U.K. (14 days). Lt HOARE.T.H.B. sent to hospital whilst on leave to U.K.	M.B
	16/10/18	09.00	Training. Cable Cart instruction, Visual & Rifle practice. Out Stations Visual Signal Scheme E. Visited Brigades and M.G. Battn.	P.B
	17/10/18	09.00	Training. Cable Cart practice and Visual. M/T Sections proceeded to Nos 2 and 3 Sections	P.B
	18/10/18	09.00	Training. Cable Cart, Visual, Rifle practice	M.B
	19/10/18	09.30	Training. Cable Cart instruction, Visual. Recreational Training. Attended 60th Bde Communication Scheme.	P.B
	20/10/18		Normal. Lt WENHAM.G. proceeded on leave to U.K. 14 days	P.B

C.M.C.O. 20TH DIVISIONAL SIGNAL CO.

Army Form C. 2118.

WAR DIARY
or
INTELLIGENCE SUMMARY
(Erase heading not required.)

2nd Divl SIGNAL CO R.E.

Place	Date	Hour	Summary of Events and Information	Remarks and references to Appendices
VILLERS CHATEL	21/10/19	09.00	Training Visual, Rifle Practice Physical Drill, Route Marching. Communication Scheme by Sig: R de (L.E. NO. MES)	R.S.
	22/10/19	09.00	Training Visual, Rifle Practice Physical Drill. Route Marching	R.S.
	23/10/19	09.00	Training Visual practice Physical Exercises	R.S.
	24/10/19	09.00	Training Visual practice Route March	R.S.
	25/10/19	09.10	Training Rifle Practice Physical Exercises. 2/Lt WALKER G.A. Joined for temporary duty	R.S.
	26/10/19	09.00	Training Visual practice. Cable Cart Drill	R.S.
	27/10/19	09.00	Training Visual practice. 14.00 Shooting Competition	R.S.
	28/10/19	09.00 14.30	Recreational Training 11.00 Night Visual Scheme 600k Rdv Communication Scheme	R.S.
	29/10/19	09.00	Training Cable Cart Instruction Visual. Packing up	R.S.
	30/10/19	14.30 23.15	Advance Party (Sgt DENTON 7/c) left for HN on 4.Q. CAMBRAI Transport + dismounted personnel left VILLERS CHATEL for Entrainment	R.S.

P Chase
MAJOR, A.E.
CMDG 2nd DIVISIONAL SIGNAL CO

WAR DIARY

INTELLIGENCE SUMMARY

(Erase heading not required.)

Army Form C. 2118.

20th Divisional Signal Coy.

Place	Date	Hour	Summary of Events and Information	Remarks and references to Appendices
CAMBRAI	31/10/18	10.00	XVII CORPS - 3rd ARMY. All Units of Div and Brigades stationed in CAMBRAI. Div H.Q. Office opened at CAMBRAI 10.00 and closed at VILLERS CHATEL 09.30	AB
"	1/11/18		Normal	AB
"	2/11/18	23:59	Normal Signal Dump of surplus Stores Kits arranged at CAMBRAI. Orders received for Div HQ to move on 3rd.	AB
AVESNES-LEZ AUBERT	3/11/18	08.00	Advance Party left for AVESNES-LEZ-AUBERT. Capt H.S.L. PORTER i/c	AB
		10.00	Div HQ opened at AVESNES-LEZ-AUBERT and closed at CAMBRAI same hour. Relieved 19th Div. 59 Bde at CAURIOR - 60 Bde at RIEUX - 61 Bde at CAGNONCLES	AB
Do	4/11/18	22.00	Bde Moves:- 59th to ST AUBERT; 60th 6 VENDEGIES; 61st to ST AUBERT. M.G. Bn to VENDEGIES. Div under 2 hours notice to move. 2/Lt LASSEN & 7 Brs proceed to UK on leave (in lorry). 2/Lt SMITH R.C. to 60 Bde Signal Section.	AB
Do	5/11/18		Div H.Q. & Bdes remained as on 4th inst.	AB
Do	6/11/18		Bde Moves: 59th remained at ST AUBERT. 60th to SEPMERIES; 61st to SOMMAING. M.G. Bn to SOMMAING. Div H.Q. opened at VENDEGIES 11.0.0. Transport to VENDEGIES by Road. Lt WENHAM G. returned from leave to U.K.	AB
VENDEGIES	7/11/18	13.00	Bde Moves: 59th to VENDEGIES and SOMMAING; 60th to JENLAIN; 61st to SEPMERIES; M.G. Bn to MARESCHES. Reconnoitre of ST JENLAIN AREA in afternoon. 2 Miles D5 cable recovered in VENDEGIES	AB
Do VENDEGIES	8/11/18	11.30	Div HQ moved to new HQ WAGNIES-LE-GRAND at 11.30. Transport moved by Road 2½/Lt HOLMES i/c	
WAGNIES-LE GRAND		09.00	Advance party proceeded to near HQ at 08.00. Capt PORTER. Cable Detachment proceeded in advance to lay new Wet Day lines. Roads getting very bad. 19th Div moved out of WAGNIES-LE-GRAND to lay new to ST WAAST. 61st to WAGNIES-LE-PETIT. M.G. Bn to JENLAIN	AB
WAGNIES-LE-GRAND BAVAY	9/11/18	16.00	Div under orders to move at ½ hours notice from 08.30. Bde Moves: 59th remained at JENLAIN. 60th to FIEGNIES. 61st remained at WAGNIES-LE-PETIT. M.G. Bn to FIEGNIES. Div HQ closed WAGNIES-LE-GRAND 16.00 and opened at BAVAY same hour.	AB
BAVAY	10/11/18	13.00	Bde Moves: 59th remained at JENLAIN: 60th moved into line- GRISOELLE - coming under orders of 24th Division; 61st to ST WAAST; M.G.Bn into line CRISOELLE. Cable Detachment left for FIEGNIES. 13.20 Advance Party left BAVAY for FIEGNIES.	AB
BAVAY FEIGNIES	11/11/18	10.00	Div moved to FEIGNIES. opened office 10.00	AB
		11.00	HOSTILITIES CEASED.	
		13.00	Div take over Command from 24th Div. Cable Detachment laid line forward to 60th Adv line under 2/Lt HOLMES. BDE Moves: 59th at ST WAAST: 60th in the line MONS-MAUBEUGE ROAD; 61st to FEIGNIES. M.G. Bn in line.	

MAJOR R.E.
C.M.D.G. 20th DIVISIONAL SIGNAL CO

Army Form C. 2118.

WAR DIARY

~~INTELLIGENCE SUMMARY~~

(Erase heading not required.)

20th Div Signal Co. C.E.

Place	Date	Hour	Summary of Events and Information	Remarks and references to Appendices
FEIGNIES	12/11/18	08.00	Bde Moves: 59th to THAISNIERES - MALPLAQUET AREA. 60th Bde. and M.G. Bn no change. Artillery at FEIGNIES.	PPB
		09.00	Improvements & testing of 60th Bde line. Lines laid from CORPS EXCHANGE BAVAY to 59 Bde at THAISNIERES.	PPB
		09.00	Tidying up local lines. Salving cable.	PPB
	13/11/18	09.00	Work: Cleaning up & cleaning Transport. Raising in Cable around Div. H.Q. Dispositions as for previous	PPB
	14/11/18	09.00	Work. Cleaning & overhauling cable carts. Dispositions unchanged.	PPB
	15/11/18	09.00	Work. Cleaning Transport. 60th Bde moved from GRISOELLE to BELLIGNIES - BETTRECHIES - LA FLAMENGERIE Area. Communication via CORPS thence by D.R.	PPB
	16/11/18	08.30	Work. Cleaning Transport and Bicycles.	PPB
		10.00	Thanksgiving Service held in Bakery, Div. I.Q.	PPB
	17/11/18		Normal	PPB
	18/11/18		Normal	PPB
	19/11/18		Normal	PPB
	20/11/18		Normal	PPB
	21/11/18		Normal. Lt LASSEN E.T. returned from leave to U.K. & proceeded to 60th Bde. 2/Lt SMITH P.C. returned to Div. H.Q. from 60th Bde. Capt PARSONS J.S. O.16 Sigr 20 Div D.R. proceeded on leave to U.K. 14 days.	PPB
	22/11/18	09.00	Reeling in local lines + Cable. Packing Transport.	PPB
	23/11/18	11.00	Div H.Q. closed FEIGNIES & opened MAGNIES-LE-GRAND 11.00. Bde MOVES:- 59 Bn from THAISNIERES to MAGNIES-LE-PETIT: 60 Bn to ETH + BRY Area: 61 & 2 STH&EST: 20 K BgN M.G. to LE PISSOTIAU	PPB
MAGNIES-LE-GRAND	24/11/18		Bde Moves:- 59th to MARESCHES-SEPMERIES Area: 60th to VENDEGIES 61 to MAGNIES-LE-PETIT: 20 M.G.Bn to VILLERS POL.	PPB
Do.	25/11/18		Preparations for Move. Packing Transport etc. Load of Technical Stores sent to Signal Dump at CAMBRAI.	PPB
Do.	26/11/18	10.00	Arrived to near A.Q. RIEUX. Bde moves. 59th at ST AUBERT: 60th at RIEUX: 61st at VENDEGIES: M.G. Bn at AVESNES-LE-AUBERT.	PPB
RIEUX	27/11/18		Div Bde dispositions - No change from 26th inst. Artillery moved from CAMBRAI to BEUGNATRE	PPB

R. Place
CMDG. 20th DIV. SIGNAL CO.

Army Form C. 2118.

WAR DIARY

~~INTELLIGENCE~~ SUMMARY

(Erase heading not required)

20th Divisional Signal Coy R.E.

Place	Date	Hour	Summary of Events and Information	Remarks and references to Appendices
CAMBRAI	28/11/18	10.30	Div H.Q. closed at CAMBRAI and opened at CAMBRAI same hour. Bdes moves: 59th from ST AUBERT to CAMBRAI: 60th from RIEUX to CAMBRAI: 61st from VENDEGIES to CAGNONCLES: M.G.Bn from AVESNES to CAMBRAI. Lt NENHAM + party proceeded to New Area for Billeting purposes &c.	WD
CAMBRAI	29/11/18	09.00	Transport moved by Road to New Area under Capt PORTER - with Div transport.	WD
		10.0	Signal Stores at CAMBRAI Signal Dump proceeded to new area by lorry.	
		10.00	Advance Party (Office Staff Sgt DENTON &c) proceeded by lorry to new Area. A.d. Dispositions as for 28th unit. Artillery established in New Area.	

F.J.Thomas

Army Form C. 2118.

WAR DIARY
or
INTELLIGENCE SUMMARY.
(Erase heading not required.)

20th DIVISIONAL SIGNAL Cy. R.E. Vol 4 2

Place	Date	Hour	Summary of Events and Information	Remarks and references to Appendices
CAMBRAI	31/12/18		Transport on Road to PAS	App
CAMBRAI	1/1/19		Company at CAMBRAI embarked for PAS. 0930 Rear Office Left for CAMBRAI until 2nd inst.	App
		0830	P.E.L + Company Lorries proceeded at 0830	App
PAS.		1000	Rear Office at CAMBRAI closed. Electric Wiring in Village: Wiring local offices; Improving + Cleaning Billets	App
			59th & 60th Bde at TOUTENCOURT: 61st Bde at AUTHIE: 61st Bde at VAUCHELLES: M.G. Bn. at MARIEUX	App
PAS.	2/1/19		Arty. at HENU: Communication by wire and —	App
"	3/1/19		Improvements to Billets and Offices.	App
"	4/1/19		Work on Billets and new Signal Office continued	App
"	5/1/19		Work. Patrol of cleaning party to 61st Bde Lines; Improvements (building bunks) at billets continued:	App
"	6/1/19		Demobilisation: Personal Interviews of N.C.O.'s + O.R.'s by the O.C. commenced.	App
"	7/1/19		Work. Improvements of Billets and Hoto Lines.	App
"	8/1/19		Normal	App
"	9/1/19		Capt. PARSONS returned from Leave to U.K.	App
"	10/1/19		Work continued on Billets - Shelters and Duck boarding.	App
"	11/1/19		Portion of No 4 Section returns to Div. HQ.	App
"	12/1/19		No. 5 Section returns to Div. HQ.	App
"	13/1/19		Work on Canteen - Mess Room - Standings continued	App
"			Lt. PARSON G.R. returned from Leave to U.K. Lt. SHERMAN from 3rd Army Signal Co.	App
			Lt. DONFIELD S.W. R.W.F. (R.S.) attached to Company from Sub-enumerary; Duck boarding. Recreation Hut existing
			Lt. HOLMES, R.E. proceeded on leave to U.K. 14/1/19 ST. Work continued on Mess Room. Duck boarding,
			commenced: Lt. DONALDSON to 61st Bde. Sub-Section.
"	14/1/19		Work on Recreation Hut + Standings continued	App
"	15/1/19		Recreation Hut + Mess Solving + Cable; Lieut. R.H. DONALDSON sent to 91st Bde. R.F.A.	App
			Sub-section for duty vice Lieut. T.H.B. HOARE (sick in England.)

R.P. River
MAJOR R.E.
CMDG. 20th DIVISIONAL SIGNAL Co.

WAR DIARY
INTELLIGENCE SUMMARY

Army Form C. 2118.

20th DIVISIONAL SIGNAL Coy. R.E.

Place	Date	Hour	Summary of Events and Information	Remarks and references to Appendices
PAS.	16/12/18		WORK: Recreation Hut and Drainage. Salving Cable.	APB
	17/12/18		WORK: Salving Cable + erection of E.L. Cable: Recreation Hut + Drainage continued	APB
	18/12/18		WORK: Recreation Hut. Drainage Standings continued. demobilization of Miners.	APB
	19/12/18		WORK on Recreation Hut. Lgt: Railway + Duckboards continued. Improvement of E.L. Circuit.	APB
	20/12/18		WORK on Recreation Hut, Light Rly, Drainage + E.L. Circuit continued	APB
	21/12/18		2/Lt. SMITH, P.C. proceeded on leave to UK 14 days.	APB
	22/12/18		Normal.	APB
	23/12/18		Work on Recreation Hut completed.	APB
	24/12/18		WORK: Reconnoitring Area preparatory to taking over from L. of C.	APB
	25/12/18		XMAS DAY. Mens Xmas Dinner 12.30 followed by Tea + a Whist Drive.	APB
	26/12/18		NORMAL. RE Recreation Meeting to elect Committee. Sqn. Bde. H.Q. ordered to LONGPRÉ for Demobilization Duties	APB
	27/12/18		NORMAL. Linemen to ACHEUX Test Station. 200 yd range settled. Practice Rifle Shoot.	APB
	28/12/18		NORMAL. Electric Light put in for Village Sisters. Maintenance of Permanent Routes. Reconnoitring Linemen to TOUTENCOURT Test Station	APB
	29/12/18		Rifle Practice. Move of 59th Bde. H.Q. cancelled.	APB
	30/12/18		NORMAL – Reconnoitring new Area.	APB

R.F.Power
MAJOR, R.E.
OMDG 20th DIVISIONAL SIGNAL Coy

WAR DIARY
or
INTELLIGENCE SUMMARY
(Erase heading not required.)

Army Form C. 2118.

20th Divisional Signal Coy. R.E.

Place	Date	Hour	Summary of Events and Information	Remarks and references to Appendices
PAS.	31/8	09:00	Work - Drainage and Ablution Room - Dismantling Huts at SOUASTRE & erecting huts at GAUDIEMPRE. for Test Station. Lt. Cork joined from 17th Corps. Sig. Coy. as Supernumerary officer.	APB
	1/9		Lt. H. Donaldson posted to Command of 63rd R.Sgt. Signal Subsection.	APB
	2/9		Work - Screening mule standings, continued work on drainage & ablution benches & Test House, also on Test Station Hut at GAUDIEMPRE.	APB
	3/9		Work - Drainage to the house & continuing work on Test Hut at GAUDIEMPRE, Latter now completed.	APB
	4/9		Work - Light Rly. Latrines, Drainage re. Salving Cable in HENU & SOUASTRE.	APB
	5/9		Capt. H.E.L. PORTER M.C. left unit for Demobilization E. Sartin worked on this daily except Sundays after this date). Salving Cable continued -	APB
	6/9		Improvements to billets continued also Baths. horses.	APB
	7/9		Normal.	APB
	8/9		Educational Classes commenced in morning in Recreation Hut. & mason	APB
	9/9		Dismantling Air Line Route THIEVES - PAS. Recreation - Football Match.	APB
	10/9		Dismantling Route in THIEVES. Tile Shoot.	APB
	11/9		R.A. subsection transfered to Div. H.Qs. Leaving very Office Shift. Work. Dismantling Cable route & repairing floor in Stables. Classification of horses.	APB
	12/9		Baths. Normal.	APB
	13/9		Completed mule standings - Tile Shoot practice.	APB
	14/9		Improvements to billets. Recreation Football Match.	APB
	15/9.		Working on Football ground. Tile Shoot practice - Work on Ockham's Track.	APB Trace Ing. to R.E.

WAR DIARY

INTELLIGENCE SUMMARY

(Erase heading not required.)

Army Form C. 2118.

Instructions regarding War Diaries and Intelligence Summaries are contained in F. S. Regs., Part II. and the Staff Manual respectively. Title pages will be prepared in manuscript.

Place	Date	Hour	Summary of Events and Information	Remarks and references to Appendices
PAS.	16/9		Dismantling permanent Routes. Football match Duckboard track completed. Rifle short practice.	App
	17/9		Dismantling Cable routes. Cleaning transport & witnessing on football ground. Damaged permanent route repaired at THIEVRES.	App
	18/9		Continue dismantling Air Line routes. Baths. Football match.	App
	19/9		Normal.	App
	20/9		Continue dismantling Air Line routes. Potato picking	App
	21/9		H. handover to Bedford Training Centre Bedford. Football match. Continue Dismantling Air Line Route	App
	22/9		Cleaning Transport. Recreation Football. Coff Parson ~~~~ with Div. H.Q. Arm R.A.H.Q.	App
	23/9		Potato picking Normal.	App
	24/9		Dismantling Air Line route.	App
	25/9		Dismantling Air Line routes. Inoculation of Horses. Classes Y. Rifle short practice	App
	26/9		Normal.	App
	27/9		Dismantling Air Line Routes.	App
	28/9		Dismantling Air Line Routes. - Rifle Short Practice.	App
	29/9		Dismantling Air Line Routes. Salving Cable. Reerecting St. route.	App
	30/9		Dismantling Air Line Routes. Rifle short Practice.	App

R.P. Price MAJOR, R.E.
OMDG. 20th DIVISIONAL SIGNAL CO

Army Form C. 2118.

WAR DIARY
INTELLIGENCE SUMMARY.
(Erase heading not required)

20th Div Signal Co RE

V8 44

Place	Date	Hour	Summary of Events and Information	Remarks and references to Appendices
PAS	3/1/19		Dismantling Airline Routes SOUASTRE and PAS.	PPB
	1/2/19		Dismantling Air Line Routes ST AMAND	PPB
	2/2/19		Normal	PPB
	3/2/19		Dismantling Airline Routes ST AMAND Salvage of cable between SOUASTRE and ST AMAND	PPB
	4/2/19		Dismantling Air Line Route. Salvage of cable in FAMECHON.	PPB
	5/2/19		Dismantling Air Line Route. Lecture by the OC in Recreation hut explanatory of New Army Order of the Army of Occupation & its effects on Demobilization	PPB
	6/2/19		2/Lt BURTON. C. left Unit for Demobilization Dismantling Air Line Route.	PPB
	7/2/19		Dismantling Cable Route. Dismantling Air Line Route at HENU Salvage of cable.	PPB
	8/2/19		Dismantled a cable Route continued. Dismantling Air Line Route between HENU & SOUASTRE Stove built in Bath Route. Bath.	PPB
	9/2/19		Normal	PPB
	10/2/19		Dismantling Air Line & Cable Route between HENU and SOUASTRE.	PPB
	11/2/19		Work on ACHEUX - TOUTENCOURT Route	PPB
	12/2/19		Dismantling Air line Routes continued.	PPB
	13/2/19		Dismantling Air line Routes continued	PPB
	14/2/19		Dismantling Air line Route at GRINCOURT	PPB
	15/2/19		Work continued at GRINCOURT Baths.	PPB

PPK Knee Major RE
Aug 20th Div Sigmal Coy RE

WAR DIARY

INTELLIGENCE SUMMARY

Army Form C. 2118.

20th Div Signal Co. R.E.

Place	Date	Hour	Summary of Events and Information	Remarks and references to Appendices
PAS	16/9		Normal.	PPB
	17/9		Repairing Top Pole Route between PAS and THIEVRES. 2/Lt J.T HADDEN (T.F.) M.C. to be Act/Capt dated 9/9/19 & absorbed 2nd in Command of Company	PPB
	18/9		2/Lt J.R. PATTEN proceeded on leave to U.K. 2/Lt WALKER J.H. returned from leave to U.K. Dismantling Air line Routes at GAUDIEMPRE and MONDECOURT.	PPB
	19/9		Work continued at MONDECOURT. Dismantling Poles on Dump (PAS)	PPB
	20/9		Dismantling PAS-HENU Airline Route.	PPB
	21/9		Dismantling PAS-HENU Route continued	PPB
	22/9		Dismantling Poles on PAS Dump. Baths. Work on lines at AUTHIEULE.	PPB
	23/9		Collection of Cable from HENU to Central Dump at PAS	PPB
	24/9		Dismantled Cable Route between HURTEBISE FARM and HALLOY. Reeling in Cable on GAUDIEMPRE ROAD	PPB
	25/9		Salvage of Cable in PAS VILLAGE. Trees felled by French - breakdown on Main Route - considerable delay to traffic in consequence	PPB
	26/9		Salvage of Cable in PAS VILLAGE continued Dismantling Poles on Dump.	PPB
	27/9		Salvage of cable in PAS and HALLOY.	PPB

P.P.Palmer MAJOR. R.E.
Commanding 20 Div Signal Co R.E.

WAR DIARY

INTELLIGENCE SUMMARY

Army Form C. 2118.

20th Divisional Signal Coy RE

WW 45

Place	Date	Hour	Summary of Events and Information	Remarks and references to Appendices
PAS-EN-ARTOIS	28/9	09.00	Salvage of cable in HUMBERCAMP.	WB
	1/10	09.00	Salvage of cable at HUMBERCAMP - also on AUTHIE ROUTE. 23.00 Summer Time into force	WB
	2/10		Normal.	WB
	3/10	09.00	Salvage of cable at HUMBERCAMP continued. Dismantling Poles on PAS DUMP.	WB
	4/10	09.00	Reeling in cable from GRINCOURT to DOULLENS-ARRAS Road. ACHEUX TEST STATION closed.	WB
	5/10	09.00	Reeling in cable work continued at GRINCOURT. TEST STATION formed at MARIEUX	WB
	6/10	09.00	Work continued at GRINCOURT.	WB
	7/10	09.00	Salvage of cable at LA HERLIERE.	WB
	8/10	09.00	Salvage of cable at LA HERLIERE continued. Company Baths.	WB
	9/10		Normal. N O.C. proceeded on leave, Capt. J. HADDEN, R.E., Second in Command assumed Command of Company. Lt J.S. PATTEN returned from leave to U.K.	WB
	10/10	09.00	2/Lt COOK I A F proceeded on leave to U.K. Improvements at Waggon Lines	WB
	11/10	09.00	Salvage of cable in MONDICOURT.	WB
	12/10	09.00	Cleaning Waggons and Harness.	WB
	13/10	09.30	Cable baths complete to will No8 STORES & loc did TRANSPORT proceeded to MONDICOURT WAGON PARK. Harness cleaning continued.	WB
	14/10	09.00	Dismantling at PAS DUMP.	WB
	15/10	09.00	Work at PAS DUMP continued	WB
	16/10		Normal.	WB
	17/10	09.00	Work at PAS DUMP continued. Wagon cleaning	WB
	18/10	09.00	Work at PAS DUMP continued. Cleaning up camp at Transport Lines & Vicinity	WB

RWPhiney Major

Army Form C. 2118.

WAR DIARY

INTELLIGENCE SUMMARY

(Erase heading not required.)

20th Divisional Signal Coy. R.E.

Place	Date	Hour	Summary of Events and Information	Remarks and references to Appendices
PAS-EN-ARTOIS	19/3/19		Normal - Recreation Six-a-side football competition.	APB
"	20/3/19		Normal	APB
"	21/3/19		Normal - Capt. J.S. PARSONS, R.E. and Lieut. G.R. PARKIN, R.E. left Unit for demobilisation	APB
"	22/3/19	09.00	Dismantling on PAS DUMP. Cleaning & packing Saddlery	APB
"	23/3/19		Normal. O.C returned from leave	APB
"	24/3/19	09.00	Work continued on PAS DUMP	APB
"	25/3/19	09.00	Work continued on PAS DUMP	APB
"	26/3/19		Normal. A/Capt J. HADDEN proceeded on leave to U.K. 2/Lieut COOK, A.F. returned from leave to U.K.	APB
"	27/3/19	09.00	Clearing up ground in camp	APB
"	28/3/19	09.00	Work on Artillery lines. 2/Lieut J.A. WALKER, R.E. left Unit for demobilisation	APB
"	29/3/19	09.00	Overhaul of Technical Stores at MONDICOURT WAGON PARK. Clearing-up of Billets & vicinity. Work continued on Artillery lines	APB
"	30/3/19	09.00	Work continued at MONDICOURT WAGON PARK.	APB

RPhase Major
Cmd. 20 Dn Signal Coy.

Army Form C. 2118.

WAR DIARY

~~INTELLIGENCE SUMMARY~~
(Erase heading not required.)

20th Divisional Signal Co. R.E.

Vol 46

Instructions regarding War Diaries and Intelligence Summaries are contained in F.S. Regs., Part II. and the Staff Manual respectively. Title pages will be prepared in manuscript.

Place	Date	Hour	Summary of Events and Information	Remarks and references to Appendices
PAS-EN-ARTOIS	31/3/19	09.00	XVII CORPS. Wagons at MONDICOURT WAGON PARK.	PPS
	1/4/19	09.00	Cleaning Wagons at MONDICOURT WAGON PARK.	PPR
	2/4/19	09.00	Wagon Cleaning continued at MONDICOURT WAGON PARK.	PPR
	3/4/19	15.00	Inspection of Cattle Carts & pack Transport by G.O.C. 20th Divisional Parked at MONDICOURT WAGON PARK.	PPR
	4/4/19		Normal	PPR
	5/4/19	09.00	Salvage of Cable at PAS	PPR
	6/4/19		Normal	PPR
	7/4/19	09.00	Work on T.H.-P.S. Route	PPR
			Lt. J.R. PATTEN, M.C. posted to 95th Bde R.F.A. as O.C. Signal Subsection.	PPR
	8/4/19		Normal	PPR
	9/4/19		Normal	PPR
	10/4/19		Capt JADDEN T.M.O returned from leave to U.K.	PPR
	11/4/19		Normal	PPR
	12/4/19	09.00	Work on test Ne at HENU	PPR
	13/4/19	14.00	Inter Company (R.E.) Sports preliminary 6 Div CADRE SPORTS MEETING	PPR
	14/4/19	15.00	Football Match V 10th Div SIGNAL Co R.E.	PPR
	15/4/19	14.30	Preliminary Sports Meeting (R.E.) for Div CADRE SPORTS MEETING.	PPR
	16/4/19		Normal	PPR
	17/4/19		Normal	PPR
	18/4/19	09.00	Dismantling lines in CHATEAU PAS	PPR
	19/4/19		Normal	PPR

R.P.Rnee Major Co.
Cofg 20 Div Signal Co R.E.

Army Form C. 2118.

WAR DIARY

~~INTELLIGENCE SUMMARY~~

(Erase heading not required.)

20th Divisional Signal Co R.E.

Place	Date	Hour	Summary of Events and Information	Remarks and references to Appendices
PAS-EN-ARTOIS	20/10		Normal	PPB
"	21/19	04.00	Work on lines & Poles at FAMECHON.	PPB
"	22/19	13.00	Dn CADRE SPORTS MEETING - Lui-a-side football Competitions	PPB
"	23/19	13.00	Dn CADRE SPORTS MEETING.	PPB
"	24/19		Normal	PPB
"	25/19		Normal	PPB
"	26/19		Normal	PPB
"	27/19		Normal	PPB
"	28/19	09.00	Work - Repairing HV. P5 Route	PPB
"	29/19	09.00	Work continued on HV. P5 Route	PPB

R.H.Moore Major R.E.
Cmdg 20 Dn Signal Co R.E.

History of 77th Bn Durham L. Infantry.
The BN commenced to form at WOKING in Surrey in August 1914 and formed part of the 20th Light Division.
During Nov 1914 the BN moved to Pirbright, the strength being 900 all ranks. Owing to the BN being composed of 95% Miners it was converted into a Pioneer BN in Jany 1915 and trained as such.
Bt Colonel J.N. Davison was in Command Major Howe 2nd in Command and Captain G. Hayes Adjutant.
During the time the BN was at Pirbright all ranks were trained in Musktry and route marching.
The end of Feby 1915 the BN moved to billets in NORTHCHAPEL, Sussex and whilst at this place did hard training in route marching and engineer work
The next move was to Larkhill Camp, Salisbury Plain in April 1915, it was in this Place the BN was fully equipped and fully trained in Musktry.

Plenty of hard work was put in during the stay of the BN at Larkhill.
July   the BN entrained for Southampton arriving in the afternoon and embarked for France, Bt Col J.N. Davison being in Command with Major A.E. Collins D.S.O 2nd in Command.
July   BN arrived at Havre and proceeded to Rest Camp, we remained here 2 days and then entrained for LUMBRES from this place we marched to billets at ESQNERDES where we remained for 7 days, during this period route marching and over-hauling equipment was carried out. Our next move was to MERRIS by march route, at this place we halted 4 days.
Bt Col J.N Davison was in Command, Major A.E. Collins D.S.O. 2nd in Command and Captain A.W. Dawson, Adjt.
From MERRIS "A" and "B" Companies under the Command of Major A.E. Collins D.S.O. moved forward to ESTAIRES

where they were employed on defences and improvement of trenches in the LAVENTIE Sector. "C" and "D" Companies moved to billets at LA MOTTE in Bois de NIEPPE here the Companies did very good work making Fascines and hurdles for the forward Area.

In October 1915 the BN was at ESTAIRES and were ordered into the line to strengthen the 12th R.B. who had had heavy Casualties the BN were in and out of the line for over 2 months and did real good work the whole time.

During December 1915 the BN was transferred to the FLEURBAIX Sector and there continued Pioneer work. At this Period Lieut Col A.E. Collins D.S.O was in Command, Bt Col Davison haveing gone to England Sick.

Major. G. Hayes was 2nd in Command Xmas 1915 was spent in BAC st MAUR and ROUGE de BOUT, the men had a very Cheery time and were very Keen

January 1916 the BN proceeded to LA BELLE HOTESSE near STEENBECQUE for rest and training.

The next move was to ZERMEZEELE on forming part of the 14th Corps from here we again moved to WINNEZEELE and from here to ELVERDINGHE where we arrived in Feby 1916.

From Elverdinghe "B" Company moved to dugouts in the Canal bank opposite St Jean. "D" Company moved to BRIELEN HQs and 2 Companies remaining in the Chateau at Elverdinghe, these 2 Companies marched out nightly to work in the forward area.

The BN remained in Elverdinghe and forward area till the 16th April 1916. During the period Feb to April the BN was continually under shell fire in the Chateau grounds and in the forward area, casualties were never very high, men remained as keen as ever but all ranks were looking forward to a rest.

1916

On Sunday April 16th the Battalion left Elverdinghe
Chateau for rest at Rodezelle, where a
very pleasant three weeks were spent.
Training in morning - sports in afternoon.
Battalion sports held Saturday April 29th.
Horse Show held Friday May 5th.
~~H H H Kenble and J H Smyth Pigott~~
~~joined Battalion during this period~~

On Tuesday May 9th left Rodezelle for H Camp.
Two Companies on detachment at Burgomaster and
Machine Gun Farm for work in line under
6th Division. Remaining Companies occupied
in improving Camp and a certain amount
of Training. ~~H R D Pickering joined Battalion~~
~~on May 17th~~

May 20th relieved 4th Batt. Coldstream Guards at
Brandhoek. Work on C.Ts. Garden Street,
Haymarket & West Lane - also defence of White Chateau
Defences. May 25th One Company went to
live in the Ramparts at Ypres.
Battalion relieved Sunday July 16th.
~~Reinforcement~~

~~Capt Higgins left Bn to take over Salvage Coy~~
~~Capt ~~~~~~~ to supply transferred to H. Q.C.~~

On night of June 26/27 the Battalion lost its first officer killed. 2Lt Clough being killed during heavy shell fire on the ST JEAN ROAD.

Our casualties during this period May 10th – July 16th as follows —

    Officers 1 killed
    O.R.   1   "   45 wounded

July 16th. Battalion relieved by 11th Leicesters & proceeded to Winnezeele where we stayed until the 19th.

July 19th proceeded to M Camp and next day left for 24th Divisional School near Bailleul where we bivouacked.

July 23rd moved to St SYLVESTRE CAPEL
     25th   "   DOULLENS
     26th   "   COUIN
     28th relieved 19th Bn. Welsh Fusiliers at
         THE DELL SAILLY-AU-BOIS

Worked on BLUE LINE; & making Bay onto our support line.

Aug 11th moved to ORVILLE
     12   BERNEUIL

Aug 19	Lt. Col. Collins to Hospital.
	Major J. Hayes resumed command.
	Capt. H.P. Lloyd second in command
" 20	Marched to GANDAS Station entrained for
	Mericourt L'Abbée. Marched to MOLANCOURT.
" 21	Moved to THE CITADEL CAMP
	Capt Seison left Battalion for M.G. Corps.
22	Bivouacked near CARNOY.
23	Occupied trenches near CARNOY - old German front line. Battalion attempted to dig "jumping off" trench for attack of 59th Brigade on Guillemont. but were unable to get near the job owing to the enemy barrage. The same thing recurred the following night but on the night of the 25th and succeeding nights the work was completed. On night of 1st September Lieut Harples wounded.
Sept 3rd	Division attacked GUILLEMONT & Battalion took part in the operation as under:-
	A Coy went over at ZERO + 10 to assist 59th Brigade in consolidating positions and making strong points.

	D Coy assisted 47th (Irish) Brigade to consolidate	
	B + C Coys carried wire up for R.E's & dug new trench east of GUILLEMONT STATION.	
Sept 7th	Battalion moved to BOIS-DE-TAILLES	
8	Moved to MERICOURT – bivouacked	
12	" " Sand-pits	
14	" " CITADEL	
15	" into CORPS RESERVE at TALUS BOIS	
17	" " BERNAFAY WOOD	
	Two Companies repairing track from BERNAFAY – TRONES WOOD	
18, 19 and 20th	Battalion working on assembly trenches in front of our lines west of LES BOEUFS	
20	Moved to sandpits. 2/Lts Lovell, Baskell, Kemp, Ingles, and Gillingham reported.	
22	Moved to MEAULT	
23	3 2 0 Officers and O.R proceeded to CARNOY for road making	
25	2/Lts Dennis + Brown reported	
26	Moved to MALTZ-HORN VALLEY	
27	" TALUS-BOIS	
	Lieut Sears reported	

Sept 29   Bivouacked near Trones Wood.
     30   Two Companies occupied TATLER TRENCH
          and two Coys. at WATERLOW FARM.
nights of 1st & 2nd Oct. Battalion working consolidating the
          positions won by infantry on the afternoon of the 1st.
          on the right of GUEUDECOURT. Following nights spent
          digging assembly trenches for the attack on the 7th.
          At push on 7th Battalion went forward and
          consolidated positions captured by 60th & 61st Bdes.
          Our casualties during this seven days were Killed 14
          Wounded 60.
     On 9th marched out to MEAULTE & from here went to
          Méaulte VILLE on the 15th & to the CITADEL camp
          on the 18th. Lt. Col Collins arrived about this time and
          took over command. At CITADEL battalion worked
          under orders of C.E. Corps. until Nov. 1st when entrained
          at Saleux at EDGE HILL for SALEUX - marched from to
          BOURDON on the 2nd. Here the Batt rested until the 8th.
          when moved to PICQUIGNY.
16th Nov. Battalion moved to CORBIE and on 25th to CITADEL
     26th took over camp from 18th Middlesex at MONTAUBAN.
     29th moved into MUD CAMP MONTAUBAN - filthy camp - worked
          under C.E. CORPS. Nov 30th Col. COLLINS to HOSPITAL
          Major Hays commanding.

Dec. 11 B 3 Coys went forward ~~under~~ ~~occupied~~ Hq 2 Coys in
HOGSBACK and one in sunken road behind MORVAL.
Worked on FLANK AVENUE and OZONE Trench

20 Capt. Dawson returned and appointed Adjt.

21 + 22nd. Dug intermediate line across Div. Front

23 Coys returned to MONTAUBAN - working under C.E. XIV Corps.
Xmas morning spent digging Decauville track through
Hun graveyard on Quadrilateral - filthy work.

30 Relieved by 1st Coldstreams who refused to take over camp
on a/c of Mud. — we moved to VILLE

1917
Jan. 1 Capt & Adjt Dawson sick to hospital - relieved by 2/Lt Dennis

3 Batt moved to WEDGE WOOD near COMBLES.
One Coy in Combles, + one at FREGICOURT.
~~A Coy~~ ~~in cellars at~~ COMBLES 6 Coy MORVAL COPSE
Work on C.Ts ~~in~~ and later support line BREAD +
BEAN TRENCH dug.

28 Relieved by York & Lancs. moved to Mansel Camp, next
day to MEAULTE.

Feb. 8 Moved forward - H.Q at MONTAUBAN. A Coy GUILLEMONT
B Coy to HOGSBACK   C + D Coys behind MORVAL
Battalion working in sunken road West of LES BOEUFS
making deep dug outs, and also parties working in front line under Bde.
March 9 2/Lt Fletcher killed

17 Sgt Gardner awarded Italian Bronze medal for meritorious action
23 Moved to GUILLEMONT.

March 25 Moved to Le Transloy.

April 10 H.Q. moved to Buss. Coys in YTRES and LECHELLE.

15 One Coy having own mess in house in YTRES blown up by delay-action mine. Fortunately all officers out at time but several batmen + signallers killed + wounded.

From this time the enemy retired to the Hindenburg line until end of April Batt. engaged on repairing roads in Divisional area - and very useful work was accomplished filling in craters etc.

May 2. Wiring reserve line across Divisional front.

10. Battalion bivouacked in Haverincourt Wood. From May 2nd to May 20 Battalion chiefly engaged on C.T.s, three C.Ts from front line.

21 Moved back to Ytres.

22 " " Barastre.

23 " to camp behind Vaulx Vraucourt. relieved 5th Australian Pioneers.

During this tour in the line excellent C.T. "SIDNEY AVENUE" dug making it possible to get to front line in daylight. Worked also on "DUNELM AVENUE" and on roads etc.

June 28. March to BIHUCOURT (March past G.O.C. at Monument).

June 30.	Entrained ACHIET-LE-GRAND for CANDAS.	
	Marched from CANDAS to DOMART	
	Here we spent a very pleasant time resting until 19th July	
July 19.	Marched to Doullens.	
" 20.	Entrained for HOROUTRE near POPERINGHE & march to camp at PROVEN.	
21.	One Coy on detachment for work with Railway Troops.	
30.	Moved to "G" Camp.	
31.	Battalion moved up shortly after zero to make plank road from BARDS CAUSEWAY forward towards (HUDDLESTON ROAD) PILKEM. This work was continued for several days. In addition to a 6 hours task the men had a walk of 14 miles to & from work.	
Aug. 6.	HQ + 2 Coys billeted in Canal Bank. remaining Coy bivouacked near DAWSONS CORNER Work on Plank Road continued.	
18.	Relieved by 38th Divisional Pioneers. (Welsh)	
19.	Moved to SEATON CAMP ("S" Camps) Resting	
28.	3 Officers + 225 O.R. on detachment for work under 38th Div. R.E.s near DAWSONS CORNER	
Sept 5.	Paraded with 60th Bde for presentation of medals by G.O.C.	

Sept. 9. Relieved 38th Div. Pioneers HQ & 2 Coys in Canal Bank. One Coy near DAWSONS CORNER. Remaining Coy still detached.

10. 11, 12, 13, & 14th. Battalion employed wiring GREEN LINE in LANGEMARCK and carrying material for same.

14 & succeeding nights engaged on repair of tramways duckboard tracks etc.

20. 2 Coys Pioneers working with R.E.s went up at night to construct dugouts strong points in area captured by 59th & 60th Brigades. Battalion Lewis Gunners in line in A.A. Duties assisted infantry in the attack.

LANGEMARCK

21, 22, & 23. Employed on roads leading to Steenbeek & through

24. Support line dug.

Work on Support line & roads continued until 28th when relieved by 21st West Yorks. Pioneers of 4th Div. & marched to Seaton Camp.

During this tour in the line the greatest difficulty was experienced in getting to & from work on account of heavy shell fire. Crossing the Steenbeek twice a night was exceptionally difficult.

Oct. 2. Moved by train to BAPAUME & marched to BARASTRE

Oct 5 Moved to YPRES.

Oct 9 The Coy Battalion relieved 12th Yorkshire Regt.
(Pioneers of 40 Div.). HQ + 1 Coy in PIONEER CAMP
midway between FINS + GOUZEAUCOURT. 1 Coy at
HEUDECOURT, 1 Coy at GOUZEAUCOURT + 1 Coy at GOUZEAUCOURT
WOOD.

Work. Maintenance of trenches — dug outs — wiring of
front + support lines — roads etc.

Nov 19 HQ + 2 Coys moved to GOUZEAUCOURT 2 Coys near VILLERS PLUICH
Nov 20 2 Companies went over just after Zero making Cavalry Track from VILLERS PLUICH to MARCOING working with Tanks that pulled away the wire.
2 Companies digging a C.T. into LA VACQUERIE +
late working on roads. LT. INGIS KILLED

21 & following days WORK on roads continued filling
craters etc.

29 Two Coys started work on new C.T in line.

1/12/1917

On the morning of Dec 1st the BN was still holding the positions it had occupied the night previous and was eventually relieved at night.

Dec. 2. Battalion moved back to BROWN LINE behind
SOUZEAUCOURT and took up defensive position.
3. 10.30 p.m. march out to FINS – billeted there for the night
4. moved to SOREL
5, 6 & 7. working on new Reserve Line
8. Entrained at SOREL for HESDEN marched into
billets at BOUIN – AUBYN ST VAST and ECQUEMICOURT.
11. moved to WARDRECQUES
16. Entrained at EBBLINGHEM for DICKEBUSH.
19. Batt Coys proceeded by light railway to SPOIL BANK
and CANTON SIDING for work carrying wiring materials
to forward dumps.
This work of wiring reserve line on IX CORPS
front in front of OBSERVATORY RIDGE until 5th January.
Xmas Day & New Years Day battalion did not proceed
to work. A very pleasant Xmas day was spent.

1918
Jany 5. Relieved 11th South Lancs (Parnells) at ~~Zillebeke~~
ZILLEBEKE BUND)
Battalion working on ~~duckboards~~ plank roads, mule tracks,
duckboard tracks, – wiring PERTH AVENUE and digging
CULLEY'S TRAIL.

Feb 8. Draft of 6 off and 118 O.R. joined from 14th I.D.L.I
17. Batt. relieved by 9th Batt. North Staffs Regiment

Mar. 21 Batt concentrated at JOUAN COURT & moved to VILLERS ST CHRISTOPHE
one Coy reported to 61st Inf Bde. Details moved to MATIGNY.

22 Details (6 Off + 130 O.R.) dug in a line N. of MATIGNY – DOUILLY ROAD
+ retired to VOYENNES midnight
Batt. attached itself to 59th Bde + occupied trench system covering
GERMAINE. Later orders received to report to 60th Bde. Moved back
and took up a position on the right of K.S.L.I. + left of
12th Kings. About midnight Batt was rushed from
the right + some fighting took place. Later Batt. ordered to proceed to
OFFOY to hold the bridge head there.

23 Dug in on line of canal and on right obtained touch with
30th Entrenching Batt. + on left with 12th KRRC. Quiet day till
evening.

24 Retired after dk to western edge of canal from DUVERCHY to
BREUIL + thereupon dug in.

25 Fought rearguard action through CRESSY + reformed at ROYE.

26 Dug in at ARVILLERS

27 KRRC on left but touch could not be obtained on right
French making arrangements for relief when enemy attacked
on right.

28 Orders received to retire on FRESNOY and took up position
behind MEZIERES.

29 Enemy attacked MEZIERES. Batt in reserve with YORKS LI

over

		entrained at DICKEBUSCH for EBBLINGHEM and marched to RACQUINGHEM
	19	Battalion formed into 3 Companies, in common with other Pioneer Battalions. "C" Coy moved to east
	21	Entrained from STEENBECQUE Station
	22	Arrived at NESLE & marched to GOLANCOURT one Coy at MOULLE LOUVETTE
	27	Commenced work on HAM - NOYEN railway 18% training
Mar	14	One Coy on detachment at VOYENNES.

April 1 Battalion relieved by troops of 14th Division & entrained for QUEVAUVILLERS.
  7 Proceeded by march route to LINCHEUX
 10   HUPPY
 11   REAUX
 17 Lt. Col. R E BOULTON took command of Batt vice Lt. Col Hayes. (sick)
 18 Marched to GAMACHES, embussed for SAVY, marched

Mar.	At 3.15 p.m. Batt ordered to attack MEZIERES.
	attacked at 4.0 p.m. but owing to heavy shell & M.G. fire
	only a handful of men reached the village &
	were compelled to withdraw
	Batt. ordered to take up a line between THENNES and
	HOURGES
30	Day uneventful.
31	Enemy broke through on right & Batt proceeded to hill
	S.E of THENNES & joined cavalry.
	At 4 p.m. Boche enemy attacked but was driven off.

     to FREVILLERS
     Training.
April 26. CAPT H.F. LAING M.C. joined + assumed duties of
    2nd in command.
May 2. marched to CANADA CAMP, CHATEAU-DE-LA-HAIE
 4. Bn H.Q & 1 Coy moved to RATATA CAMP, CARENCY
   + two Coys into LIEVEN.
 5. Worked on CYRIL C.T. GLUCAS C.T + BROWN LINE.
   Work continued following days.
 23. Battalion parties working with special Company
   R.E. pushing trucks containing gas cylinders
   for launching Gas Beam Attack. First time this
   method of launching Gas was used. Trucks pushed up
   light railway into outpost line + detonators on
   cylinders fired electrically which allows gas to escape.
   Operation very successful.
 25. Two Companies working on defences (small strong
   points) in BOIS DE L'HIRONDELLE, remaining Coy
   on Red Line.
June 1. CAPTAIN P.V. KEMP died in hospital from gas
   received night of May 26/27 d.
 3. Coys in Lieven had to leave on a/c of heavy gas
   shelling — one Company returned to H.Q at RATATA CAMP

		+ other Coy went into CAMP at JENKS SIDING SOUCHEZ.
June	5	Just after returning from work at 3.30 a.m. order received "Test: man Battle Stations" Batt. proceeded to and took up positions in posts on BROWN LINE.
	6	Work continued as usual.
	10	One Coy on RIAUMONT defences, two Coys on BROWN LINE.
	17	Work on CASKETT C.T. CAVALRY TRENCH + RIAUMONT Defences.
July	13	Battalion again assisted special Coy R.E. to carry out GAS BEAM attack. Operation very successful.
	31	Bn. Transport Horse Show held.
Aug	3	8.45 p.m "Test Man Battle Stations" received All posts in Brown line manned.
	14	Lt. Col. I.H. Carlisle D.S.O., M.C., R.E assumed command of Batt. vice Lt Col Boulton. Work on Defences + C.Ts continued
	31	New C.T. commenced from BOIS DE L'HIRONDELLE One Coy moved to NEUVILLE ST VAAST
Sept	9	One Company commenced work on KINGSTON ROAD from No 2 ARCH forward.
	4	Working on Kingston Road and LA COULOTTE ROAD. and new C.T.
Oct	3	Enemy retired on Divisional front. Battalion

~~[crossed out]~~ working on KINGSTON & QUEBEC ROADS and also on a track through ARDON.

Very good work was done on these roads - Batt complimented by C.E. Corps.

6 ~~moved by march route to ESTREE CAUCHIE~~

During September Battalion Headquarters at RATATA CAMP was frequently shelled by German long range guns, and it became necessary to clear the camp at dusk, every night. On two occasions the camp was shelled by a 10.4" gun, and every hut was riddled with splinters.

6 Moved out by march route to ESTREE CAUCHIE.
   Training.
30 Marched to TINQUES & bivouacked for the night.
31 Entrained at TINQUES for FREMICOURT.
   Embussed at FREMICOURT for CAMBRAI.

Nov 3 Moved to RIEUX.
   4   "   MONTRECOURT.
   7   "   SEPMERIES
   8   "   JENLAIN
   9   "   ST WAAST
  11   "   FEIGNIES. Armistice day.
  12 Two Coys on detachment one at BERSILLIES & one at GOEGNIES. Work on roads.

Nov. 23 Moved to PISSOTIAU
    24   "   MARESCHES
    25   "   St. AUBERT
    27   "   CAMBRAI
Dec 1 182 miners left Batt for demob.
    2 Moved to THIÉVRES
    9   "   GRENAS

www.ingramcontent.com/pod-product-compliance
Lightning Source LLC
Chambersburg PA
CBHW080847230426
43662CB00013B/2045